CCNP SWITCH
Lab Manual

Cisco Networking Academy

Cisco Press

800 East 96th Street

Indianapolis, Indiana 46240 USA

CCNA SWITCH Lab Manual
Cisco Networking Academy

Copyright© 2011 Cisco Systems, Inc.

Published by:
Cisco Press
800 East 96th Street
Indianapolis, IN 46240 USA

Printed in the United States of America

First Printing   November 2010

Library of Congress Cataloging-in-Publication Data available upon request.

ISBN-13: 978-1-58713-304-6

ISBN-10: 1-58713-304-0

Warning and Disclaimer

This book is designed to provide information about networking. Every effort has been made to make this book as complete and as accurate as possible, but no warranty or fitness is implied.

The information is provided on an "as is" basis. The authors, Cisco Press, and Cisco Systems, Inc. shall have neither liability nor responsibility to any person or entity with respect to any loss or damages arising from the information contained in this book or from the use of the discs or programs that may accompany it.

The opinions expressed in this book belong to the author and are not necessarily those of Cisco Systems, Inc.

Trademark Acknowledgments

All terms mentioned in this book that are known to be trademarks or service marks have been appropriately capitalized. Cisco Press or Cisco Systems, Inc., cannot attest to the accuracy of this information. Use of a term in this book should not be regarded as affecting the validity of any trademark or service mark.

Corporate and Government Sales

The publisher offers excellent discounts on this book when ordered in quantity for bulk purchases or special sales, which may include electronic versions and/or custom covers and content particular to your business, training goals, marketing focus, and branding interests. For more information, please contact: U.S. Corporate and Government Sales   1-800-382-3419   corpsales@pearsontechgroup.com

For sales outside the U.S. please contact: International Sales   international@pearsoned.com

Feedback Information

At Cisco Press, our goal is to create in-depth technical books of the highest quality and value. Each book is crafted with care and precision, undergoing rigorous development that involves the unique expertise of members from the professional technical community.

Readers' feedback is a natural continuation of this process. If you have any comments regarding how we could improve the quality of this book, or otherwise alter it to better suit your needs, you can contact us through email at feedback@ciscopress.com. Please make sure to include the book title and ISBN in your message.

We greatly appreciate your assistance.

Publisher	Paul Boger
Associate Publisher	Dave Dusthimer
Cisco Representative	Erik Ullanderson
Cisco Press Program Manager	Anand Sundaram
Executive Editor	Mary Beth Ray
Managing Editor	Sandra Schroeder
Editorial Assistant	Vanessa Evans
Cover Designer	Louisa Adair

Americas Headquarters	Asia Pacific Headquarters	Europe Headquarters
Cisco Systems, Inc.	Cisco Systems (USA) Pte. Ltd.	Cisco Systems International BV
San Jose, CA	Singapore	Amsterdam, The Netherlands

Cisco has more than 200 offices worldwide. Addresses, phone numbers, and fax numbers are listed on the Cisco Website at **www.cisco.com/go/offices.**

CCDE, CCENT, Cisco Eos, Cisco HealthPresence, the Cisco logo, Cisco Lumin, Cisco Nexus, Cisco StadiumVision, Cisco TelePresence, Cisco WebEx, DCE, and Welcome to the Human Network are trademarks; Changing the Way We Work, Live, Play, and Learn and Cisco Store are service marks; and Access Registrar, Aironet, AsyncOS, Bringing the Meeting To You, Catalyst, CCDA, CCDP, CCIE, CCIP, CCNA, CCNP, CCSP, CCVP, Cisco, the Cisco Certified Internetwork Expert logo, Cisco IOS, Cisco Press, Cisco Systems, Cisco Systems Capital, the Cisco Systems logo, Cisco Unity, Collaboration Without Limitation, EtherFast, EtherSwitch, Event Center, Fast Step, Follow Me Browsing, FormShare, GigaDrive, HomeLink, Internet Quotient, IOS, iPhone, iQuick Study, IronPort, the IronPort logo, LightStream, Linksys, MediaTone, MeetingPlace, MeetingPlace Chime Sound, MGX, Networkers, Networking Academy, Network Registrar, PCNow, PIX, PowerPanels, ProConnect, ScriptShare, SenderBase, SMARTnet, Spectrum Expert, StackWise, The Fastest Way to Increase Your Internet Quotient, TransPath, WebEx, and the WebEx logo are registered trademarks of Cisco Systems, Inc. and/or its affiliates in the United States and certain other countries.

All other trademarks mentioned in this document or website are the property of their respective owners. The use of the word partner does not imply a partnership relationship between Cisco and any other company. (0812R)

Contents

About This Lab Manual

This is the only authorized Lab Manual for the Cisco Networking Academy CCNP version 6 SWITCH course

A CCNP certification equips students with the knowledge and skills needed to plan, implement, secure, maintain, and troubleshoot converged enterprise networks. The CCNP certification requires candidates to pass three 120-minute exams—ROUTE #642-902, SWITCH #642-813, and TSHOOT #642-832—that validate the key competencies of network engineers.

The Cisco Networking Academy curriculum consists of three experience-oriented courses that employ industry-relevant instructional approaches to prepare students for professional-level jobs: CCNP ROUTE: Implementing IP Routing, CCNP SWITCH: Implementing IP Switching, and CCNP TSHOOT: Maintaining and Troubleshooting IP Networks.

CCNP SWITCH: Implementing IP Switching

This course teaches students how to implement, monitor, and maintain switching in converged enterprise campus networks. Students will learn how to plan, configure, and verify the implementation of complex enterprise switching solutions. The course also covers the secure integration of VLANs, WLANs, voice, and video into campus networks. Comprehensive labs emphasize hands-on learning and practice to reinforce configuration skills.

The 19 comprehensive labs in this manual emphasize hands-on learning and practice to reinforce configuration skills.

Command Syntax Conventions

The conventions used to present command syntax in this book are the same conventions used in the IOS Command Reference. The Command Reference describes these conventions as follows:

- Boldface indicates commands and keywords that are entered literally as shown. In actual configuration examples and output (not general command syntax), boldface indicates commands that are manually input by the user (such as a show command).
- Italic indicates arguments for which you supply actual values.
- Vertical bars (|) separate alternative, mutually exclusive elements.
- Square brackets ([ ]) indicate an optional element.
- Braces ({ }) indicate a required choice.
- Braces within brackets ([{ }]) indicate a required choice within an optional element

Chapter 1 Analyzing the Cisco Enterprise Campus Architecture

Lab 1-1, Clearing a Switch

Topology

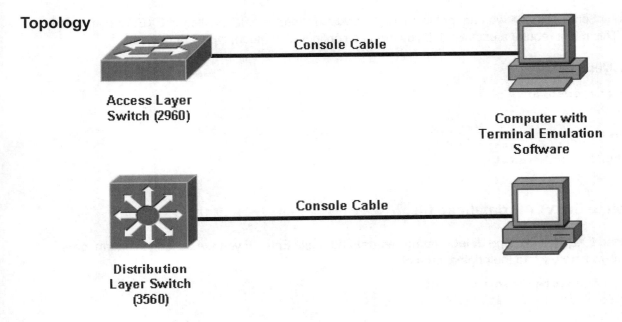

Access Layer
Switch (2960)

Console Cable

Computer with
Terminal Emulation
Software

Console Cable

Distribution
Layer Switch
(3560)

Objective

- Clear the configuration of a standalone switch to prepare it for a new lab.

Background

When working with a switch that has been previously configured, any new commands entered will be merged with the existing configuration, causing unpredictable results. In this lab you prepare a Catalyst 2960 or 3560 switch for use with a lab. This is accomplished by erasing the startup configuration from NVRAM and deleting the VLAN database.

Note: This lab uses the Cisco WS-C2960-24TT-L switch with the Cisco IOS image c2960-lanbasek9-mz.122-46.SE.bin and the Catalyst 3560-24PS switch with the Cisco IOS image c3560-advipservicesk9-mz.122-46.SE.bin. Other switches (such as a 2950 or a 3550), and Cisco IOS Software versions can be used if they have comparable capabilities and features. Depending on the switch model and Cisco IOS Software version, the commands available and output produced might vary from what is shown in this lab.

Required Resources

You may use one of the following switches or a comparable one with this lab:

- Cisco 2960 with the Cisco IOS Release 12.2(46)SE C2960-LANBASEK9-M image or comparable
- Cisco 3560 with the Cisco IOS Release 12.2(46)SE C3560-ADVIPSERVICESK9-M image or comparable
- Console cable

Step 1: Connect to the switch console port and enter privileged EXEC mode.

From a computer running a terminal emulation program, connect to the console port of the switch that you want to clear using a console cable. You should see a console prompt that includes the switch's hostname, followed by a **>** or **#**. The default switch hostname is "Switch."

```
Switch>
```

or

```
Switch#
```

If the prompt ends with a **>**, you are not in privileged EXEC mode. To enter privileged EXEC mode, type **enable**. This might require a password. If you are in a configuration mode, type **exit** or **end**.

If not enabled:

```
Switch> enable
Switch#
```

If in global configuration mode:

```
Switch(config)# exit
Switch#
```

Step 2: Delete the VLAN database file.

In privileged EXEC mode, type **delete flash:vlan.dat** and press Enter. If you are asked to confirm, press Enter until you are back to the original prompt.

```
Switch# delete flash:vlan.dat
Delete flash:vlan.dat? [confirm]
Switch#
```

Step 3: Erase the startup config from NVRAM.

After deleting the vlan.dat file, you can erase the startup configuration on the switch by typing **erase startup-config**. You again have to press Enter to confirm.

```
Switch# erase startup-config
Erasing the nvram filesystem will remove all configuration files! Continue?
[confirm]
[OK]
Erase of nvram: complete
Switch#
```

Step 4: Reload the device, but do *not* save the system configuration if prompted.

After clearing the switch configuration, reload the switch by typing **reload** and pressing Enter. If you are asked whether to save the current configuration, answer **no**. Press Enter to confirm. The switch starts reloading. Your output might look different depending on the switch model that you are using. This step might take a few minutes, because the switch needs time to reload.

```
Switch# reload

System configuration has been modified. Save? [yes/no]: no
Proceed with reload? [confirm]

%SYS-5-RELOAD: Reload requested by console. Reload Reason: Reload command.
```

```
Base ethernet MAC Address: 00:1b:0c:6d:8f:00
Xmodem file system is available.
The password-recovery mechanism is enabled.
Initializing Flash...
flashfs[0]: 606 files, 20 directories
flashfs[0]: 0 orphaned files, 0 orphaned directories
flashfs[0]: Total bytes: 32514048
flashfs[0]: Bytes used: 10336256
flashfs[0]: Bytes available: 22177792
flashfs[0]: flashfs fsck took 10 seconds.
...done Initializing Flash.
Boot Sector Filesystem (bs) installed, fsid: 3
done.
Loading "flash:/c2960-lanbase-mz.122-46.SE/c2960-lanbasek9-mz.122-46.SE.bin"..
.@@@@@@@@@@@@@@@@@@@@@@@@@@@@@@@@@@@@@@@@@@@@@@@@@@@@@@@@@@@@@@@@@@@@@@@@@@@@@@@@@
@@@@@@@@@@@@@@@@@@@@@@@@@@@@@@@@@@@@@@@@@@@@@@@@@@@@@@@@@@@@@@@@@@@@@@@@@@@@@@@@@@@
@@@@@@@@@@@@@@@@@@@@@@@@@@@@@@@@@@@@@@@@@@@@@@@@@@@@@@@@@@@@@@@@@@@@@@@@@@@@@@@@@@@
@@@@@@@@@@@@@@@@@@@@@@@@@@@@@@@@@@@@@@@@@@@@@@@@@@@@@@@@@@@@@@@@@@@@@@@@@@@@@@@@@@@
@@@@@@@@@@@@@@@@@@@@@@@@@@@@@@@@@@@@@@@@@@@@@@@@@@@@@@@@@@@@@@@@@@@@@@@@@@@@@@@@@@@
@@@@@@@@@@@@@@@@@@@@@@@@@@@@@@@@@@@@@@@@@@@@@@@@@@@@@@@@@@@@@@@@@@@@@@@@@@@@@@@@@@@
@@@@@@@@@@@@@@@@@@@@@@@@@@@@@@@@@@@@@@@@@@@@@@@@@@@@@@@@@@@@@@@@@@@@@@@@@@@@@@@@@@@
@@@@@@@@@@@@@@@@@@@@@@@@@@@@@@@@@@@@@@@@@@@@@@@@@@@@@@@@@@@@@@@@@@@@@@@@@@@@@@@@@@@
@@@@@@@@@@@@@@@@@@@@@@@@@@@@@@@@@@@@@@@@@@@@@@@@@@@@@@@@@@@@@@@@@@@@@@@@@@@@@@@@@@@
@@@@@@@@@@@@@@@@@@@@@@@@@@@@@@@@@@@@@@@@@@@@@@@@@@@@@@@@@@@@@@@@@@@@@@@@@@@@@@@@@@@
@@@@@@@@@@@@@@@@@@@@@@@@@@@@@@@@@@@@@@@@@@@@@@@@@@@@@@@@@@@@@@@@@@@@@@@@@@@@@@@@@@@
@@@@@@@@@@@@@@@@@@@@@@@@@@@@@@@@@@@@@@@@@@@@@@@@@@@@@@@@@@@@@@@@@@@@@@@@@@@@@@@@@@@
@@@@@@@@@@@@@@@@@@@@@@@@@@@@@@@@@@@@@@@@@@@@@@@@@@@@@@@@@@@@@@@@@@@@@@@@@@@@@@@@@@@
@@@@@@@@@@@@@@@@@@@@@@@@@@@@@@@@@@@@@@@@@@@@@@@@@@@@@@@@@@@@@@@@@@@@@@@@@@@@@@@@@@@
@@@@@@@@@@@@@@@@@@@@@@@@@@@@@@@@@@@@@@@@@@@@@@@@@@@@@@@@@@@@@@@@@@@@@@@@@@@@@@@@@@@
@@@@@@@@@@@@@@@@@@@@@@@@@@@@@@@@@@@@@@@@@@@@@@@@@@@@@@@@@@@@@@@@@@@@@@@@@@@@@@@@@@@
@@@@@@@@@@@@@@@@@@@@@@@@@@@@@@@@@@@@@@@@@@@@@@@@@@@@@@@@@@@@@@@@@@@@@@@@@@@@@@@@@@@
@@@@@@@@@@@@@@@@@@@@@@@@@@@@@@@@@@@@@@@@@@@@@@@@@@@@@@@@@@@@@@@@@@@@@@@@@@@@@@@@@@@
@@@@@@@@@@@@@@@@@@@@@@@@@@@@@@@@@@@@@@@@@@@@@@@@@@@@@@@@@@@@@@@@@@@@@@@@@@@@@@@@@@@
@@@@@@@@@@@@@@@@@@@@@@@@@@@@@@@@@@@@@@@@@@@@@@@@@@@@@@@@@@@@@@@@@@@@@@@@@@@@@@@@@@@
@@@@@@@@@@@@@@@@@@@@@@@@@@@@@@@@@@@@@@@@@@@@@@@@@@@@@@@@@@@@@@@@@@@@@@@@@@@@@@@@@@@
@@@@@@@@
File "flash:/c2960-lanbase-mz.122-46.SE/c2960-lanbasek9-mz.122-46.SE.bin" unco
mpressed and installed, entry point: 0x3000
executing...


                  Restricted Rights Legend


Use, duplication, or disclosure by the Government is
subject to restrictions as set forth in subparagraph
(c) of the Commercial Computer Software - Restricted
Rights clause at FAR sec. 52.227-19 and subparagraph
(c) (1) (ii) of the Rights in Technical Data and Computer
Software clause at DFARS sec. 252.227-7013.

             cisco Systems, Inc.
             170 West Tasman Drive
             San Jose, California 95134-1706
```

```
Cisco IOS Software, C2960 Software (C2960-LANBASEK9-M), Version 12.2(46)SE,
RELE
ASE SOFTWARE (fc2)
Copyright (c) 1986-2008 by Cisco Systems, Inc.
Compiled Thu 21-Aug-08 15:59 by nachen
Image text-base: 0x00003000, data-base: 0x01200000

Initializing flashfs...

flashfs[1]: 606 files, 20 directories
flashfs[1]: 0 orphaned files, 0 orphaned directories
flashfs[1]: Total bytes: 32514048
flashfs[1]: Bytes used: 10336256
flashfs[1]: Bytes available: 22177792
flashfs[1]: flashfs fsck took 1 seconds.
flashfs[1]: Initialization complete....done Initializing flashfs.

POST: CPU MIC register Tests : Begin
POST: CPU MIC register Tests : End, Status Passed

POST: PortASIC Memory Tests : Begin
POST: PortASIC Memory Tests : End, Status Passed

POST: CPU MIC interface Loopback Tests : Begin
POST: CPU MIC interface Loopback Tests : End, Status Passed

POST: PortASIC RingLoopback Tests : Begin
POST: PortASIC RingLoopback Tests : End, Status Passed

POST: PortASIC CAM Subsystem Tests : Begin
POST: PortASIC CAM Subsystem Tests : End, Status Passed

POST: PortASIC Port Loopback Tests : Begin
POST: PortASIC Port Loopback Tests : End, Status Passed

Waiting for Port download...Complete
```

This product contains cryptographic features and is subject to United
States and local country laws governing import, export, transfer and
use. Delivery of Cisco cryptographic products does not imply
third-party authority to import, export, distribute or use encryption.
Importers, exporters, distributors and users are responsible for
compliance with U.S. and local country laws. By using this product you
agree to comply with applicable laws and regulations. If you are unable
to comply with U.S. and local laws, return this product immediately.

A summary of U.S. laws governing Cisco cryptographic products may be found at:
http://www.cisco.com/wwl/export/crypto/tool/stqrg.html

If you require further assistance please contact us by sending email to
export@cisco.com.

```
cisco WS-C2960-24TT-L (PowerPC405) processor (revision B0) with 61440K/4088K
byt
es of memory.
Processor board ID FOC1104W0G0
Last reset from power-on
1 Virtual Ethernet interface
24 FastEthernet interfaces
2 Gigabit Ethernet interfaces
The password-recovery mechanism is enabled.

64K bytes of flash-simulated non-volatile configuration memory.
Base ethernet MAC Address       : 00:1B:0C:6D:8F:00
Motherboard assembly number     : 73-10390-03
Power supply part number        : 341-0097-02
Motherboard serial number       : FOC11036013
Power supply serial number      : AZS1103015V
Model revision number           : B0
Motherboard revision number     : C0
Model number                    : WS-C2960-24TT-L
System serial number            : FOC1104W0G0
Top Assembly Part Number        : 800-27221-02
Top Assembly Revision Number    : C0
Version ID                      : V02
CLEI Code Number                : COM3L00BRA
Hardware Board Revision Number  : 0x01


Switch Ports Model              SW Version        SW Image
------ ----- -----              ----------        ----------
*    1 26    WS-C2960-24TT-L     12.2(46)SE        C2960-LANBASEK9-M
```

Step 5: When the switch restarts, do not enter the initial configuration dialog, but terminate autoinstall.

The switch might log messages to the console, such as interfaces coming up and down. When you see the "Press RETURN to get started!" prompt, press Enter.

If you are asked to enter an initial configuration dialog, type **no**. This places you at the user EXEC prompt. If you accidentally type yes, you can break out of the initial configuration dialog at any time by pressing Ctrl-C. If you are asked whether you want to terminate autoinstall, press Enter for "yes."

```
Press RETURN to get started! Enter


        --- System Configuration Dialog ---

Would you like to enter the initial configuration dialog? [yes/no]: no

Would you like to terminate autoinstall? [yes]: Enter
```

Lab 1-2, Clearing a Switch Connected to a Larger Network

Topology

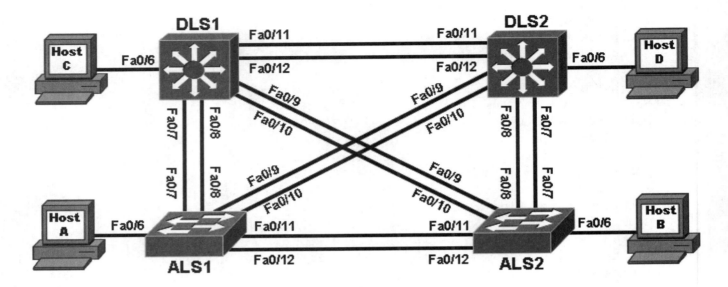

Objective

- Clear the configuration of a switch that is connected to other switches and prepare it for a new lab.

Background

When working with a switch that has been previously configured, any new commands entered are merged with the existing configuration, causing unpredictable results. Additionally, if the switch is connected to other switches in the network, you can remove the VLANs but they might be relearned from another switch via VTP. In this lab, you prepare a Catalyst 2960 or 3560 switch for use with a lab by erasing the startup configuration from NVRAM and deleting the VLAN database. You also ensure that VLANs will not be relearned from another switch after the VLAN database has been deleted.

Note: This lab uses the Cisco WS-C2960-24TT-L switch with the Cisco IOS image c2960-lanbasek9-mz.122-46.SE.bin, and the Catalyst 3560-24PS switch with the Cisco IOS image c3560-advipservicesk9-mz.122-46.SE.bin. You can use other switches (such as a 2950 or a 3550) and Cisco IOS Software versions if they have comparable capabilities and features. Depending on the switch model and Cisco IOS Software version, the commands available and output produced might vary from what is shown in this lab.

Required Resources

- 2 switches (Cisco 2960 with the Cisco IOS Release 12.2(46)SE C2960-LANBASEK9-M image or comparable)
- 2 switches (Cisco 3560 with the Cisco IOS Release 12.2(46)SE C3560-ADVIPSERVICESK9-M image or comparable)
- Console and Ethernet cables

Step 1: Connect to the switch console port and enter privileged EXEC mode.

This lab assumes that you have completed Lab 1-1, Clearing a Switch.

Step 2: Delete the VLAN database file.

In privileged EXEC mode, type **delete vlan.dat** and press Enter. If you are asked to confirm, press Enter until you are back to the original prompt.

```
Switch# delete vlan.dat
Delete flash:vlan.dat? [confirm]
Switch#
```

Step 3: Erase the startup config from NVRAM.

After deleting the vlan.dat file, you can erase the startup configuration on the switch by typing **erase startup-config**. You again have to press Enter to confirm. Reload the switch.

```
Switch# erase startup-config
Erasing the nvram filesystem will remove all configuration files! Continue?
[confirm]
[OK]
Erase of nvram: complete
Switch#
Switch# reload
```

Step 4: Display the existing configured VLANs.

The difficulty with clearing a switch that is cabled to other switches is removing the VLANs. When the switch is finished reloading, it is possible for it to relearn VLANs from another connected switch that is in VTP server or client mode.

To determine if the VLANs have been relearned, use the **show vlan** command.

```
Switch# show vlan brief

VLAN Name                             Status    Ports
---- -------------------------------- --------- ------------------------------
--
1    default                          active    Fa0/1, Fa0/2, Fa0/3, Fa0/4
                                                 Fa0/5, Fa0/6, Fa0/7, Fa0/8
                                                 Fa0/9, Fa0/10, Fa0/11, Fa0/12
                                                 Fa0/13, Fa0/14, Fa0/15, Fa0/16
                                                 Fa0/17, Fa0/18, Fa0/19, Fa0/20
                                                 Fa0/21, Fa0/22, Fa0/23, Fa0/24
                                                 Gi0/1, Gi0/2

1002 fddi-default                     act/unsup
1003 token-ring-default               act/unsup
1004 fddinet-default                  act/unsup
1005 trnet-default                    act/unsup
```

In this sample output, the switch has not learned any VLANs from another switch. You are finished clearing both the configuration and VLANs from the switch.

However, if the **show vlan** command displays nondefault VLANs after you have deleted the vlan.dat file, your switch has learned the VLANs dynamically from another switch. For example:

```
Switch# show vlan brief

VLAN Name                             Status    Ports
---- -------------------------------- --------- -----------------------------
--
1    default                          active    Fa0/1, Fa0/2, Fa0/3, Fa0/4
                                                 Fa0/5, Fa0/6, Fa0/7, Fa0/8
                                                 Fa0/9, Fa0/10, Fa0/11, Fa0/12
                                                 Fa0/13, Fa0/14, Fa0/15, Fa0/16
                                                 Fa0/17, Fa0/18, Fa0/19, Fa0/20
                                                 Fa0/21, Fa0/22, Fa0/23, Fa0/24
                                                 Gi0/1, Gi0/2
10   OFFICE                           active
20   VOICE                            active
30   GUEST                            active
50   SERVERS                          active
100  MGMT                             active
200  TRANS                            active
900  NATIVE                           active
999  UNUSED                           active

1002 fddi-default                     act/unsup
1003 token-ring-default               act/unsup
1004 fddinet-default                  act/unsup
1005 trnet-default                    act/unsup
```

Step 5: Shut down interfaces and remove the VLANs.

To eliminate these VLANS, shut down all interfaces and remove the existing VLANs.

```
Switch(config)# interface range FastEthernet 0/1 - 24
Switch(config-if-range)# shutdown
Switch(config-if-range)#
15:44:06: %LINK-5-CHANGED: Interface FastEthernet0/1, changed state to
administratively down
15:44:06: %LINK-5-CHANGED: Interface FastEthernet0/2, changed state to
administratively down
15:44:06: %LINK-5-CHANGED: Interface FastEthernet0/3, changed state to
administratively down
15:44:06: %LINK-5-CHANGED: Interface FastEthernet0/4, changed state to
administratively down
15:44:06: %LINK-5-CHANGED: Interface FastEthernet0/5, changed state to
administratively down
15:44:06: %LINK-5-CHANGED: Interface FastEthernet0/6, changed state to
administratively down
<output omitted>

Switch(config-if-range)# interface range GigabitEthernet 0/1 - 2
Switch(config-if-range)# shutdown
Switch(config-if-range)#
15:45:59: %LINK-5-CHANGED: Interface GigabitEthernet0/1, changed state to
```

```
administratively down
15:45:59: %LINK-5-CHANGED: Interface GigabitEthernet0/2, changed state to
administratively down


Switch(config-if-range)# exit
Switch(config)# no vlan 2-999
Switch(config)#exit

Switch# show vlan brief

VLAN Name                                Status    Ports
---- -------------------------------- --------- ------------------------------
--
1    default                          active    Fa0/1, Fa0/2, Fa0/3, Fa0/4
                                                 Fa0/5, Fa0/6, Fa0/7, Fa0/8
                                                 Fa0/9, Fa0/10, Fa0/11, Fa0/12
                                                 Fa0/13, Fa0/14, Fa0/15, Fa0/16
                                                 Fa0/17, Fa0/18, Fa0/19, Fa0/20
                                                 Fa0/21, Fa0/22, Fa0/23, Fa0/24
                                                 Gi0/1, Gi0/2
1002 fddi-default                     act/unsup
1003 token-ring-default               act/unsup
1004 fddinet-default                  act/unsup
1005 trnet-default                    act/unsup
```

Step 6: (Optional) Configure transparent VTP mode.

Now that both the startup configuration and the VLANs have been erased, you are ready to start a new lab. For interfaces that need to be up, use the **no shutdown** command in the new lab. If you want to do some configuration before the switch learns VLANs from the network, put it into VTP transparent mode until you are ready.

```
Switch# conf t
Enter configuration commands, one per line.  End with CNTL/Z.
Switch(config)# vtp mode transparent
Setting device to VTP TRANSPARENT mode.
```

Chapter 2 Implementing VLANs in Campus Networks

Lab 2-1, Static VLANS, VLAN Trunking, and VTP Domains and Modes

Topology

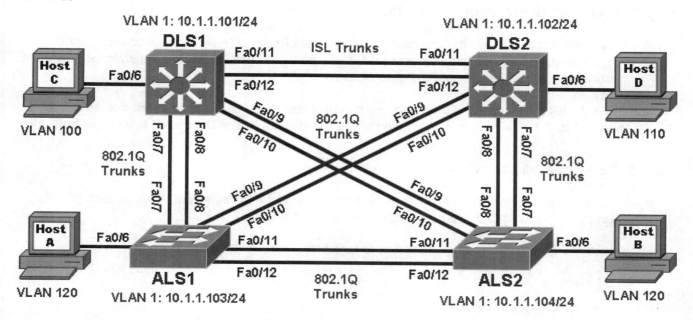

Objectives

- Set up a VTP domain.
- Create and maintain VLANs.
- Configure ISL and 802.1Q trunking.

Background

VLANs logically segment a network by function, team, or application, regardless of the physical location of the users. End stations in a particular IP subnet are often associated with a specific VLAN. VLAN membership on a switch that is assigned manually for each interface is known as static VLAN membership.

Trunking, or connecting switches, and the VLAN Trunking Protocol (VTP) are technologies that support VLANs. VTP manages the addition, deletion, and renaming of VLANs on the entire network from a single central switch.

Note: This lab uses Cisco WS-C2960-24TT-L switches with the Cisco IOS image c2960-lanbasek9-mz.122-46.SE.bin, and Catalyst 3560-24PS with the Cisco IOS image c3560-advipservicesk9-mz.122-46. SE.bin. You can use other switches (such as a 2950 or 3550) and Cisco IOS Software versions if they have comparable capabilities and features. Depending on the switch model and Cisco IOS Software version, the commands available and output produced might vary from what is shown in this lab.

Required Resources

- 2 switches (Cisco 2960 with the Cisco IOS Release 12.2(46)SE C2960-LANBASEK9-M image or comparable)
- 2 switches (Cisco 3560 with the Cisco IOS Release 12.2(46)SE C3560-ADVIPSERVICESK9-M image or comparable)
- 4 PCs (optional)
- Ethernet and console cables

Step 1: Prepare the switches for the lab.

Power up the switches and use the standard process for establishing a HyperTerminal console connection from a workstation to each switch in your pod. If you are connecting remotely to the switches, follow the instructions that have been supplied by your instructor.

Remove all VLAN information and configurations that may have been previously entered into the switches. Refer to Lab 1-1, "Clearing a Switch," and Lab 1-2, "Clearing a Switch Connected to a Larger Network."

Step 2: Configure basic switch parameters.

Assign each switch a hostname and configure an IP address on the management VLAN according to the diagram. By default, VLAN 1 is used as the management VLAN.

Enter basic configuration commands on each switch according to the diagram.

DLS1 example:

```
Switch# configure terminal
Enter configuration commands, one per line.  End with CNTL/Z.
Switch(config)# hostname DLS1
DLS1(config)# interface vlan 1
DLS1(config-if)# ip address 10.1.1.101 255.255.255.0
DLS1(config-if)# no shutdown
```

(Optional) On each switch, create an enable secret password and configure the vty lines to allow remote access from other network devices.

DLS1 example:

```
DLS1(config)# enable secret cisco
DLS1(config)# line vty 0 15
DLS1(config-line)# password cisco
DLS1(config-line)# login
```

Step 3: Display the switch default VLAN information.

Use the **show vlan** command in privileged mode on any switch. The following output is for a 2960 switch.

```
ALS1# show vlan

VLAN Name                             Status    Ports
---- -------------------------------- --------- ---------------------------
--
1    default                          active    Fa0/1, Fa0/2, Fa0/3, Fa0/4
```

```
                                                Fa0/5, Fa0/6, Fa0/7, Fa0/8
                                                Fa0/9, Fa0/10, Fa0/11, Fa0/12
                                                Fa0/13, Fa0/14, Fa0/15, Fa0/16
                                                Fa0/17, Fa0/18, Fa0/19, Fa0/20
                                                Fa0/21, Fa0/22, Fa0/23, Fa0/24
                                                Gi0/1, Gi0/2
1002 fddi-default                    act/unsup
1003 token-ring-default              act/unsup
1004 fddinet-default                 act/unsup
1005 trnet-default                   act/unsup
```

VLAN	Type	SAID	MTU	Parent	RingNo	BridgeNo	Stp	BrdgMode	Trans1	Trans2
1	enet	100001	1500	-	-	-	-	-	0	0
1002	fddi	101002	1500	-	-	-	-	-	0	0
1003	tr	101003	1500	-	-	-	-	-	0	0
1004	fdnet	101004	1500	-	-	-	ieee	-	0	0
1005	trnet	101005	1500	-	-	-	ibm	-	0	0

```
Remote SPAN VLANs
------------------------------------------------------------------------------


Primary Secondary Type             Ports
------- --------- ---------------- ------------------------------------------
```

The following output is for a 3560 switch.

```
DLS1# show vlan

VLAN Name                             Status    Ports
---- -------------------------------- --------- ------------------------------
--
1    default                          active    Fa0/1, Fa0/2, Fa0/3, Fa0/4
                                                Fa0/5, Fa0/6, Fa0/7, Fa0/8
                                                Fa0/9, Fa0/10, Fa0/11, Fa0/12
                                                Fa0/13, Fa0/14, Fa0/15, Fa0/16
                                                Fa0/17, Fa0/18, Fa0/19, Fa0/20
                                                Fa0/21, Fa0/22, Fa0/23, Fa0/24
                                                Gi0/1, Gi0/2
1002 fddi-default                     act/unsup
1003 token-ring-default               act/unsup
1004 fddinet-default                  act/unsup
1005 trnet-default                    act/unsup
```

VLAN	Type	SAID	MTU	Parent	RingNo	BridgeNo	Stp	BrdgMode	Trans1	Trans2
1	enet	100001	1500	-	-	-	-	-	0	0
1002	fddi	101002	1500	-	-	-	-	-	0	0
1003	tr	101003	1500	-	-	-	-	-	0	0
1004	fdnet	101004	1500	-	-	-	ieee	-	0	0
1005	trnet	101005	1500	-	-	-	ibm	-	0	0

```
Remote SPAN VLANs
-----------------------------------------------------------------------


Primary Secondary Type             Ports
------- --------- ----------------- ---------------------------------------
```

Note the default VLAN numbers, names, and associated types, and that all switch ports are automatically assigned to VLAN 1.

You can use the **show vlan** command to determine the mode of a port. Ports configured for a particular VLAN are shown in that VLAN. Ports configured for trunk mode are not associated with a specific VLAN, and so are not included in the output.

Step 4: Examine VTP information.

A VTP domain, also called a VLAN management domain, consists of trunked switches that are under the administrative responsibility of a switch or switches in server VTP mode. A switch can be in only one VTP domain with the same VTP domain name. The default VTP mode for the 2960 and 3560 switches is server mode. VLAN information is not propagated until a domain name is specified and trunks are set up between the devices.

The following table describes the three VTP modes.

VTP Mode	Description
VTP server	You can create, modify, and delete VLANs and specify other configuration parameters, such as VTP version and VTP pruning, for the entire VTP domain. VTP servers advertise their VLAN configuration to other switches in the same VTP domain and synchronize their VLAN configuration with other switches based on advertisements received over trunk links. VTP server is the default mode.
VTP client	VTP clients behave the same way as VTP servers, but you cannot create, change, or delete VLANs on a VTP client.
VTP transparent	VTP transparent switches do not participate in VTP. A VTP transparent switch does not advertise its VLAN configuration nor synchronize its VLAN configuration based on received advertisements. Transparent switches do forward VTP advertisements that they receive out their trunk ports in VTP Version 2.

Use the **show vtp status** command on any switch. The output should be similar to the following sample for DLS1.

```
DLS1# show vtp status
VTP Version                     : running VTP1 (VTP2 capable)
Configuration Revision          : 0
Maximum VLANs supported locally : 1005
Number of existing VLANs        : 5
VTP Operating Mode              : Server
```

```
VTP Domain Name                    :
VTP Pruning Mode                   : Disabled
VTP V2 Mode                        : Disabled
VTP Traps Generation               : Disabled
MD5 digest                         : 0x57 0xCD 0x40 0x65 0x63 0x59 0x47 0xBD
Configuration last modified by 0.0.0.0 at 0-0-00 00:00:00
Local updater ID is 10.1.1.101 on interface Vl1 (lowest numbered VLAN
interface
found)
```

Because no VLAN configurations were made, all settings are the defaults. Notice that the VTP mode is server mode. The number of existing VLANs is the five built-in VLANs. The 3560 switch supports 1,005 maximum VLANs locally. The 2960 switch supports 255 VLANs. The configuration revision is 0, and the default VTP version is 1. All switches in the VTP domain must run the same VTP version.

The importance of the configuration revision number is that the switch with the highest revision number in VTP server mode propagates VLAN information over trunked ports. Every time VLAN information is modified and saved in the VLAN database or vlan.dat file, the revision number is increased by one when the user exits from VLAN configuration mode.

Multiple switches in the VTP domain can be in VTP server mode. These switches can be used to manage all other switches in the VTP domain. This is suitable for small-scale networks where the VLAN information is small and easily stored in all switches. In a large network, the administrator must determine which switches make the best VTP servers. The network administrator should select switches to function as VTP servers. The other switches in the VTP domain can be configured as clients. The number of VTP servers should be consistent based on the amount of redundancy desired in the network.

Step 5: Configure VTP on the switches.

Change the VTP domain name on DLS1 to SWLAB using the **vtp domain** command. If the VTP version defaults to 1, set it manually to version 2 using the **vtp version** command.

```
DLS1(config)# vtp domain SWLAB
Changing VTP domain name from NULL to SWLAB

DLS1(config)# vtp version 2
```

Note: The newest VTP version, VTPv3, is not supported by the IOS used on the switches in this lab. However, it is supported in IOS versions 12.2(52)SE and newer on all platforms eligible for this IOS (2960, 3560, 3750, etc.). VTPv3 has improvements in three major areas.

Better administrative control over which device is allowed to update other devices' view of the VLAN topology. The chance of unintended and disruptive changes is significantly reduced, and availability is increased.

Functionality for the VLAN environment has been significantly expanded. In addition to supporting the earlier ISL VLAN range from 1 to 1001, the new version supports the whole IEEE 802.1Q VLAN range up to 4095. In addition to supporting the concept of normal VLANs, VTP version 3 can transfer information regarding Private VLAN (PVLAN) structures.

The third area of major improvement is support for databases other than VLAN (for example, MST).

Set up the switches so that the distribution layer switches are in VTP server mode, and the access layer switches are in VTP client mode. Set the version number to 2 on the DL switches.

```
DLS1(config)# vtp mode server
Device mode already VTP SERVER.
```

Because the default mode is server, you receive a message on DLS1 stating that the device mode is already VTP server.

```
ALS1(config)# vtp mode client
Setting device to VTP CLIENT mode.
```

Note: You cannot modify the version in VTP client mode

Use the **show vtp status** command on either of the AL switches. The output should be similar to the following sample for ALS1.

```
ALS1# show vtp status
VTP Version                        : running VTP1 (VTP2 capable)
Configuration Revision      : 0
Maximum VLANs supported locally : 255
Number of existing VLANs    : 5
VTP Operating Mode          : Client
VTP Domain Name             :
VTP Pruning Mode            : Disabled
VTP V2 Mode                 : Disabled
VTP Traps Generation        : Disabled
MD5 digest                  : 0x57 0xCD 0x40 0x65 0x63 0x59 0x47 0xBD
Configuration last modified by 0.0.0.0 at 0-0-00 00:00:00
```

Notice that you do not see the VTP domain name that you set up on DLS1. Because no trunks are set up between the switches, they have not started to distribute any VLAN information. There is no IP address (0.0.0.0) or time listed for the last configuration modification.

Step 6: Configure trunking.

The **show interfaces switchport** command lists the configured mode of each port in detail. The following partial sample output is for a 2960 switch on Fa0/7.

```
ALS1# show interfaces fastEthernet 0/7 switchport
Name: Fa0/7
Switchport: Enabled
Administrative Mode: dynamic auto
Operational Mode: static access
Administrative Trunking Encapsulation: dot1q
Operational Trunking Encapsulation: native
Negotiation of Trunking: On
Access Mode VLAN: 1 (default)
Trunking Native Mode VLAN: 1 (default)
Administrative Native VLAN tagging: enabled
Voice VLAN: none
Administrative private-vlan host-association: none
Administrative private-vlan mapping: none
Administrative private-vlan trunk native VLAN: none
Administrative private-vlan trunk Native VLAN tagging: enabled
Administrative private-vlan trunk encapsulation: dot1q
Administrative private-vlan trunk normal VLANs: none
Administrative private-vlan trunk private VLANs: none
```

```
Operational private-vlan: none
Trunking VLANs Enabled: ALL
Pruning VLANs Enabled: 2-1001
Capture Mode Disabled
Capture VLANs Allowed: ALL

Protected: false
Unknown unicast blocked: disabled
Unknown multicast blocked: disabled
Appliance trust: none
```

Ports on the 2960 and 3560 switches are set to dynamic auto by default. This means that they are willing to negotiate a trunk with the neighbor; however, if both sides are set to dynamic auto, the link will remain in access mode. This can be done by configuring one end of the trunk using the **switchport mode trunk** command. On the 3560 switches, you also need to configure the trunk encapsulation with the **switchport trunk encapsulation** command. The 3560 switch can use either Inter-Switch Link (ISL) or 802.1Q encapsulation, whereas the 2960 switch only supports 802.1Q.

Refer to the lab diagram for which ports to set up as trunks and the type of encapsulation to use.

Configure only the interfaces on DLS1 and ALS1 with the **switchport mode trunk** command, and leave DLS2 and ALS2 as the default port types for Fast Ethernet interfaces 0/9–0/12. Fast Ethernet 0/7 and 0/8 of DLS2 also need to be configured with the **switchport mode trunk** command for the trunks connecting DLS2 and ALS2.

The 2960 and 3560 switches have a **range** command that you can use to designate multiple individual ports or a continuous range of ports for an operation. Use the **interface range** command to configure all trunk ports at once for trunking.

The following is a sample configuration for the 802.1Q and ISL trunk ports on DLS1.

```
DLS1(config)# interface range fastEthernet 0/7 - 10
DLS1(config-if-range)# switchport trunk encapsulation dot1q
DLS1(config-if-range)# switchport mode trunk

DLS1(config)# interface range fastEthernet 0/11 - 12
DLS1(config-if-range)# switchport trunk encapsulation isl
DLS1(config-if-range)# switchport mode trunk
```

The following is a sample configuration for the trunk ports on ALS1.

```
ALS1(config)# interface range fastEthernet 0/7 - 12
ALS1(config-if)# switchport mode trunk
```

The following is a sample configuration for the trunk ports on DLS2.

```
DLS2(config)# interface range fastEthernet 0/7 - 8
DLS2(config-if-range)# switchport trunk encapsulation dot1q
DLS2(config-if-range)# switchport mode trunk
```

Note: This lab uses dynamic trunking protocol (DTP) to negotiate trunking, which can lead to security issues. In general, when configuring trunks, it is a good practice to deactivate DTP using the **switchport nonegotiate** command and configure all trunks statically.

Step 7: Verify trunk configuration.

Use the show interfaces fastEthernet 0/7 switchport command on ALS2.

```
ALS2# show interfaces fastEthernet 0/7 switchport
Name: Fa0/7
Switchport: Enabled
Administrative Mode: dynamic auto
Operational Mode: trunk
Administrative Trunking Encapsulation: dot1q
Operational Trunking Encapsulation: dot1q
Negotiation of Trunking: On
Access Mode VLAN: 1 (default)
Trunking Native Mode VLAN: 1 (default)
Administrative Native VLAN tagging: enabled
Voice VLAN: none
Administrative private-vlan host-association: none
Administrative private-vlan mapping: none
Administrative private-vlan trunk native VLAN: none
Administrative private-vlan trunk Native VLAN tagging: enabled
Administrative private-vlan trunk encapsulation: dot1q
Administrative private-vlan trunk normal VLANs: none
Administrative private-vlan trunk private VLANs: none
Operational private-vlan: none
Trunking VLANs Enabled: ALL
Pruning VLANs Enabled: 2-1001
Capture Mode Disabled
Capture VLANs Allowed: ALL

Protected: false
Unknown unicast blocked: disabled
Unknown multicast blocked: disabled
Appliance trust: none
```

Notice that administrative mode on Fa0/7 is still the default dynamic auto. Fa0/7 on ALS2 is operating as a trunk, because port Fa0/7 of DLS2 was configured using the switchport mode trunk command. Once this command was issued, trunking was negotiated between the two switch ports.

Use the **show interfaces trunk** command on DLS1.

```
DLS1# show interfaces trunk
```

Port	Mode	Encapsulation	Status	Native vlan
Fa0/7	on	802.1q	trunking	1
Fa0/8	on	802.1q	trunking	1
Fa0/9	on	802.1q	trunking	1
Fa0/10	on	802.1q	trunking	1
Fa0/11	on	isl	trunking	1
Fa0/12	on	isl	trunking	1

Port	Vlans allowed on trunk
Fa0/7	1-4094
Fa0/8	1-4094
Fa0/9	1-4094
Fa0/10	1-4094

```
Fa0/11          1-4094
Fa0/12          1-4094


Port            Vlans allowed and active in management domain
Fa0/7           1
Fa0/8           1
Fa0/9           1
Fa0/10          1
Fa0/11          1


Port            Vlans allowed and active in management domain
Fa0/12          1


Port            Vlans in spanning tree forwarding state and not pruned
Fa0/7           1
Fa0/8           1
Fa0/9           1
Fa0/10          1
Fa0/11          1
Fa0/12          none
```

Note: By default, all VLANs are allowed on all trunks. You can explicitly control which VLANs are allowed on a trunk by using the **switchport trunk allowed vlan** *vlan-id* command on the interface at each end of the trunk. In addition, you can specify a native VLAN other than the default VLAN 1, using the **switchport trunk native vlan** *vlan-id* command. These two measures can help reduce the possibility of VLAN attacks.

Use the **show interfaces trunk** command on DLS2.

```
DLS2# show interfaces trunk
```

Port	Mode	Encapsulation	Status	Native vlan
Fa0/7	on	802.1q	trunking	1
Fa0/8	on	802.1q	trunking	1
Fa0/9	auto	n-802.1q	trunking	1
Fa0/10	auto	n-802.1q	trunking	1
Fa0/11	auto	n-isl	trunking	1
Fa0/12	auto	n-isl	trunking	1

```
Port            Vlans allowed on trunk
Fa0/7           1-4094
Fa0/8           1-4094
Fa0/9           1-4094
Fa0/10          1-4094
Fa0/11          1-4094
Fa0/12          1-4094


Port            Vlans allowed and active in management domain
Fa0/7           1
Fa0/8           1
Fa0/9           1
Fa0/10          1
Fa0/11          1
```

```
Port          Vlans allowed and active in management domain
Fa0/12        1

Port          Vlans in spanning tree forwarding state and not pruned
Fa0/7         1
Fa0/8         1
Fa0/9         1
Fa0/10        1
Fa0/11        1
Fa0/12        1
```

Notice the highlighted portion of the above output from DLS2 where it indicates that these ports became trunks by negotiation. For example, port Fa0/9 mode is Auto and encapsulation is n-802.1q. The "n" indicates the 802.1q encapsulation was negotiated. The connected ports of the respective switches were configured using the **switchport mode trunk** command.

Step 8: Configure access ports.

A port on the 2960 switch can operate in one of three modes, and a port on the 3560 switch can operate in one of five modes. Use the **switchport mode ?** command for interface Fast Ethernet 0/6 in interface configuration mode to view the modes.

The following command output is for a 2960 switch.

```
ALS1(config)# interface fastEthernet 0/6
ALS1#(config-if)# switchport mode ?
  access   Set trunking mode to ACCESS unconditionally
  dynamic  Set trunking mode to dynamically negotiate access or trunk mode
  trunk    Set trunking mode to TRUNK unconditionally
```

The following command output is for a 3560 switch.

```
DLS1(config)# interface fastEthernet 0/6
DLS1(config-if)# switchport mode ?
  access        Set trunking mode to ACCESS unconditionally
  dot1q-tunnel  set trunking mode to TUNNEL unconditionally
  dynamic       Set trunking mode to dynamically negotiate access or trunk
mode
  private-vlan  Set the mode to private-vlan host or promiscuous
  trunk         Set trunking mode to TRUNK unconditionally
```

The Fast Ethernet ports connected to the hosts on the network can be set up as static access because they are not to be used as trunk ports. Use the **switchport mode access** command to set the access mode on the Fast Ethernet 0/6 port on all four switches in the pod.

The following is a sample configuration for the access port on ALS1.

```
ALS1(config)# interface fastEthernet 0/6
ALS1(config-if)# switchport mode access
```

Use the **show interfaces** command for Fast Ethernet 0/6 to verify the configuration.

The following command is for a 3560 switch.

```
DLS1# show interfaces fastEthernet 0/6 switchport
Name: Fa0/6
```

```
Switchport: Enabled
Administrative Mode: static access
Operational Mode: down
Administrative Trunking Encapsulation: negotiate
Negotiation of Trunking: Off
Access Mode VLAN: 1 (default)
Trunking Native Mode VLAN: 1 (default)
Administrative Native VLAN tagging: enabled
Voice VLAN: none
Administrative private-vlan host-association: none
Administrative private-vlan mapping: none
Administrative private-vlan trunk native VLAN: none
Administrative private-vlan trunk Native VLAN tagging: enabled
Administrative private-vlan trunk encapsulation: dot1q
Administrative private-vlan trunk normal VLANs: none
Administrative private-vlan trunk private VLANs: none
Operational private-vlan: none
Trunking VLANs Enabled: ALL
Pruning VLANs Enabled: 2-1001
Capture Mode Disabled
Capture VLANs Allowed: ALL

Protected: false
Unknown unicast blocked: disabled
Unknown multicast blocked: disabled
Appliance trust: none
```

Note that administrative mode has now changed to static access and that trunking negotiation is off. The Fast Ethernet 0/6 ports on all four switches are now statically set to connect to a host device.

Step 9: Verify VTP configuration.

Before configuring the VLANs, verify the VTP configuration within the domain by using the **show vtp status** command on ALS1 and ALS2.

The following sample output is from ALS1.

```
ALS1# show vtp status
VTP Version                       : running VTP2
Configuration Revision       : 1
Maximum VLANs supported locally : 255
Number of existing VLANs      : 5
VTP Operating Mode            : Client
VTP Domain Name               : SWLAB
VTP Pruning Mode              : Disabled
VTP V2 Mode                   : Enabled
VTP Traps Generation          : Disabled
MD5 digest                    : 0xD1 0xC0 0x36 0xF9 0xC4 0x3E 0x73 0xA0
Configuration last modified by 10.1.1.101 at 3-1-93 00:12:43
```

The following sample output is from ALS2.

```
ALS2# show vtp status
VTP Version                       : running VTP2
Configuration Revision       : 1
```

```
Maximum VLANs supported locally : 255
Number of existing VLANs        : 5
VTP Operating Mode              : Client
VTP Domain Name                 : SWLAB
VTP Pruning Mode                : Disabled
VTP V2 Mode                     : Enabled
VTP Traps Generation            : Disabled
MD5 digest                      : 0xD1 0xC0 0x36 0xF9 0xC4 0x3E 0x73 0xA0
Configuration last modified by 10.1.1.101 at 3-1-93 00:12:43
```

At this point, all switches in the lab are in VTP domain SWLAB and have five existing VLANs. All are running VTP version 2. DLS1 and DLS2 are configured as VTP servers, and ALS1 and ALS2 are configured as clients.

Note: You can limit the VLAN traffic passed between switches using VTP pruning. Pruning increases available bandwidth by restricting flooded traffic to those trunk links that the traffic must use to access the destination devices. You can enable VTP pruning on a switch in VTP server mode using the **vtp pruning** command. For example, if a VLAN is not defined on access switch ALS1 but is defined on distribution switches DLS1 and DLS2, the VLAN will be pruned from the trunk links between ALS1 and the distribution switches but not from the link between the two distribution switches.

Step 10: Configure VLANs by assigning port membership.

VLANs can be configured on a switch in different ways, depending on the type of switch used and the Cisco IOS version.

An older way to configure VLANs is to use the VLAN database. This method is being deprecated and is no longer recommended. However, the VLAN database is still accessible for those who choose to use it. For example, the following command is for a 3560 switch.

```
DLS1# vlan database
% Warning: It is recommended to configure VLAN from config mode,
    as VLAN database mode is being deprecated. Please consult user
    documentation for configuring VTP/VLAN in config mode.
```

A more current method to create a VLAN is to assign a port to a VLAN that does not yet exist. If the switch is in VTP Server or Transparent mode, it automatically creates the VLAN to the port that it has been assigned to.

VLAN 1 is the management VLAN by default. By default, all ports are set to dynamic mode and their access VLAN is set to 1. There is no need to create a VLAN 1, assign ports to it, or to set the mode of each port.

According to the lab diagram, VLANs 100, 110, and 120 must be created, and port 6 must be assigned to each VLAN. You will create VLANs 100 and 110 on the distribution switches using the port assignment method. You will create VLAN 120 for the access switches using global configuration commands and then assign ports to those VLANs.

Use the **switchport access vlan** command to assign port 6 on DLS1 and DLS2, according to the diagram. Port Fast Ethernet 0/6 of DLS1 will be assigned to VLAN 100, and Fast Ethernet 0/6 on DLS2 will be assigned to VLAN 110.

The following command is for the 3560 switches.

```
DLS1(config)# interface FastEthernet 0/6
DLS1(config-if-range)# switchport access vlan 100
% Access VLAN does not exist. Creating vlan 100
```

VLAN 100 was created at the same time port 6 was assigned to it.

Configure DLS2 in the manner similar to DLS1, but this time use VLAN 110.

```
DLS2(config)# interface FastEthernet 0/6
DLS2(config-if-range)# switchport access vlan 110
% Access VLAN does not exist. Creating vlan 110
```

Issue the **show vlan** command on DLS1 to verify that VLANs 100 and 110 have been created. The output should be similar to the following output.

```
DLS1# show vlan
```

VLAN	Name	Status	Ports
1	default	active	Fa0/1, Fa0/2, Fa0/3, Fa0/4
			Fa0/5, Fa0/13, Fa0/14
			Fa0/15, Fa0/16, Fa0/17, Fa0/18
			Fa0/19, Fa0/20, Fa0/21, Fa0/22
			Fa0/23, Fa0/24, Gi0/1, Gi0/2
100	VLAN0100	active	Fa0/6
110	VLAN0110	active	1002 fddi-default
act/unsup			
1003	token-ring-default	act/unsup	
1004	fddinet-default	act/unsup	
1005	trnet-default	act/unsup	

VLAN	Type	SAID	MTU	Parent	RingNo	BridgeNo	Stp	BrdgMode	Trans1	Trans2
1	enet	100001	1500	–	–	–	–	–	0	0
100	enet	100100	1500	–	–	–	–	–	0	0
110	enet	100110	1500	–	–	–	–	–	0	0
1002	fddi	101002	1500	–	–	–	–	–	0	0

VLAN	Type	SAID	MTU	Parent	RingNo	BridgeNo	Stp	BrdgMode	Trans1	Trans2
1003	tr	101003	1500	–	–	–	–	–	0	0
1004	fdnet	101004	1500	–	–	–	ieee	–	0	0
1005	trnet	101005	1500	–	–	–	ibm	–	0	0

```
Remote SPAN VLANs
------------------------------------------------------------------------


Primary Secondary Type              Ports
------- --------- ----------------- ------------------------------------------
```

Because VLAN 100 and 110 were not named, the switch automatically assigns default names, which are VLAN0100 and VLAN0110.

Note that on DLS1, port Fa0/6 is active in VLAN 100. A **show vlan** command issued on DLS2 should show port Fa0/6 active in VLAN 110.

Step 11: Configure VLANs in configuration mode.

Another way of creating VLANs is to create them in configuration mode without assigning port membership.

You can create a VLAN in global configuration mode using the **vlan** command. Because ALS1 and ALS2 are configured for VTP client mode and it is not possible to create a VLAN when a switch is in client mode, you must create the VLAN on the switch that is acting as a server for the network. The VLAN then propagates to the other switches that are in client mode.

Issue the **vlan** command in global configuration mode on DLS1.

```
DLS1(config)# vlan 120
```

Ports still need to be assigned to VLAN 120. Port assignment to a VLAN is an interface configuration operation. Use the **switchport access vlan** command on Fast Ethernet 0/6 of ALS1 and ALS2 to configure ports for VLAN 120.

```
ALS1(config)# interface fastEthernet 0/6
ALS1(config-if)# switchport access vlan 120

ALS2(config)# interface fastEthernet 0/6
ALS2(config-if)# switchport access vlan 120
```

Use the **show vlan** command to verify the creation of VLAN 120, with port Fa0/6 assigned to it. The output should be similar to the following.

```
ALS1# show vlan
```

VLAN	Name	Status	Ports
1	default	active	Fa0/1, Fa0/2, Fa0/3, Fa0/4
			Fa0/5, Fa0/13, Fa0/14, Fa0/15
			Fa0/16, Fa0/17, Fa0/18, Fa0/19
			Fa0/20, Fa0/21, Fa0/22, Fa0/23
			Fa0/24, Gi0/1, Gi0/2
100	VLAN0100	active	
110	VLAN0110	active	
120	VLAN0120	active	Fa0/6
1002	fddi-default	act/unsup	
1003	token-ring-default	act/unsup	
1004	fddinet-default	act/unsup	
1005	trnet-default	act/unsup	

VLAN	Type	SAID	MTU	Parent	RingNo	BridgeNo	Stp	BrdgMode	Trans1	Trans2
1	enet	100001	1500	-	-	-	-	-	0	0
100	enet	100100	1500	-	-	-	-	-	0	0
110	enet	100110	1500	-	-	-	-	-	0	0
120	enet	100120	1500	-	-	-	-	-	0	0
1002	fddi	101002	1500	-	-	-	-	-	0	0

VLAN	Type	SAID	MTU	Parent	RingNo	BridgeNo	Stp	BrdgMode	Trans1	Trans2
1003	tr	101003	1500	-	-	-	-	srb	0	0
1004	fdnet	101004	1500	-	-	-	ieee	-	0	0
1005	trnet	101005	1500	-	-	-	ibm	-	0	0

```
Remote SPAN VLANs
-----------------------------------------------------------------------------


Primary Secondary Type              Ports
------- --------- ---------------- ----------------------------------------
```

Step 12: Change the VLAN names.

The VLANs have not been named yet. Naming VLANs can help network administrators identify the functionality of those VLANs. To add names, use the **name** command in VLAN configuration mode.

The following is a sample configuration for naming the three VLANs created in the domain.

```
DLS1(config)# vlan 100
DLS1(config-vlan)# name Server-Farm-1
DLS1(config-vlan)# exit
DLS1(config)# vlan 110
DLS1(config-vlan)# name Server-Farm-2
DLS1(config-vlan)# exit
DLS1(config)# vlan 120
DLS1(config-vlan)# name Net-Eng
DLS1(config-vlan)# exit
```

Use the **show vlan** command on DLS1 to verify that the new names have been added.

```
DLS1# show vlan
```

```
VLAN Name                             Status    Ports
---- -------------------------------- --------- -------------------------------
1    default                          active    Fa0/1, Fa0/2, Fa0/3, Fa0/4
                                                Fa0/5, Fa0/7, Fa0/8, Fa0/9
                                                Fa0/10, Fa0/11, Fa0/12, Fa0/13
                                                Fa0/14, Fa0/15, Fa0/16, Fa0/17
                                                Fa0/18, Fa0/19, Fa0/20, Fa0/21
                                                Fa0/22, Fa0/23, Fa0/24, Gi0/1
                                                Gi0/2
100  Server-Farm-1                    active    Fa0/6
110  Server-Farm-2                    active
120  Net-Eng                          active
1002 fddi-default                     act/unsup
1003 token-ring-default               act/unsup
1004 fddinet-default                  act/unsup
1005 trnet-default                    act/unsup
```

VLAN	Type	SAID	MTU	Parent	RingNo	BridgeNo	Stp	BrdgMode	Trans1	Trans2
1	enet	100001	1500	–	–	–	–	–	0	0
100	enet	100100	1500	–	–	–	–	–	0	0
110	enet	100110	1500	–	–	–	–	–	0	0

VLAN	Type	SAID	MTU	Parent	RingNo	BridgeNo	Stp	BrdgMode	Trans1	Trans2

```
120   enet  100120     1500  -      -     -         -     -       0      0
1002  fddi  101002     1500  -      -     -         -     -       0      0
1003  tr    101003     1500  -      -     -         -     -       0      0
1004  fdnet 101004     1500  -      -     -         ieee  -       0      0
1005  trnet 101005     1500  -      -     -         ibm   -       0      0


Remote SPAN VLANs
------------------------------------------------------------------------



Primary Secondary Type              Ports
------- --------- ----------------- ------------------------------------
```

Step 13: Change the VLAN status to deactivate ports.

The default status of VLAN 1 and user-created VLANs is "active". A VLAN can be made locally inactive in the VLAN configuration mode by entering the command **shutdown** for the particular VLAN (does not apply to an SVI). This will cause all ports on a switch in a particular VLAN to stop transmitting data. Shutting down the VLAN on a switch does not influence its state on other switches in a VTP domain.

Shutdown the Net-Eng VLAN 120 on ALS1, wait a few moments, exit vlan configuration mode and then issue the **show vlan brief** command. The status should change to "act/lshut".

```
ALS1(config)# vlan 120
ALS1(config-vlan)# shutdown

ALS1# show vlan brief

VLAN Name                             Status    Ports
---- -------------------------------- --------- ----------------------------
--
1    default                          active    Fa0/1, Fa0/2, Fa0/3, Fa0/4
                                                Fa0/5, Fa0/7, Fa0/8, Fa0/9
                                                Fa0/10, Fa0/11, Fa0/12, Fa0/13
                                                Fa0/14, Fa0/15, Fa0/16, Fa0/17
                                                Fa0/18, Fa0/19, Fa0/20, Fa0/21
                                                Fa0/22, Fa0/23, Fa0/24, Gi0/1
                                                Gi0/2
100  Server-Farm-1                    active    Fa0/6
110  Server-Farm-2                    active
120  Net-Eng                          act/lshut
1002 fddi-default                     act/unsup
1003 token-ring-default               act/unsup
1004 fddinet-default                  act/unsup
1005 trnet-default                    act/unsup
```

Reactivate all ports in ALS1 Net-Eng VLAN 120 using the **no shutdown** command in VLAN configuration mode..

```
ALS1(config)# vlan 120
ALS1(config-vlan)# no shutdown
```

You can also put a VLAN into "suspend" status. The "suspend" state is configured in the VLAN configuration mode using the command state suspend. Suspending a VLAN causes all ports in that VLAN throughout the VTP domain to stop transferring data.

Suspend Net-Eng VLAN 120 on ALS1, wait a few moments, exit VLAN configuration mode and then issue the **show vlan brief** command. The status should change to "suspended".

```
ALS1(config)# vlan 120
ALS1(config-vlan)# state suspend

ALS1# show vlan brief

VLAN Name                          Status    Ports
---- ------------------------------ --------- ------------------------------
--
1    default                       active    Fa0/1, Fa0/2, Fa0/3, Fa0/4
                                             Fa0/5, Fa0/7, Fa0/8, Fa0/9
                                             Fa0/10, Fa0/11, Fa0/12, Fa0/13
                                             Fa0/14, Fa0/15, Fa0/16, Fa0/17
                                             Fa0/18, Fa0/19, Fa0/20, Fa0/21
                                             Fa0/22, Fa0/23, Fa0/24, Gi0/1
                                             Gi0/2
100  Server-Farm-1                 active    Fa0/6
110  Server-Farm-2                 active
120  Net-Eng                       suspended
1002 fddi-default                  act/unsup
1003 token-ring-default            act/unsup
1004 fddinet-default               act/unsup
1005 trnet-default                 act/unsup
```

Reactivate VLAN 120 using the **state active** command in VLAN configuration mode..

```
ALS1(config)# vlan 120
ALS1(config-vlan)# state active
```

Note: The suspend state is advertised by VTP while the lshut state is not. The **state suspend** command can be issued on any switch in the VTP domain. It does not have to be issued on the VTP server.

Both options can be used to temporarily take a particular VLAN out of operation which can be useful in certain scenarios - especially for guests, infrequently used conference rooms and similar deployments.

Step 14: Prepare for the next lab.

Prepare for the next lab by removing all the VLAN information and configurations. The VLAN database and startup configuration need to be deleted.

Note: Traffic between VLANs must be routed. Inter-VLAN routing will be covered in a later lab.

Lab 2-2, Configuring EtherChannel

Topology

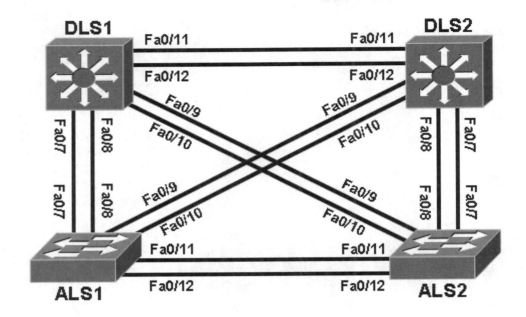

Objective

- Configure EtherChannel.

Background

Four switches have just been installed. The distribution layer switches are Catalyst 3560 switches, and the access layer switches are Catalyst 2960 switches. There are redundant uplinks between the access layer and distribution layer. Usually, only one of these links could be used; otherwise, a bridging loop might occur. However, using only one link utilizes only half of the available bandwidth. EtherChannel allows up to eight redundant links to be bundled together into one logical link. In this lab, you configure Port Aggregation Protocol (PAgP), a Cisco EtherChannel protocol, and Link Aggregation Control Protocol (LACP), an IEEE 802.3ad open standard version of EtherChannel.

Note: This lab uses Cisco WS-C2960-24TT-L switches with the Cisco IOS image c2960-lanbasek9-mz.122-46.SE.bin, and Catalyst 3560-24PS with the Cisco IOS image c3560-advipservicesk9-mz.122-46. SE.bin. You can use other switches (such as a 2950 or 3550) and Cisco IOS Software versions if they have comparable capabilities and features. Depending on the switch model and Cisco IOS Software version, the commands available and output produced might vary from what is shown in this lab.

Required Resources

- 2 switches (Cisco 2960 with the Cisco IOS Release 12.2(46)SE C2960-LANBASEK9-M image or comparable)
- 2 switches (Cisco 3560 with the Cisco IOS Release 12.2(46)SE C3560- ADVIPSERVICESK9-M image or comparable)
- Ethernet and console cables

Step 1: Prepare the switches for the lab.

Delete vlan.dat, erase the startup configuration, and reload all your switches. Refer to Lab 1-1, "Clearing a Switch," and Lab 1-2, "Clearing a Switch Connected to a Larger Network."

Step 2: Configure basic switch parameters.

a. Assign each switch a hostname according to the topology diagram.

b. Configure ports Fa0/7 through Fa0/12 as trunks. On the 3560 switches, you must first set the trunk encapsulation to 802.1Q. On the 2960s, only dot1q is supported, therefore the **switchport trunk encapsulation** command is unavailable, but the mode still needs to be changed to trunk.

Note: If the ports are configured with dynamic auto mode and you do not set the mode of the ports to trunk, the links do not form trunks and remain access ports. The default mode on a 3560 or 2960 switch is dynamic auto. The default mode on a 3550 or 2950 switch is dynamic desirable.

DLS1 example:

```
DLS1# configure terminal
Enter configuration commands, one per line.  End with CNTL/Z.
DLS1(config)# interface range fastEthernet 0/7 - 12
DLS1(config-if-range)# switchport trunk encapsulation dot1q
DLS1(config-if-range)# switchport mode trunk
```

Step 3: Configure an EtherChannel with Cisco PAgP.

Note: When configuring EtherChannels, it is a recommended best practice to shutdown the physical ports being grouped on both devices before configuring them into channel groups. Otherwise, the EtherChannel Misconfig Guard may place these ports into err-disabled state. The ports and port channel can be re-enabled after the EtherChannel is configured.

a. The first EtherChannel created for this lab aggregates ports Fa0/11 and Fa0/12 between ALS1 and ALS2. Make sure that you have a trunk link active for those two links with the **show interfaces trunk** command.

```
ALS1# show interfaces trunk
```

Port	Mode	Encapsulation	Status	Native vlan
Fa0/7	on	802.1q	trunking	1
Fa0/8	on	802.1q	trunking	1
Fa0/9	on	802.1q	trunking	1
Fa0/10	on	802.1q	trunking	1
Fa0/11	on	802.1q	trunking	1
Fa0/12	on	802.1q	trunking	1

```
<output omitted>
```

b. On both switches, add ports Fa0/11 and Fa0/12 to port channel 1 with the **channel-group 1 mode desirable** command. The **mode desirable** option indicates that you want the switch to actively negotiate to form a PAgP link.

```
ALS1(config)# interface range fastEthernet 0/11 - 12
ALS1(config-if-range)# channel-group 1 mode desirable
Creating a port-channel interface Port-channel 1
```

c. Configure the logical interface to become a trunk by first entering the **interface port-channel** *number* command and then the **switchport mode trunk** command. Add this configuration to both switches.

```
ALS1(config)# interface port-channel 1
ALS1(config-if)# switchport mode trunk
```

d. Verify that EtherChannel is working by issuing the **show etherchannel summary** command on both switches. This command displays the type of EtherChannel, the ports utilized, and port states.

```
ALS1# show etherchannel summary
Flags:  D - down         P - in port-channel
        I - stand-alone  s - suspended
        H - Hot-standby (LACP only)
        R - Layer3       S - Layer2
        U - in use       f - failed to allocate aggregator
        u - unsuitable for bundling
        w - waiting to be aggregated
        d - default port


Number of channel-groups in use: 1
Number of aggregators:           1

Group  Port-channel  Protocol    Ports
------+-------------+-----------+-----------------------------------------
1      Po1(SU)       PAgP        Fa0/11(P)    Fa0/12(P)


ALS2# show etherchannel summary
Flags:  D - down         P - in port-channel
        I - stand-alone  s - suspended
        H - Hot-standby (LACP only)
        R - Layer3       S - Layer2
        U - in use       f - failed to allocate aggregator
        u - unsuitable for bundling
        w - waiting to be aggregated
        d - default port


Number of channel-groups in use: 1
Number of aggregators:           1

Group  Port-channel  Protocol    Ports
------+-------------+-----------+-----------------------------------------
1      Po1(SU)       PAgP        Fa0/11(P)    Fa0/12(P)
```

e. If the EtherChannel does not come up, you might want to try "flapping" the physical interfaces on both ends of the EtherChannel. This involves using the **shut** command on those interfaces, followed by a **no shut** command a few seconds later.

The **show interfaces trunk** and **show spanning-tree** commands also show the port channel as one logical link.

```
ALS1# show interfaces trunk

Port       Mode       Encapsulation  Status       Native vlan
Fa0/7      on         802.1q         trunking     1
Fa0/8      on         802.1q         trunking     1
Fa0/9      on         802.1q         trunking     1
```

```
Fa0/10          on              802.1q          trunking        1
Po1             on              802.1q          trunking        1
```

`<output omitted>`

```
ALS1# show spanning-tree
VLAN0001
  Spanning tree enabled protocol ieee
  Root ID    Priority    32769
             Address     0017.5a53.a380
             Cost        19
             Port        9 (FastEthernet0/9)
             Hello Time   2 sec  Max Age 20 sec  Forward Delay 15 sec

  Bridge ID  Priority    32769  (priority 32768 sys-id-ext 1)
             Address     001d.4635.0c80
             Hello Time   2 sec  Max Age 20 sec  Forward Delay 15 sec
             Aging Time 300

Interface          Role Sts Cost      Prio.Nbr Type
------------------ ---- --- --------- -------- ----------------------------

Fa0/7              Altn BLK 19        128.7    P2p
Fa0/8              Altn BLK 19        128.8    P2p
Fa0/9              Root FWD 19        128.9    P2p
Fa0/10             Altn BLK 19        128.10   P2p
Po1                Desg FWD 12        128.56   P2p
```

Step 4: Configure an 802.3ad LACP EtherChannel.

a. In 2000, the IEEE passed 802.3ad, which is an open standard version of EtherChannel. Using the previous commands, configure the link between DLS1 and ALS1 on ports Fa0/7 and Fa0/8 as an LACP EtherChannel. You must use a different port channel number on ALS1 than 1, because you already used that in the previous step. To configure a port channel as LACP, use the interface-level command **channel-group** *number* **mode active**. Active mode indicates that the switch actively tries to negotiate that link as LACP, as opposed to PAgP.

```
ALS1(config)# interface range fastEthernet 0/7 - 8
ALS1(config-if-range)# channel-group 2 mode active
Creating a port-channel interface Port-channel 2

ALS1(config-if-range)# interface port-channel 2
ALS1(config-if)# switchport mode trunk
```

b. Apply a similar configuration on DLS1. Verify the configuration with the **show etherchannel summary** command.

```
ALS1# show etherchannel summary
Flags:  D - down         P - in port-channel
        I - stand-alone  s - suspended
        H - Hot-standby (LACP only)
        R - Layer3       S - Layer2
        U - in use       f - failed to allocate aggregator
        u - unsuitable for bundling
```

```
            w - waiting to be aggregated
            d - default port


Number of channel-groups in use: 2
Number of aggregators:            2

Group  Port-channel  Protocol    Ports
------+-------------+----------+-------------------------------------
1      Po1(SU)       PAgP        Fa0/11(P)   Fa0/12(P)
2      Po2(SU)       LACP        Fa0/7(P)    Fa0/8(P)
```

Step 5: Configure a Layer 3 EtherChannel.

In the previous steps, you configured EtherChannels as Layer 2 trunk connections between switches. You can also configure EtherChannels as Layer 3 (routed) connections on switches that support routed ports. Because DLS1 and DLS2 are both multilayer switches, they can support routed ports.

a. Use the **no switchport** command on Fa0/11 and Fa0/12 to make them Layer 3 ports, and then add them to the channel group with the **channel-group** *number* **mode desirable** command. On the logical interface, issue the **no switchport** command to make it a Layer 3 port. Add the IP address 10.0.0.1 for DLS1 and 10.0.0.2 for DLS2. Configure both with a /24 subnet mask.

```
DLS1(config)# interface range fastEthernet 0/11 - 12
DLS1(config-if-range)# no switchport
DLS1(config-if-range)# channel-group 3 mode desirable
Creating a port-channel interface Port-channel 3
DLS1(config-if-range)# interface port-channel 3
DLS1(config-if)# no switchport
DLS1(config-if)# ip address 10.0.0.1 255.255.255.0
```

b. Verify that you have Layer 3 connectivity by attempting to ping the other side of the link.

```
DLS1# ping 10.0.0.2

Type escape sequence to abort.
Sending 5, 100-byte ICMP Echos to 10.0.0.2, timeout is 2 seconds:
!!!!!
Success rate is 100 percent (5/5), round-trip min/avg/max = 1/1/1 ms
```

c. If you look at the output of the **show etherchannel summary** command, you see that it lists the port channel as a routed port, not a switched port. The RU in parentheses next to the name means routed and up, as opposed to switched and up (SU).

```
DLS1# show etherchannel summary
Flags:  D - down         P - in port-channel
        I - stand-alone  s - suspended
        H - Hot-standby (LACP only)
        R - Layer3       S - Layer2
        U - in use       f - failed to allocate aggregator
        u - unsuitable for bundling
        w - waiting to be aggregated
        d - default port


Number of channel-groups in use: 2
```

```
Number of aggregators:              2

Group   Port-channel   Protocol     Ports
------+-------------+-----------+----------------------------------------
2        Po2(SU)        LACP        Fa0/7(P)      Fa0/8(P)
3        Po3(RU)        PAgP        Fa0/11(P)     Fa0/12(P)
```

Step 6: Configure load balancing.

The switches can use different methods to load-balance traffic going through a port channel. The available methods as well as the default method used varies by hardware platform. By default, Cisco Catalyst 3560 and Catalyst 2960 switches load-balance using the source MAC address.

a. You can view the current load-balancing configuration with the **show etherchannel load-balance** command.

```
DLS1# show etherchannel load-balance
EtherChannel Load-Balancing Operational State (src-mac):
Non-IP: Source MAC address
   IPv4: Source MAC address
   IPv6: Source IP address
```

Other methods of load balancing are based on the destination MAC address, both source and destination MAC addresses, source IP address, destination IP address, and both source and destination IP addresses. Some older platforms, such as the Cisco Catalyst 2950 and Catalyst 3550 switches, may not support all of these methods.

b. For this scenario, configure ALS1 to load-balance by both source and destination MAC addresses using the global configuration command **port-channel load-balance** *method*, where the method is **src-dst-mac**.

```
ALS1(config)# port-channel load-balance src-dst-mac
```

c. Verify the configuration with the **show etherchannel load-balance** command.

```
ALS1# show etherchannel load-balance
EtherChannel Load-Balancing Operational State (src-dst-mac):
Non-IP: Source XOR Destination MAC address
   IPv4: Source XOR Destination MAC address
   IPv6: Source XOR Destination IP address
```

Challenge

The topology still has redundant links that you can aggregate. Experiment with the other port channel modes using the question mark on the interface-level command **channel-group** *number* **mode ?**. Look at the descriptions and implement some port channels in different ways. If The port mode is set to desirable, auto, active or passive (when PAgP or LACP are used), the command **channel-protocol** can be used. It cannot be used with **channel-group** *number* **mode on** command. The "on" mode statically sets the EtherChannel protocol without negotiation.

Chapter 3 Implementing Spanning Tree

Lab 3-1, Spanning Tree Protocol (STP) Default Behavior

Topology

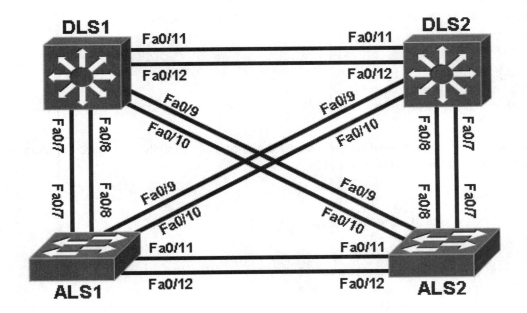

Objective

- Observe the default behavior of STP.

Background

Four switches have just been installed. The distribution layer switches are Catalyst 3560s, and the access layer switches are Catalyst 2960s. There are redundant uplinks between the access layer and distribution layer. Because of the possibility of bridging loops, spanning tree logically removes any redundant links. In this lab, you will observe what spanning tree does and why.

Note: This lab uses Cisco WS-C2960-24TT-L switches with the Cisco IOS image c2960-lanbasek9-mz.122-46.SE.bin and Catalyst 3560-24PS switches with the Cisco IOS image c3560-advipservicesk9-mz.122-46.SE.bin. Other switches (such as a 2950 or 3550), and Cisco IOS Software versions can be used if they have comparable capabilities and features. Depending on the switch model and Cisco IOS Software version, the commands available and output produced might vary from what is shown in this lab.

Required Resources

- 2 switches (Cisco 2960 with the Cisco IOS Release 12.2(46)SE C2960-LANBASEK9-M image or comparable)
- 2 switches (Cisco 3560 with the Cisco IOS Release 12.2(46)SE C3560-ADVIPSERVICESK9-M image or comparable)

- Ethernet and console cables

Step 1: Prepare the switches for the lab.

Refer to Lab 1-1 Clearing a Switch and Lab 1-2 Clearing a Switch Connected to a Larger Network to prepare all four switches for this lab. Cable the equipment as shown. If you are accessing your equipment remotely, ask your instructor for instructions on how to do this.

Step 2: Configure basic switch parameters.

a. Configure the four switches as shown in the diagram with a hostname.

ALS1 example:

```
Switch> enable
Switch# configure terminal
Switch(config)# hostname ALS1
```

b. Optionally, configure an enable secret password and console security. Configure the console line with **logging synchronous** and no timeout.

ALS1 example:

```
ALS1(config)# enable secret class
ALS1(config)# line console 0
ALS1(config-line)# logging synchronous
ALS1(config-line)# exec-timeout 0 0
ALS1(config-line)# password cisco
ALS1(config-line)# login
```

Note: After the cables are connected spanning tree is initiated and the switch detects the redundant links.

By default, spanning tree runs on every port. When a new link becomes active, the port goes through the IEEE 802.1D spanning tree listening and learning states before transitioning to forwarding state. During this period, the switch discovers if it is connected to another switch or an end-user device.

One of the switches is elected as the root bridge for the tree. Then an agreement is established as to which links to keep active and which links to logically remove from the spanning tree (disable) if multiple links exist.

What type of frame does STP use to communicate with other switches?

_____

The results in this lab will vary. Spanning tree operation is based on the MAC addresses of the switches.

c. Observe the LEDs on the switch to check the status of the link. For access ports a bright green light indicates an active link. An amber light indicates an inactive link.

Step 3: Display default spanning tree information for all switches.

a. Verify IEEE 802.1D STP with the **show spanning-tree** command on DLS1.

Note: Your output may differ, based on the root bridge selected in your topology. The sample output below may also differ from those in your lab, because they were generated with a different set of switches.

```
DLS1# show spanning-tree

VLAN0001
  Spanning tree enabled protocol ieee
  Root ID    Priority    32769
             Address     000a.b8a9.d680
             Cost        19
             Port        13 (FastEthernet0/11)
             Hello Time   2 sec  Max Age 20 sec  Forward Delay 15 sec

  Bridge ID  Priority    32769  (priority 32768 sys-id-ext 1)
             Address     000a.b8b3.d780
             Hello Time   2 sec  Max Age 20 sec  Forward Delay 15 sec
             Aging Time 300

Interface        Role Sts Cost      Prio.Nbr Type
---------------- ---- --- --------- -------- --------------------------------
Fa0/7            Desg FWD 19        128.9    P2p
Fa0/8            Desg FWD 19        128.10   P2p
Fa0/9            Desg FWD 19        128.11   P2p
Fa0/10           Desg FWD 19        128.12   P2p
Fa0/11           Root FWD 19        128.13   P2p
Fa0/12           Altn BLK 19        128.14   P2p
```

b. Verify STP with the **show spanning-tree** command on DLS2.

```
DLS2# show spanning-tree

VLAN0001
  Spanning tree enabled protocol ieee
  Root ID    Priority    32769
             Address     000a.b8a9.d680
             This bridge is the root
             Hello Time   2 sec  Max Age 20 sec  Forward Delay 15 sec

  Bridge ID  Priority    32769  (priority 32768 sys-id-ext 1)
             Address     000a.b8a9.d680
             Hello Time   2 sec  Max Age 20 sec  Forward Delay 15 sec
             Aging Time 300

Interface        Role Sts Cost      Prio.Nbr Type
---------------- ---- --- --------- -------- --------------------------------
Fa0/7            Desg FWD 19        128.9    P2p
Fa0/8            Desg FWD 19        128.10   P2p
Fa0/9            Desg FWD 19        128.11   P2p
Fa0/10           Desg FWD 19        128.12   P2p
Fa0/11           Desg FWD 19        128.13   P2p
```

```
Fa0/12            Desg FWD 19         128.14    P2p
```

c. Verify STP with the **show spanning-tree** command on ALS1.

```
ALS1# show spanning-tree

VLAN0001
  Spanning tree enabled protocol ieee
  Root ID    Priority    32769
             Address     000a.b8a9.d680
             Cost        19
             Port        11 (FastEthernet0/9)
             Hello Time   2 sec  Max Age 20 sec  Forward Delay 15 sec

  Bridge ID  Priority    32769  (priority 32768 sys-id-ext 1)
             Address     0019.0635.5780
             Hello Time   2 sec  Max Age 20 sec  Forward Delay 15 sec
             Aging Time 300

Interface         Role Sts Cost      Prio.Nbr Type
---------------- ---- --- --------- -------- ------------------------------
Fa0/7             Altn BLK 19         128.9     P2p
Fa0/8             Altn BLK 19         128.10    P2p
Fa0/9             Root FWD 19         128.11    P2p
Fa0/10            Altn BLK 19         128.12    P2p
Fa0/11            Desg FWD 19         128.13    P2p
Fa0/12            Desg FWD 19         128.14    P2p

Fa0/11            Altn BLK 19         128.11    P2p
Fa0/12            Altn BLK 19         128.12    P2p·
```

d. Verify STP with the **show spanning-tree** command on ALS2.

```
ALS2# show spanning-tree

VLAN0001
  Spanning tree enabled protocol ieee
  Root ID    Priority    32769
             Address     000a.b8a9.d680
             Cost        19
             Port        9 (FastEthernet0/7)
             Hello Time   2 sec  Max Age 20 sec  Forward Delay 15 sec

  Bridge ID  Priority    32769  (priority 32768 sys-id-ext 1)
             Address     0019.068d.6980
             Hello Time   2 sec  Max Age 20 sec  Forward Delay 15 sec
             Aging Time 300

Interface         Role Sts Cost      Prio.Nbr Type
---------------- ---- --- --------- -------- ------------------------------
Fa0/7             Root FWD 19         128.9     P2p
Fa0/8             Altn BLK 19         128.10    P2p
Fa0/9             Altn BLK 19         128.11    P2p
Fa0/10            Altn BLK 19         128.12    P2p
```

```
Fa0/11              Altn BLK 19          128.13    P2p
Fa0/12              Altn BLK 19          128.14    P2p
```

Notice that between each pair of switches, at least one of the two ports is blocking. Blocking can occur on the access layer switch or the distribution layer switch. If all ports have their default setting, the higher interface number of the two ports will block.

A port is placed in the blocking state because the switch detects two links between the same switches. A bridging loop would result if one of the switches did not logically disable a redundant link.

e. Display the spanning tree information for DLS2 again.

```
DLS2# show spanning-tree

VLAN0001
  Spanning tree enabled protocol ieee
  Root ID    Priority    32769
             Address     000a.b8a9.d680
             This bridge is the root
             Hello Time   2 sec  Max Age 20 sec   Forward Delay 15 sec

  Bridge ID  Priority    32769   (priority 32768 sys-id-ext 1)
             Address     000a.b8a9.d680
             Hello Time   2 sec  Max Age 20 sec   Forward Delay 15 sec
             Aging Time 300

Interface         Role Sts Cost      Prio.Nbr Type
----------------  ---- --- --------- -------- ----------------------------
Fa0/7             Desg FWD 19        128.9    P2p
Fa0/8             Desg FWD 19        128.10   P2p
Fa0/9             Desg FWD 19        128.11   P2p
Fa0/10            Desg FWD 19        128.12   P2p
Fa0/11            Desg FWD 19        128.13   P2p
Fa0/12            Desg FWD 19        128.14   P2p
```

After reviewing the spanning tree output, answer the following questions.

Which switch is the root of the spanning tree?

_____

How can the root switch be identified?

_____

Why was that switch selected as the root?

_____

What caused one port to be in blocking state over another?

_____

_____

What caused one link to be blocked over another?

_____

_____

f.   Another useful STP command is **show spanning-tree root**. This command displays a summary listing of the VLANs defined, the Root (bridge) ID for each one, the Root Cost and the Root Port that the switch uses to reach the root bridge. In this lab the only active VLAN is default VLAN 1. Issue the **show spanning-tree root** command on ALS1. The output shows the priority and MAC address of DLS2 as the Root ID for VLAN 1. The Root Cost is 19 and ALS1 uses port Fa0/9 to reach DLS2.

```
ALS1# show spanning-tree root
```

		Root	Hello	Max	Fwd	
Vlan	Root ID	Cost	Time	Age	Dly	Root Port
---	---	---	---	---	---	---
VLAN0001	32769 0017.5a53.a380	19	2	20	15	Fa0/9

g.   Issue the **show spanning-tree root** command on DLS2. The output shows the priority and MAC address of DLS2 as the Root ID for VLAN 1. The Root Cost is 0 and there is no Root Port listed because DLS2 is the root bridge.

```
DSL2# show spanning-tree root
```

		Root	Hello	Max	Fwd	
Vlan	Root ID	Cost	Time	Age	Dly	Root Port
---	---	---	---	---	---	---
VLAN0001	32769 0017.5a53.a380	0	2	20	15	

Step 4: Diagram the STP topology for VLAN 1.

Diagram the spanning tree topology for VLAN 1. With Cisco Catalyst switches, there is a different spanning tree state for each VLAN. Identify the root bridge, root forwarding ports, designated forwarding ports, and alternate blocking ports.

On the lab diagram provided below, indicate which switch is the root and the STP port role and state for the switch ports. Place the letter R (Root FWD), D (Desg FWD) or A (Altn BLK) next to each port identified in the topology.

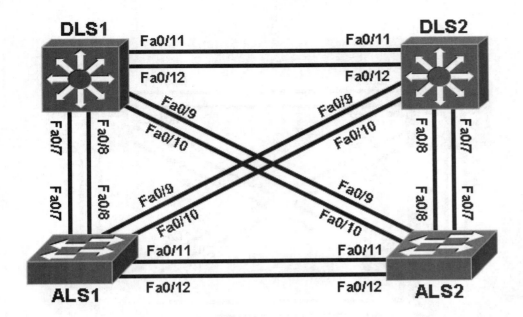

In this lab, the default operation of IEEE 802.1D spanning tree was observed. Since no bridge priorities were specified, the switch with the lowest MAC address was elected as the root. The link providing the lowest root path cost was chosen as the active link. If costs were equal, the tie was broken first by the lowest sender BID of the BPDU, then by the lowest sending port priority and last by the lowest sending port number.

In the next lab, the default STP behavior will be modified so that spanning tree works according to specifications.

Challenge

Try to guess how your topology would look if you completely removed the root switch. Remember that the switch with the lowest MAC address becomes the root.

a.   Shut down all the ports on your current root switch.

```
Switch# conf t
Switch(config)# interface range fastEthernet 0/1-24
Switch(config-if-range)# shutdown
```

Note: If you are on a 48 port switch, use interface range Fa0/1 – 48. If there are Gigabit Ethernet ports on the switch, they are not used with this lab, so it is not necessary to shut them down.

b.   Issue the **show spanning-tree** command on the other switches. Did the topology converge the way you thought it would?

_____

_____

Lab 3-2, Modifying Default Spanning Tree Behavior

Topology

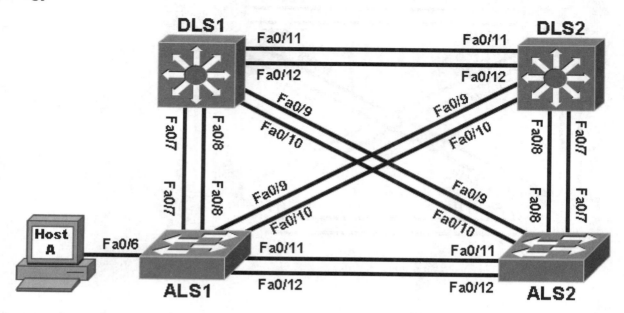

Objective

- Observe what happens when the default spanning tree behavior is modified.

Background

Four switches have just been installed. The distribution layer switches are Catalyst 3560s, and the access layer switches are Catalyst 2960s. There are redundant uplinks between the access layer and distribution layer. Because of the possibility of bridging loops, spanning tree logically removes any redundant links. In this lab, you will see what happens when the default spanning tree behavior is modified.

Note: This lab uses Cisco WS-C2960-24TT-L switches with the Cisco IOS image c2960-lanbasek9-mz.122-46.SE.bin and Catalyst 3560-24PS switches with the Cisco IOS image c3560-advipservicesk9-mz.122-46.SE.bin. Other switches (such as a 2950 or 3550) and Cisco IOS Software versions can be used if they have comparable capabilities and features. Depending on the switch model and Cisco IOS Software version, the commands available and output produced might vary from what is shown in this lab.

Required Resources

- 2 switches (Cisco 2960 with the Cisco IOS Release 12.2(46)SE C2960-LANBASEK9-M image or comparable)
- 2 switches (Cisco 3560 with the Cisco IOS Release 12.2(46)SE C3560-ADVIPSERVICESK9-M image or comparable)
- 1 PC (optional) attached to switch ALS1.
- Ethernet and console cables

Note: Configuring PortFast in Step 5 requires a PC attached to one of the access switches.

Step 1: Prepare the switches for the lab.

a. Delete vlan.dat, erase the startup configuration, and reload all switches. You can find detailed instructions in Lab 1-1 or 1-2.

b. Give each switch a hostname according to the topology diagram.

c. Configure ports Fa0/7 through Fa0/12 on all switches to be trunks. On the 3560s, first set the trunk encapsulation to dot1q. On the 2960s, only dot1q is supported, therefore the **switchport trunk encapsulation** command is unavailable, but the mode still needs to be changed to trunk. If you do not set the mode of the ports to trunk, they will negotiate the operational mode according to their default DTP settings.

Note: The default mode on a 3560 or 2960 is dynamic auto; the default mode on a 3550 or 2950 is dynamic desirable.

DLS1 example:

```
DLS1(config)# interface range fastEthernet 0/7 - 12
DLS1(config-if-range)# switchport trunk encapsulation dot1q
DLS1(config-if-range)# switchport mode trunk
```

Step 2: Display default spanning tree information for all switches.

a. Use the **show spanning-tree** command to check how the non-configured switches created a spanning tree. Verify which switch became the root bridge. In the topology used in this lab, DLS2 is the root bridge.

```
DLS1# show spanning-tree


VLAN0001
  Spanning tree enabled protocol ieee
  Root ID    Priority    32769
             Address     000a.b8a9.d680
             Cost        19
             Port        13 (FastEthernet0/11)
             Hello Time   2 sec  Max Age 20 sec  Forward Delay 15 sec

  Bridge ID  Priority    32769  (priority 32768 sys-id-ext 1)
             Address     000a.b8a9.d780
             Hello Time   2 sec  Max Age 20 sec  Forward Delay 15 sec
             Aging Time 300

Interface        Role Sts Cost      Prio.Nbr Type
---------------- ---- --- --------- -------- ----------------------------
Fa0/7            Desg FWD 19        128.9    P2p
Fa0/8            Desg FWD 19        128.10   P2p
Fa0/9            Desg FWD 19        128.11   P2p
Fa0/10           Desg FWD 19        128.12   P2p
Fa0/11           Root FWD 19        128.13   P2p
Fa0/12           Altn BLK 19        128.14   P2p


DLS2# show spanning-tree
```

```
VLAN0001
  Spanning tree enabled protocol ieee
  Root ID    Priority    32769
             Address     000a.b8a9.d680
             This bridge is the root
             Hello Time   2 sec  Max Age 20 sec  Forward Delay 15 sec

  Bridge ID  Priority    32769  (priority 32768 sys-id-ext 1)
             Address     000a.b8a9.d680
             Hello Time   2 sec  Max Age 20 sec  Forward Delay 15 sec
             Aging Time 300

Interface        Role Sts Cost      Prio.Nbr Type
---------------- ---- --- --------- -------- ----------------------------
Fa0/7            Desg FWD 19        128.9    P2p
Fa0/8            Desg FWD 19        128.10   P2p
Fa0/9            Desg FWD 19        128.11   P2p
Fa0/10           Desg FWD 19        128.12   P2p
Fa0/11           Desg FWD 19        128.13   P2p
Fa0/12           Desg FWD 19        128.14   P2p


ALS1# show spanning-tree


VLAN0001
  Spanning tree enabled protocol ieee
  Root ID    Priority    32769
             Address     000a.b8a9.d680
             Cost        19
             Port        11 (FastEthernet0/9)
             Hello Time   2 sec  Max Age 20 sec  Forward Delay 15 sec

  Bridge ID  Priority    32769  (priority 32768 sys-id-ext 1)
             Address     0019.0635.5780
             Hello Time   2 sec  Max Age 20 sec  Forward Delay 15 sec
             Aging Time 300

Interface        Role Sts Cost      Prio.Nbr Type
---------------- ---- --- --------- -------- ----------------------------
Fa0/7            Altn BLK 19        128.9    P2p
Fa0/8            Altn BLK 19        128.10   P2p
Fa0/9            Root FWD 19        128.11   P2p
Fa0/10           Altn BLK 19        128.12   P2p
Fa0/11           Desg FWD 19        128.13   P2p
Fa0/12           Desg FWD 19        128.14   P2p


ALS2# show spanning-tree


VLAN0001
  Spanning tree enabled protocol ieee
  Root ID    Priority    32769
             Address     000a.b8a9.d680
```

```
                Cost          19
                Port          9 (FastEthernet0/7)
                Hello Time    2 sec   Max Age 20 sec   Forward Delay 15 sec

        Bridge ID  Priority    32769   (priority 32768 sys-id-ext 1)
                   Address     0019.068d.6980
                   Hello Time    2 sec   Max Age 20 sec   Forward Delay 15 sec
                   Aging Time 300


Interface           Role Sts Cost      Prio.Nbr Type
---------------     ---- --- --------- -------- -----------------------------
Fa0/7               Root FWD 19          128.9    P2p
Fa0/8               Altn BLK 19          128.10   P2p
Fa0/9               Altn BLK 19          128.11   P2p
Fa0/10              Altn BLK 19          128.12   P2p
Fa0/11              Altn BLK 19          128.13   P2p
Fa0/12              Altn BLK 19          128.14   P2p
```

b. If you receive the following message "No spanning tree instance exists", issue the **no shutdown** command on all interfaces.

```
Switch# show spanning-tree

No spanning tree instance exists.

Switch# conf t
Switch(config)# interface range fastEthernet 0/1-24
Switch(config-if-range)# no shutdown
Switch(config-if-range)# end
Switch# show spanning-tree
```

Now that the switch is communicating with the other switches in the topology, you should receive spanning tree output.

c. Issue the **show interfaces trunk** command on DLS1 to verify the trunking mode, encapsulation and status for the trunk links.

```
DSL1# show interfaces trunk

Port        Mode          Encapsulation   Status       Native vlan
Fa0/7       on            802.1q          trunking     1
Fa0/8       on            802.1q          trunking     1
Fa0/9       on            802.1q          trunking     1
Fa0/10      on            802.1q          trunking     1
Fa0/11      on            802.1q          trunking     1
Fa0/12      on            802.1q          trunking     1

Port        Vlans allowed on trunk
Fa0/7       1-4094
Fa0/8       1-4094
Fa0/9       1-4094
Fa0/10      1-4094
Fa0/11      1-4094
Fa0/12      1-4094
```

```
<output omitted>
```

Are BPDUs propagated without trunk links?

_____

_____

Step 3: Configure specific switches to be primary and secondary root.

In this step you configure other switches to be the primary root and secondary root. Because DLS2 is the root switch in this topology, this lab changes DLS1 to be the primary root and ALS1 to be the secondary. Do the same in your topology, regardless of which switch is the initial root. On one of the switches that you are not changing, you can use the **debug spanning-tree events** command to monitor topology changes. To change the spanning tree root status, use the global configuration commands **spanning-tree vlan** *vlan_number* **root primary** and **spanning-tree vlan** *vlan_number* **root secondary**. On a switch that you are not going to be modifying, issue the **debug** command and then watch the output.

a. Issue the **debug** command on DLS2.

```
DLS2# debug spanning-tree events
Spanning Tree event debugging is on
```

b. Change DLS1 to be the primary root switch.

```
DLS1(config)# spanning-tree vlan 1 root primary
```

c. Change ALS1 to the secondary root.

```
ALS1(config)# spanning-tree vlan 1 root secondary
```

You can see the topology changes on the switch that you enabled debugging on (your output may vary depending on your initial topology):

```
DLS2#
00:10:43: STP: VLAN0001 heard root 24577-000a.b8a9.d780 on Fa0/11
00:10:43:      supersedes 32769-000a.b8a9.d680
00:10:43: STP: VLAN0001 new root is 24577, 000a.b8a9.d780 on port Fa0/11, cost
19
00:10:43: STP: VLAN0001 sent Topology Change Notice on Fa0/11
00:10:43: STP: VLAN0001 Fa0/12 -> blocking
00:10:53: STP: VLAN0001 sent Topology Change Notice on Fa0/11
00:10:53: STP: VLAN0001 Fa0/9 -> blocking
00:10:53: STP: VLAN0001 Fa0/10 -> blocking
```

Notice the timestamps on the debugs to see the difference between changes caused by the commands done in both steps.

df. Display the running config on the new root switches, DLS1 and ALS1.

```
DLS1# show run | include span
spanning-tree mode pvst
spanning-tree extend system-id
spanning-tree vlan 1 priority 24576


ALS1# show run | include span
spanning-tree mode pvst
spanning-tree extend system-id
spanning-tree vlan 1 priority 28672
```

Notice the spanning tree commands in the running configuration. You see a different command than the one you entered. This is because **spanning-tree vlan** *vlan_number* **root** is a command that sets the priority number on that VLAN automatically rather than typing in a specific priority number. The priority number of a VLAN can be between 0 and 61440 in increments of 4096. To manually set the specific priority number, use the **spanning-tree vlan** *vlan_number* **priority** *priority_number* command.

The command **spanning-tree vlan** *vlan_number* **root primary** sets the priority to 24576 instead of the default (32768). The command **spanning-tree vlan** *vlan_number* **root secondary** sets the priority to 28672. Given this information, would a lower or higher priority number result in a switch becoming the root bridge?

_____

_____

e. You can also view the priority modification with the **show spanning-tree** command:

```
DLS1# show spanning-tree


VLAN0001
  Spanning tree enabled protocol ieee
  Root ID    Priority    24577
             Address     000a.b8a9.d780
             This bridge is the root
             Hello Time   2 sec  Max Age 20 sec  Forward Delay 15 sec

  Bridge ID  Priority    24577  (priority 24576 sys-id-ext 1)
             Address     000a.b8a9.d780
             Hello Time   2 sec  Max Age 20 sec  Forward Delay 15 sec
             Aging Time 15

Interface         Role Sts Cost      Prio.Nbr Type
----------------  ---- --- --------- -------- --------------------------
Fa0/7             Desg FWD 19        128.9    P2p
Fa0/8             Desg FWD 19        128.10   P2p
Fa0/9             Desg FWD 19        128.11   P2p
Fa0/10            Desg FWD 19        128.12   P2p
Fa0/11            Desg FWD 19        128.13   P2p
Fa0/12            Desg FWD 19        128.14   P2p
```

Step 4: Change the root port using the spanning-tree port-priority command.

With spanning tree, you can also modify port priorities to determine which ports are forwarding and which are blocking. To choose which port becomes the root on a non-root switch when faced with equal-cost redundant root paths via the same neighbor, the switch looks at the port priorities first. If the sender port priorities are the same, the switch picks the port that receives BPDUs with the lowest sender port number. On the link between DLS1 and DLS2, the default forwarding port is Fa0/11 because it is lower, and the default blocking port is Fa0/12 because it is higher. The two ports have equal costs because they have the same speed.

a. You can verify this using the **show spanning-tree** command on the non-root switch, which is DLS2.

```
DLS2# show spanning-tree


VLAN0001
  Spanning tree enabled protocol ieee
  Root ID    Priority    24577
             Address     000a.b8a9.d780
             Cost        19
             Port        13 (FastEthernet0/11)
             Hello Time   2 sec  Max Age 20 sec  Forward Delay 15 sec

  Bridge ID  Priority    32769  (priority 32768 sys-id-ext 1)
             Address     000a.b8a9.d680
             Hello Time   2 sec  Max Age 20 sec  Forward Delay 15 sec
             Aging Time 300

Interface        Role Sts Cost      Prio.Nbr Type
---------------- ---- --- --------- -------- --------------------------------
Fa0/7            Desg FWD 19        128.9    P2p
Fa0/8            Desg FWD 19        128.10   P2p
Fa0/9            Altn BLK 19        128.11   P2p
Fa0/10           Altn BLK 19        128.12   P2p
Fa0/11           Root FWD 19        128.13   P2p
Fa0/12           Altn BLK 19        128.14   P2p
```

b. For comparison, issue the **show spanning-tree** command on DLS1. Notice that all ports are forwarding because it is the root switch.

```
DLS1# show spanning-tree


VLAN0001
  Spanning tree enabled protocol ieee
  Root ID    Priority    24577
             Address     000a.b8a9.d780
             This bridge is the root
             Hello Time   2 sec  Max Age 20 sec  Forward Delay 15 sec

  Bridge ID  Priority    24577  (priority 24576 sys-id-ext 1)
             Address     000a.b8a9.d780
             Hello Time   2 sec  Max Age 20 sec  Forward Delay 15 sec
             Aging Time 15

Interface        Role Sts Cost      Prio.Nbr Type
---------------- ---- --- --------- -------- --------------------------------
Fa0/7            Desg FWD 19        128.9    P2p
Fa0/8            Desg FWD 19        128.10   P2p
Fa0/9            Desg FWD 19        128.11   P2p
```

```
Fa0/10              Desg FWD 19          128.12    P2p
Fa0/11              Desg FWD 19          128.13    P2p
Fa0/12              Desg FWD 19          128.14    P2p
```

Port priorities range from 0 to 240, in increments of 16. The default priority is 128, and a lower priority is preferred. To change port priorities, change them on the switch closer to the root.

c. To make DLS2 Fa0/12 the root port, and Fa0/11 block, change the port priority on DLS1 with the interface-level command **spanning-tree port-priority** *priority*.

```
DLS1(config)# int fastEthernet 0/12
DLS1(config-if)# spanning-tree port-priority 112
```

d. Issue the **show spanning-tree** command to verify which port is blocking on DLS2.

```
DLS2# show spanning-tree

VLAN0001
  Spanning tree enabled protocol ieee
  Root ID    Priority    24577
             Address     000a.b8a9.d780
             Cost        19
             Port        14 (FastEthernet0/12)
             Hello Time   2 sec  Max Age 20 sec  Forward Delay 15 sec

   Bridge ID  Priority    32769  (priority 32768 sys-id-ext 1)
             Address     000a.b8a9.d680
             Hello Time   2 sec  Max Age 20 sec  Forward Delay 15 sec
             Aging Time 15

Interface        Role Sts Cost      Prio.Nbr Type
---------------- ---- --- --------- -------- ------------------------------
Fa0/7            Desg FWD 19          128.9    P2p
Fa0/8            Desg FWD 19          128.10   P2p
Fa0/9            Altn BLK 19          128.11   P2p
Fa0/10           Altn BLK 19          128.12   P2p
Fa0/11           Altn BLK 19          128.13   P2p
Fa0/12           Root FWD 19          128.14   P2p
```

On DLS2, although the root port has changed, the port priorities have not. On DLS1, you can see the port priorities have changed, although all ports are still forwarding (because it is the root switch).

```
DLS1# show spanning-tree

VLAN0001
  Spanning tree enabled protocol ieee
  Root ID    Priority    24577
             Address     000a.b8a9.d780
             This bridge is the root
             Hello Time   2 sec  Max Age 20 sec  Forward Delay 15 sec

   Bridge ID  Priority    24577  (priority 24576 sys-id-ext 1)
```

```
            Address       000a.b8a9.d780
            Hello Time    2 sec  Max Age 20 sec  Forward Delay 15 sec
            Aging Time 15


Interface          Role Sts Cost      Prio.Nbr Type
---------------- ---- --- --------- -------- ----------------------------
Fa0/7              Desg FWD 19        128.9    P2p
Fa0/8              Desg FWD 19        128.10   P2p
Fa0/9              Desg FWD 19        128.11   P2p
Fa0/10             Desg FWD 19        128.12   P2p
Fa0/11             Desg FWD 19        128.13   P2p
Fa0/12             Desg FWD 19        112.14   P2p
```

Using the above output, how does DLS2 know which port to change to the root port, without changing the port priorities on DLS2?

_____

_____

Step 5: Configure PortFast on an access port.

a. (Optional) If you have a host attached to ASL1 Fa0/6 you can perform this step. If not, read through the following information to see how a port goes through the spanning tree states with and without PortFast enabled.

Another feature of spanning tree is PortFast. PortFast allows you to bypass the normal states of IEEE 802.1D spanning tree and move a port to the forwarding state as soon as it is turned on. This is useful when connecting hosts to a switch, because they can start communicating on the VLAN instantly rather than waiting for spanning tree. There is no danger of creating a spanning tree loop because you are not connecting another switch. A client that runs DHCP as soon as it starts up benefits, because the DHCP requests could be ignored if the port was not in the spanning tree forwarding state. PortFast must be used carefully to avoid inadvertently creating spanning tree loops.

b. Ensure that the port to which the host is attached (Fa0/6) on ALS1 is shut down initially.

```
ALS1(config)# interface fastEthernet 0/6
ALS1(config-if)# shutdown
```

c. Enable spanning tree debugging on ALS1.

```
ALS1# debug spanning-tree events
Spanning Tree event debugging is on
```

d. Set port Fa0/6 switchport mode to access, enable the port and observe the debug output. Notice what happens when the port is brought up. Your output may vary.

```
ALS1(config)# interface fastEthernet 0/6
ALS1(config-if)# switchport mode access
ALS1(config-if)# no shut
ALS1(config-if)# end
ALS1#
```

```
22:32:23: set portid: VLAN0001 Fa0/6: new port id 800D
22:32:23: STP: VLAN0001 Fa0/6 -> listening
22:32:25: %LINK-3-UPDOWN: Interface FastEthernet0/6, changed state to up
22:32:26: %LINEPROTO-5-UPDOWN: Line protocol on Interface FastEthernet0/6,
changed state to up
22:32:38: STP: VLAN0001 Fa0/6 -> learning
22:32:53: STP: VLAN0001 Fa0/6 -> forwarding
22:32:53: STP: VLAN0001 sent Topology Change Notice on Fa0/7
```

e. Shut down the port for the next part.

```
ALS1(config)# interface fastEthernet 0/6
ALS1(config-if)# shutdown
```

f. Activate PortFast on the port with the interface-level command **spanning-tree portfast**. The switch warns you about the possibility of creating switching loops.

```
ALS1(config)# interface fastEthernet 0/6
ALS1(config-if)# spanning-tree portfast
%Warning: portfast should only be enabled on ports connected to a single
 host. Connecting hubs, concentrators, switches, bridges, etc... to this
 interface  when portfast is enabled, can cause temporary bridging loops.
 Use with CAUTION

%Portfast has been configured on FastEthernet0/6 but will only
 have effect when the interface is in a non-trunking mode.
```

g. Now, bring up the port by issuing the **no shutdown** command on the interface.

```
ALS1(config-if)# no shutdown

22:43:23: set portid: VLAN0001 Fa0/6: new port id 800D
22:43:23: STP: VLAN0001 Fa0/6 ->jump to forwarding from blocking
22:43:25: %LINK-3-UPDOWN: Interface FastEthernet0/6, changed state to up
22:43:26: %LINEPROTO-5-UPDOWN: Line protocol on Interface FastEthernet0/6,
changed state to up
```

h. Be sure to turn off debugging before continuing:

```
ALS1(config-if)# end
ALS1#
22:55:23: %SYS-5-CONFIG_I: Configured from console by console
ALS1# undebug all
All possible debugging has been turned off
```

Why could enabling portfast on redundant switch access links be a bad idea?

_____

_____

Note: The **spanning-tree portfast trunk** interface-level command can be useful if a trunk is being connected to a router or a server. If RSTP is used, both trunk and access links can be moved to a forwarding state rapidly. The **spanning-tree portfast trunk** command is to be used only on trunks connected to non-switching devices.

Step 6: Change root port using the spanning-tree cost command.

Another way of changing which port becomes the root is to modify the port costs using the interface command **spanning-tree cost** *cost*. The default cost is 4 for a gigabit Ethernet port, 19 for a Fast Ethernet port, and 100 for a 10baseT Ethernet port. Lower cost is preferred.

Note: Each port has a default cost value based on a guideline established as part of IEEE 802.1d. In the original specification, the cost of a port cost is calculated as 1,000 Mbps (1 gigabit per second) divided by the bandwidth at which the port is functioning. A 10 Mbps connection have a cost of (1,000/10) or 100. As the speed of networks has increased beyond gigabit, the standard cost has been modified somewhat. The new cost values are:

Bandwidth	STP Cost
4 Mbps	250
10 Mbps	100
16 Mbps	62
45 Mbps	39
100 Mbps	19
155 Mbps	14
622 Mbps	6
1 Gbps	4
10 Gbps	2

a. For this scenario, change the cost of port Fa0/10 on ALS2. First, look at the current port costs using the **show spanning-tree** command.

Note: The cost shown here is for the port. The root bridge path cost is the sum of link port costs between a switch and the root bridge. The cost of traversing this path is the sum of the costs of the segments on the path. This determines how far away the root bridge is.

```
ALS2# show spanning-tree

VLAN0001
  Spanning tree enabled protocol ieee
  Root ID    Priority    24577
             Address     000a.b8a9.d780
             Cost        19
             Port        11 (FastEthernet0/9)
             Hello Time   2 sec  Max Age 20 sec  Forward Delay 15 sec

  Bridge ID  Priority    32769  (priority 32768 sys-id-ext 1)
             Address     0019.068d.6980
             Hello Time   2 sec  Max Age 20 sec  Forward Delay 15 sec
             Aging Time 300
```

Interface	Role	Sts	Cost	Prio.Nbr	Type
Fa0/7	Altn	BLK	19	128.9	P2p
Fa0/8	Altn	BLK	19	128.10	P2p
Fa0/9	Root	FWD	19	128.11	P2p
Fa0/10	Altn	BLK	19	128.12	P2p
Fa0/11	Altn	BLK	19	128.13	P2p
Fa0/12	Altn	BLK	19	128.14	P2p

Note that Fa0/9 is currently the root port.

b. Change the port cost for Fa0/10 on ALS2 to 10 and then issue the **show spanning-tree** command.

```
ALS2(config)# interface fastEthernet 0/10
ALS2(config-if-range)# spanning-tree cost 10
```

```
ALS2# show spanning-tree
```

```
VLAN0001
  Spanning tree enabled protocol ieee
  Root ID    Priority    24577
             Address     000a.b8a9.d780
             Cost        10
             Port        12 (FastEthernet0/10)
             Hello Time   2 sec  Max Age 20 sec  Forward Delay 15 sec

  Bridge ID  Priority    32769  (priority 32768 sys-id-ext 1)
             Address     0019.068d.6980
             Hello Time   2 sec  Max Age 20 sec  Forward Delay 15 sec
             Aging Time 300
```

Interface	Role	Sts	Cost	Prio.Nbr	Type
Fa0/7	Altn	BLK	19	128.9	P2p
Fa0/8	Altn	BLK	19	128.10	P2p
Fa0/9	Altn	FWD	19	128.11	P2p
Fa0/10	Root	FWD	10	128.12	P2p
Fa0/11	Altn	BLK	19	128.13	P2p
Fa0/12	Altn	BLK	19	128.14	P2p

Lab 3-3, Per-VLAN Spanning Tree Behavior

Topology

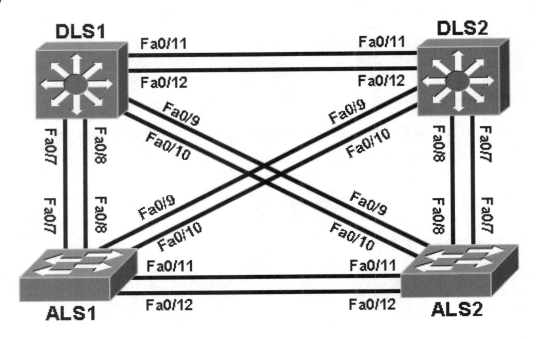

Objectives

- Observe the behavior of a separate spanning tree instance per VLAN.
- Change spanning tree mode to rapid spanning tree.

Background

Four switches have just been installed. The distribution layer switches are Catalyst 3560s, and the access layer switches are Catalyst 2960s. There are redundant uplinks between the access layer and distribution layer. Because of the possibility of bridging loops, spanning tree logically removes any redundant links. In this lab, you will see what happens when spanning tree is configured differently for different VLANs.

Note: This lab uses Cisco WS-C2960-24TT-L switches with the Cisco IOS image c2960-lanbasek9-mz.122-46.SE.bin and Catalyst 3560-24PS with the Cisco IOS image c3560-advipservicesk9-mz.122-46.SE.bin. Other switches (such as a 2950 or 3550), and Cisco IOS Software versions can be used if they have comparable capabilities and features. Depending on the switch model and Cisco IOS Software version, the commands available and output produced might vary from what is shown in this lab.

Required Resources

- 2 switches (Cisco 2960 with the Cisco IOS Release 12.2(46)SE C2960-LANBASEK9-M image or comparable)
- 2 switches (Cisco 3560 with the Cisco IOS Release 12.2(46)SE C3560-ADVIPSERVICESK9-M image or comparable)
- Ethernet and console cables

Step 1: Prepare the switches for the lab.

a. Delete the vlan.dat file, erase the startup configuration, and reload the switches.

b. Give each switch a hostname according to the topology diagram.

c. Configure ports Fa0/7 through Fa0/12 on all switches to be trunks. On the 3560s, first set the trunk encapsulation to dot1q. On the 2960s, only dot1q is supported, therefore the **switchport trunk encapsulation** command is unavailable, but the mode still needs to be changed to trunk. If you do not set the mode of the ports to trunk, they will negotiate the operational mode according to their default DTP settings.

Note: The default mode on a 3560 or 2960 is dynamic auto; the default mode on a 3550 or 2950 is dynamic desirable.

DLS1 example:

```
DLS1(config)# interface range fastEthernet 0/7 - 12
DLS1(config-if-range)# switchport trunk encapsulation dot1q
DLS1(config-if-range)# switchport mode trunk
```

Step 2: Configure VTP.

a. Configure all switches with VTP mode transparent and VTP domain CISCO. Add VLAN 10 and 20 to all of them. Use the **show vlan brief** command to view the VLAN configurations.

DLS1 example:

```
DLS1(config)# vtp mode transparent
Setting device to VTP TRANSPARENT mode.

DLS1(config)# vtp domain CISCO
Changing VTP domain name from NULL to CISCO

DLS1(config)# vlan 10,20
DLS1(config-vlan)# end
```

```
DLS1# show vlan brief

VLAN Name                             Status    Ports
---- -------------------------------- --------- -------------------------
1    default                          active    Fa0/1, Fa0/2, Fa0/3, Fa0/4
                                                Fa0/5, Fa0/6, Fa0/9, Fa0/10
                                                Fa0/13, Fa0/14, Fa0/15, Fa0/16
                                                Fa0/17, Fa0/18, Fa0/19, Fa0/20
                                                Fa0/21, Fa0/22, Fa0/23, Fa0/24
                                                Gi0/1, Gi0/2

10   VLAN0010                         active
20   VLAN0020                         active
1002 fddi-default                     act/unsup
1003 token-ring-default               act/unsup
1004 fddinet-default                  act/unsup
1005 trnet-default                    act/unsup
```

b. Issue the **show spanning-tree** command on any of the four switches. Notice that instead of just one VLAN there are three non-reserved VLANs. VLANs 1002-1005 are reserved for internal switch usage. All other VLANs shown are non-reserved.

Note: By default Cisco switches use PVST+, a Cisco-proprietary IEEE 802.1Q-compatible per-VLAN spanning tree protocol.

```
DLS1# show spanning-tree


VLAN0001
  Spanning tree enabled protocol ieee
  Root ID    Priority    32769
             Address     000a.b8a9.d680
             Cost        19
             Port        13 (FastEthernet0/11)
             Hello Time   2 sec  Max Age 20 sec  Forward Delay 15 sec

  Bridge ID  Priority    32769  (priority 32768 sys-id-ext 1)
             Address     000a.b8a9.d780
             Hello Time   2 sec  Max Age 20 sec  Forward Delay 15 sec
             Aging Time 15


Interface         Role Sts Cost      Prio.Nbr Type
----------------  ---- --- --------- -------- ----------------------------
Fa0/7             Desg FWD 19        128.9    P2p
Fa0/8             Desg FWD 19        128.10   P2p
Fa0/9             Desg FWD 19        128.11   P2p
Fa0/10            Desg FWD 19        128.12   P2p
Fa0/11            Root FWD 19        128.13   P2p
Fa0/12            Altn BLK 19        128.14   P2p



VLAN0010
  Spanning tree enabled protocol ieee
  Root ID    Priority    32778
             Address     000a.b8a9.d680
             Cost        19
             Port        13 (FastEthernet0/11)
             Hello Time   2 sec  Max Age 20 sec  Forward Delay 15 sec

  Bridge ID  Priority    32778  (priority 32768 sys-id-ext 10)
             Address     000a.b8a9.d780
             Hello Time   2 sec  Max Age 20 sec  Forward Delay 15 sec
             Aging Time 15


Interface         Role Sts Cost      Prio.Nbr Type
----------------  ---- --- --------- -------- ----------------------------
Fa0/7             Desg FWD 19        128.9    P2p
Fa0/8             Desg FWD 19        128.10   P2p
Fa0/9             Desg FWD 19        128.11   P2p
Fa0/10            Desg FWD 19        128.12   P2p
Fa0/11            Root FWD 19        128.13   P2p
```

```
Fa0/12                Altn BLK 19          128.14   P2p
```

VLAN0020
```
  Spanning tree enabled protocol ieee
  Root ID    Priority    32788
             Address     000a.b8a9.d680
             Cost        19
             Port        13 (FastEthernet0/11)
             Hello Time   2 sec  Max Age 20 sec  Forward Delay 15 sec

  Bridge ID  Priority    32788  (priority 32768 sys-id-ext 20)
             Address     000a.b8a9.d780
             Hello Time   2 sec  Max Age 20 sec  Forward Delay 15 sec
             Aging Time 15

Interface         Role Sts Cost      Prio.Nbr Type
----------------- ---- --- --------- -------- ------------------------------
Fa0/7             Desg FWD 19        128.9    P2p
Fa0/8             Desg FWD 19        128.10   P2p
Fa0/9             Desg FWD 19        128.11   P2p
Fa0/10            Desg FWD 19        128.12   P2p
Fa0/11            Root FWD 19        128.13   P2p
Fa0/12            Altn BLK 19        128.14   P2p
```

Step 3: Assign a root switch for each VLAN.

Notice that all the ports have identical spanning tree behavior for each VLAN. This is because all VLANs are running spanning tree with the default behavior. However, you can modify the default spanning tree behavior on a per-VLAN basis. The default priority is 32768. Configuring a switch with a lower priority value for a given VLAN makes it the root bridge for that VLAN. For this lab, we assign DLS1 as the root bridge for VLAN 10, and DLS2 for VLAN 20.

a. To change the priority for a given VLAN, use the **spanning-tree vlan** *number* **priority** *number* command. Configure DLS1 with priority 4096 for VLAN 10. Configure DLS2 similarly for VLAN 20.

```
DLS1(config)# spanning-tree vlan 10 priority 4096

DLS2(config)# spanning-tree vlan 20 priority 4096
```

b. If you look at the output of **show spanning-tree** on the four switches, you see that the port states and root switches vary on a per VLAN basis.

```
DLS1# show spanning-tree

VLAN0001
  Spanning tree enabled protocol ieee
  Root ID    Priority    32769
             Address     000a.b8a9.d680
             Cost        19
             Port        13 (FastEthernet0/11)
             Hello Time   2 sec  Max Age 20 sec  Forward Delay 15 sec

  Bridge ID  Priority    32769  (priority 32768 sys-id-ext 1)
```

```
              Address       000a.b8a9.d780
              Hello Time   2 sec   Max Age 20 sec   Forward Delay 15 sec
              Aging Time 300

Interface           Role Sts Cost       Prio.Nbr Type
----------------    ---- --- ---------  -------- ----------------------------
Fa0/7               Desg FWD 19         128.9    P2p
Fa0/8               Desg FWD 19         128.10   P2p
Fa0/9               Desg FWD 19         128.11   P2p
Fa0/10              Desg FWD 19         128.12   P2p
Fa0/11              Root FWD 19         128.13   P2p
Fa0/12              Altn BLK 19         128.14   P2p


VLAN0010
  Spanning tree enabled protocol ieee
  Root ID    Priority    4106
             Address       000a.b8a9.d780
             This bridge is the root
             Hello Time   2 sec   Max Age 20 sec   Forward Delay 15 sec

  Bridge ID  Priority    4106    (priority 4096 sys-id-ext 10)
             Address       000a.b8a9.d780
             Hello Time   2 sec   Max Age 20 sec   Forward Delay 15 sec
             Aging Time 300

Interface           Role Sts Cost       Prio.Nbr Type
----------------    ---- --- ---------  -------- ----------------------------
Fa0/7               Desg FWD 19         128.9    P2p
Fa0/8               Desg FWD 19         128.10   P2p
Fa0/9               Desg FWD 19         128.11   P2p
Fa0/10              Desg FWD 19         128.12   P2p
Fa0/11              Desg FWD 19         128.13   P2p
Fa0/12              Desg FWD 19         128.14   P2p


VLAN0020
  Spanning tree enabled protocol ieee
  Root ID    Priority    4116
             Address       000a.b8a9.d680
             Cost          19
             Port          13 (FastEthernet0/11)
             Hello Time   2 sec   Max Age 20 sec   Forward Delay 15 sec

  Bridge ID  Priority    32788  (priority 32768 sys-id-ext 20)
             Address       000a.b8a9.d780
             Hello Time   2 sec   Max Age 20 sec   Forward Delay 15 sec
             Aging Time 300

Interface           Role Sts Cost       Prio.Nbr Type
----------------    ---- --- ---------  -------- ----------------------------
Fa0/7               Desg FWD 19         128.9    P2p
Fa0/8               Desg FWD 19         128.10   P2p
```

```
Fa0/9                Desg FWD 19              128.11    P2p
Fa0/10               Desg FWD 19              128.12    P2p
Fa0/11               Root FWD 19              128.13    P2p
Fa0/12               Altn BLK 19              128.14    P2p


DLS2# show spanning-tree

VLAN0001
   Spanning tree enabled protocol ieee
   Root ID    Priority      32769
              Address       000a.b8a9.d680
              This bridge is the root
              Hello Time    2 sec  Max Age 20 sec  Forward Delay 15 sec

   Bridge ID  Priority      32769  (priority 32768 sys-id-ext 1)
              Address       000a.b8a9.d680
              Hello Time    2 sec  Max Age 20 sec  Forward Delay 15 sec
              Aging Time 300

Interface         Role Sts Cost        Prio.Nbr Type
---------------- ---- --- --------- -------- ----------------------------
Fa0/7             Desg FWD 19          128.9    P2p
Fa0/8             Desg FWD 19          128.10   P2p
Fa0/9             Desg FWD 19          128.11   P2p
Fa0/10            Desg FWD 19          128.12   P2p
Fa0/11            Desg FWD 19          128.13   P2p
Fa0/12            Desg FWD 19          128.14   P2p


VLAN0010
   Spanning tree enabled protocol ieee
   Root ID    Priority      4106
              Address       000a.b8a9.d780
              Cost          19
              Port          13 (FastEthernet0/11)
              Hello Time    2 sec  Max Age 20 sec  Forward Delay 15 sec

   Bridge ID  Priority      32778  (priority 32768 sys-id-ext 10)
              Address       000a.b8a9.d680
              Hello Time    2 sec  Max Age 20 sec  Forward Delay 15 sec
              Aging Time 300

Interface         Role Sts Cost        Prio.Nbr Type
---------------- ---- --- --------- -------- ----------------------------
Fa0/7             Desg FWD 19          128.9    P2p
Fa0/8             Desg FWD 19          128.10   P2p
Fa0/9             Desg FWD 19          128.11   P2p
Fa0/10            Desg FWD 19          128.12   P2p
Fa0/11            Root FWD 19          128.13   P2p
Fa0/12            Altn BLK 19          128.14   P2p
```

```
VLAN0020
  Spanning tree enabled protocol ieee
  Root ID    Priority    4116
             Address     000a.b8a9.d680
             This bridge is the root
             Hello Time   2 sec  Max Age 20 sec  Forward Delay 15 sec

  Bridge ID  Priority    4116    (priority 4096 sys-id-ext 20)
             Address     000a.b8a9.d680
             Hello Time   2 sec  Max Age 20 sec  Forward Delay 15 sec
             Aging Time 300

Interface        Role Sts Cost      Prio.Nbr Type
---------------- ---- --- --------- -------- ----------------------------
Fa0/7            Desg FWD 19        128.9    P2p
Fa0/8            Desg FWD 19        128.10   P2p
Fa0/9            Desg FWD 19        128.11   P2p
Fa0/10           Desg FWD 19        128.12   P2p
Fa0/11           Desg FWD 19        128.13   P2p
Fa0/12           Desg FWD 19        128.14   P2p


ALS1# show spanning-tree

VLAN0001
  Spanning tree enabled protocol ieee
  Root ID    Priority    32769
             Address     000a.b8a9.d680
             Cost        19
             Port        11 (FastEthernet0/9)
             Hello Time   2 sec  Max Age 20 sec  Forward Delay 15 sec

  Bridge ID  Priority    32769   (priority 32768 sys-id-ext 1)
             Address     0019.0635.5780
             Hello Time   2 sec  Max Age 20 sec  Forward Delay 15 sec
             Aging Time 300

Interface        Role Sts Cost      Prio.Nbr Type
---------------- ---- --- --------- -------- ----------------------------
Fa0/7            Altn BLK 19        128.9    P2p
Fa0/8            Altn BLK 19        128.10   P2p
Fa0/9            Root FWD 19        128.11   P2p
Fa0/10           Altn BLK 19        128.12   P2p
Fa0/11           Desg FWD 19        128.13   P2p
Fa0/12           Desg FWD 19        128.14   P2p


VLAN0010
  Spanning tree enabled protocol ieee
  Root ID    Priority    4106
             Address     000a.b8a9.d780
             Cost        19
             Port        9 (FastEthernet0/7)
```

```
                 Hello Time    2 sec  Max Age 20 sec  Forward Delay 15 sec

      Bridge ID  Priority    32778  (priority 32768 sys-id-ext 10)
                 Address      0019.0635.5780
                 Hello Time    2 sec  Max Age 20 sec  Forward Delay 15 sec
                 Aging Time 15


Interface          Role Sts Cost      Prio.Nbr Type
---------------- ---- --- --------- -------- --------------------------------
Fa0/7              Root FWD 19        128.9    P2p
Fa0/8              Altn BLK 19        128.10   P2p
Fa0/9              Altn BLK 19        128.11   P2p
Fa0/10             Altn BLK 19        128.12   P2p
Fa0/11             Desg FWD 19        128.13   P2p
Fa0/12             Desg FWD 19        128.14   P2p



VLAN0020
  Spanning tree enabled protocol ieee
  Root ID    Priority    4116
             Address      000a.b8a9.d680
             Cost         19
             Port         11 (FastEthernet0/9)
             Hello Time    2 sec  Max Age 20 sec  Forward Delay 15 sec

      Bridge ID  Priority    32788  (priority 32768 sys-id-ext 20)
                 Address      0019.0635.5780
                 Hello Time    2 sec  Max Age 20 sec  Forward Delay 15 sec
                 Aging Time 15


Interface          Role Sts Cost      Prio.Nbr Type
---------------- ---- --- --------- -------- --------------------------------
Fa0/7              Altn BLK 19        128.9    P2p
Fa0/8              Altn BLK 19        128.10   P2p
Fa0/9              Root FWD 19        128.11   P2p
Fa0/10             Altn BLK 19        128.12   P2p
Fa0/11             Desg FWD 19        128.13   P2p
Fa0/12             Desg FWD 19        128.14   P2p



ALS2# show spanning-tree

VLAN0001
  Spanning tree enabled protocol ieee
  Root ID    Priority    32769
             Address      000a.b8a9.d680
             Cost         19
             Port         9 (FastEthernet0/7)
             Hello Time    2 sec  Max Age 20 sec  Forward Delay 15 sec

      Bridge ID  Priority    32769  (priority 32768 sys-id-ext 1)
                 Address      0019.068d.6980
                 Hello Time    2 sec  Max Age 20 sec  Forward Delay 15 sec
```

```
                Aging Time 300

Interface          Role Sts Cost      Prio.Nbr Type
---------------- ---- --- --------- -------- --------------------------
Fa0/7              Root FWD 19        128.9    P2p
Fa0/8              Altn BLK 19        128.10   P2p
Fa0/9              Altn BLK 19        128.11   P2p
Fa0/10             Altn BLK 19        128.12   P2p
Fa0/11             Altn BLK 19        128.13   P2p
Fa0/12             Altn BLK 19        128.14   P2p


VLAN0010
  Spanning tree enabled protocol ieee
  Root ID    Priority    4106
             Address     000a.b8a9.d780
             Cost        19
             Port        11 (FastEthernet0/9)
             Hello Time   2 sec  Max Age 20 sec  Forward Delay 15 sec

  Bridge ID  Priority    32778  (priority 32768 sys-id-ext 10)
             Address     0019.068d.6980
             Hello Time   2 sec  Max Age 20 sec  Forward Delay 15 sec
             Aging Time 15

Interface          Role Sts Cost      Prio.Nbr Type
---------------- ---- --- --------- -------- --------------------------
Fa0/7              Altn BLK 19        128.9    P2p
Fa0/8              Altn BLK 19        128.10   P2p
Fa0/9              Root FWD 19        128.11   P2p
Fa0/10             Altn BLK 19        128.12   P2p
Fa0/11             Altn BLK 19        128.13   P2p
Fa0/12             Altn BLK 19        128.14   P2p


VLAN0020
  Spanning tree enabled protocol ieee
  Root ID    Priority    4116
             Address     000a.b8a9.d680
             Cost        19
             Port        9 (FastEthernet0/7)
             Hello Time   2 sec  Max Age 20 sec  Forward Delay 15 sec

  Bridge ID  Priority    32788  (priority 32768 sys-id-ext 20)
             Address     0019.068d.6980
             Hello Time   2 sec  Max Age 20 sec  Forward Delay 15 sec
             Aging Time 15

Interface          Role Sts Cost      Prio.Nbr Type
---------------- ---- --- --------- -------- --------------------------
Fa0/7              Root FWD 19        128.9    P2p
Fa0/8              Altn BLK 19        128.10   P2p
Fa0/9              Altn BLK 19        128.11   P2p
```

```
Fa0/10              Altn BLK 19         128.12    P2p
Fa0/11              Altn BLK 19         128.13    P2p
Fa0/12              Altn BLK 19         128.14    P2p
```

Step 4: Configure RSTP.

Other spanning tree modes besides PVST+ are available. One of these is RSTP (rapid spanning tree protocol), which greatly reduces the time for a port to transition to forwarding state while still preventing bridging loops. Cisco-proprietary per-VLAN rapid spanning tree (PVRST+) combines the functionality of RSTP and PVST.

Note: You can use the **clear spanning-tree detected-protocols** command after configuring different spanning tree modes. This can avoid a mutual deadlock between two switches when they consider themselves as 802.1D legacy bridges when in fact they were configured for RSTP.

a. To change the spanning tree mode to PVRST+, use the global configuration command **spanning-tree mode rapid-pvst**. Configure this on all four switches. During the transition period, rapid spanning tree falls back to 802.1D spanning tree on the links that have 802.1D spanning tree configured on one side.

```
DLS1(config)# spanning-tree mode rapid-pvst
```

b. After configuring all four switches with this command, use the **show spanning-tree** command to verify the configuration:

```
DLS1# show spanning-tree

VLAN0001
  Spanning tree enabled protocol rstp
  Root ID    Priority    32769
             Address     000a.b8a9.d680
             Cost        19
             Port        13 (FastEthernet0/11)
             Hello Time   2 sec  Max Age 20 sec  Forward Delay 15 sec

  Bridge ID  Priority    32769  (priority 32768 sys-id-ext 1)
             Address     000a.b8a9.d780
             Hello Time   2 sec  Max Age 20 sec  Forward Delay 15 sec
             Aging Time 300

Interface         Role Sts Cost      Prio.Nbr Type
---------------- ---- --- --------- -------- ----------------------------
Fa0/7             Desg FWD 19         128.9    P2p
Fa0/8             Desg FWD 19         128.10   P2p
Fa0/9             Desg FWD 19         128.11   P2p
Fa0/10            Desg FWD 19         128.12   P2p
Fa0/11            Root FWD 19         128.13   P2p
Fa0/12            Altn BLK 19         128.14   P2p


VLAN0010
  Spanning tree enabled protocol rstp
  Root ID    Priority    4106
             Address     000a.b8a9.d780
             This bridge is the root
```

```
                Hello Time    2 sec   Max Age 20 sec   Forward Delay 15 sec

     Bridge ID   Priority      4106     (priority 4096 sys-id-ext 10)
                 Address       000a.b8a9.d780
                 Hello Time    2 sec   Max Age 20 sec   Forward Delay 15 sec
                 Aging Time 300


  Interface         Role Sts Cost      Prio.Nbr  Type
  ---------------- ---- --- --------- ------- ----------------------------
  Fa0/7             Desg FWD 19         128.9     P2p
  Fa0/8             Desg FWD 19         128.10    P2p
  Fa0/9             Desg FWD 19         128.11    P2p
  Fa0/10            Desg FWD 19         128.12    P2p
  Fa0/11            Desg FWD 19         128.13    P2p
  Fa0/12            Desg FWD 19         128.14    P2p



VLAN0020
Spanning tree enabled protocol rstp
  Root ID     Priority      4116
              Address       000a.b8a9.d680
              Cost          19
              Port          13 (FastEthernet0/11)
              Hello Time    2 sec   Max Age 20 sec   Forward Delay 15 sec

   Bridge ID  Priority      32788   (priority 32768 sys-id-ext 20)
              Address       000a.b8a9.d780
              Hello Time    2 sec   Max Age 20 sec   Forward Delay 15 sec
              Aging Time 300


  Interface         Role Sts Cost      Prio.Nbr  Type
  ---------------- ---- --- --------- ------- ----------------------------
  Fa0/7             Desg FWD 19         128.9     P2p
  Fa0/8             Desg FWD 19         128.10    P2p
  Fa0/9             Desg FWD 19         128.11    P2p
  Fa0/10            Desg FWD 19         128.12    P2p
  Fa0/11            Root FWD 19         128.13    P2p
  Fa0/12            Altn BLK 19         128.14    P2p
```

Challenge

a. On each switch, add VLANs 50, 60, 70, 80, 90, and 100. Configure ALS1 to be the root bridge for VLANs 50, 60, and 70, and ALS2 to be the root bridge for VLANs 80, 90, and 100. Configure the root bridges with a single line on each switch.

HINT: Use the question mark when you type the global configuration command **spanning-tree vlan ?**. Notice that you can modify spanning tree attributes in ranges.

_____

_____

_____

_____

_____

b   Change the spanning tree cost of VLAN 20 on Fa0/11 and Fa0/12 between DLS1 and DLS2 to 15.

HINT: Use the question mark on the interface level command **spanning-tree vlan *number* ?**.

_____

_____

_____

_____

_____

_____

Lab 3-4, Multiple Spanning Tree

Topology

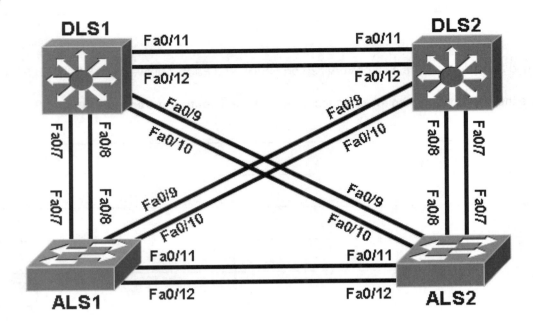

Objective

- Observe the behavior of multiple spanning tree (MST).

Background

Four switches have just been installed. The distribution layer switches are Catalyst 3560s, and the access layer switches are Catalyst 2960s. There are redundant uplinks between the access layer and distribution layer. Because of the possibility of bridging loops, spanning tree logically removes any redundant links. In this lab, we will group VLANs using MST so that we can have fewer spanning tree instances running at once to minimize switch CPU load.

Note: This lab uses Cisco WS-C2960-24TT-L with the Cisco IOS image c2960-lanbasek9-mz.122-46.SE.bin and Catalyst 3560-24PS switches with the Cisco IOS image c3560-advipservicesk9-mz.122-46.SE.bin. Other switches (such as a 2950 or 3550), and Cisco IOS Software versions can be used if they have comparable capabilities and features. Depending on the switch model and Cisco IOS Software version, the commands available and output produced might vary from what is shown in this lab.

Note: VTP version 3, is not supported by the IOS used on the switches in this lab. However, it is supported in IOS versions 12.2(52)SE and newer on all platforms eligible for this IOS (2960, 3560, 3750, etc.). VTPv3 has improvements in three major areas.

- Better administrative control over which device is allowed to update other devices' view of the VLAN topology. The chance of unintended and disruptive changes is significantly reduced, and availability is increased.

- Functionality for the VLAN environment has been significantly expanded. In addition to supporting the earlier ISL VLAN range from 1 to 1001, the new version supports the whole IEEE 802.1Q VLAN range up to 4095. In addition to supporting the concept of normal VLANs, VTP version 3 can transfer information regarding Private VLAN (PVLAN) structures.

- The third area of major improvement is support for databases other than VLAN. For example, VTPv3 supports MST mapping propagation instances, can synchronize MST configuration and be very helpful in maintaining the coherent MST configuration on all switches.

Required Resources

- 2 switch (Cisco 2960 with the Cisco IOS Release 12.2(46)SE C2960-LANBASEK9-M image or comparable)

- 2 switches (Cisco 3560 with the Cisco IOS Release 12.2(46)SE C3560-ADVIPSERVICESK9-M image or comparable)

- Ethernet and console cables

Step 1: Prepare the switches for the lab.

a. Delete vlan.dat file, erase the startup config, and reload the switches.

b. Give each switch a hostname according to the topology diagram.

c. Configure ports Fa0/7 through Fa0/12 on all switches to be trunks. On the 3560s, first set the trunk encapsulation to dot1q. On the 2960s, only dot1q is supported, therefore the **switchport trunk encapsulation** command is unavailable, but the mode still needs to be changed to trunk. If you do not set the mode of the ports to trunk, they will negotiate the operational mode according to their default DTP settings.

Note: The default mode on a 3560 or 2960 is dynamic auto; the default mode on a 3550 or 2950 is dynamic desirable.

DLS1 example:

```
DLS1(config)# interface range fastEthernet 0/7 - 12
DLS1(config-if-range)# switchport trunk encapsulation dot1q
DLS1(config-if-range)# switchport mode trunk
```

Step 2: Configure VTP and VLANs.

a. Configure all switches with VTP mode transparent and VTP domain CISCO. Add VLANs 10, 20, 30, 40, 50, 60, 70, 80, 90 and 100 to all of them.

DLS1 example:

```
DLS1# configure terminal
Enter configuration commands, one per line.  End with CNTL/Z.
DLS1(config)# vtp mode transparent
Setting device to VTP TRANSPARENT mode.
DLS1(config) #vtp domain CISCO
Changing VTP domain name from NULL to CISCO
DLS1(config)# vlan 10,20,30,40,50,60,70,80,90,100
DLS1(config-vlan)# end
```

b. Issue the **show vlan brief** command to view the VLAN configurations.

```
DLS1# show vlan brief
```

```
00:11:56: %SYS-5-CONFIG_I: Configured from console by console
```

VLAN	Name	Status	Ports
1	default	active	Fa0/1, Fa0/2, Fa0/3, Fa0/4
			Fa0/5, Fa0/6, Fa0/7, Fa0/8
			Fa0/9, Fa0/10, Fa0/11, Fa0/12
			Fa0/13, Fa0/14, Fa0/15, Fa0/16
			Fa0/17, Fa0/18, Fa0/19, Fa0/20
			Fa0/21, Fa0/22, Fa0/23, Fa0/24
			Gi0/1, Gi0/2
10	VLAN0010	active	
20	VLAN0020	active	
30	VLAN0030	active	
40	VLAN0040	active	
50	VLAN0050	active	
60	VLAN0060	active	
70	VLAN0070	active	
80	VLAN0080	active	
90	VLAN0090	active	
100	VLAN0100	active	
1002	fddi-default	act/unsup	
1003	token-ring-default	act/unsup	
1004	fddinet-default	act/unsup	
1005	trnet-default	act/unsup	

Step 3: Display spanning tree information.

Issue the **show spanning-tree** command on one of the switches. How many spanning tree instances are running?

_____

_____

```
DLS1# show spanning-tree

VLAN0001
  Spanning tree enabled protocol ieee
  Root ID    Priority    32769
             Address     000a.b8a9.d680
             Cost        19
             Port        13 (FastEthernet0/11)
             Hello Time   2 sec  Max Age 20 sec  Forward Delay 15 sec

  Bridge ID  Priority    32769  (priority 32768 sys-id-ext 1)
             Address     000a.b8a9.d780
             Hello Time   2 sec  Max Age 20 sec  Forward Delay 15 sec
             Aging Time 300
```

```
Interface           Role Sts Cost      Prio.Nbr Type
----------------    ---- --- --------- -------- ----------------------------
Fa0/7               Desg FWD 19        128.9    P2p
Fa0/8               Desg FWD 19        128.10   P2p
Fa0/9               Desg FWD 19        128.11   P2p
Fa0/10              Desg FWD 19        128.12   P2p
Fa0/11              Root FWD 19        128.13   P2p
Fa0/12              Altn BLK 19        128.14   P2p
```

VLAN0010
```
  Spanning tree enabled protocol ieee
  Root ID    Priority    32778
             Address     000a.b8a9.d680
             Cost        19
             Port        13 (FastEthernet0/11)
             Hello Time   2 sec  Max Age 20 sec  Forward Delay 15 sec

  Bridge ID  Priority    32778  (priority 32768 sys-id-ext 10)
             Address     000a.b8a9.d780
             Hello Time   2 sec  Max Age 20 sec  Forward Delay 15 sec
             Aging Time 300
```

```
Interface           Role Sts Cost      Prio.Nbr Type
----------------    ---- --- --------- -------- ----------------------------
Fa0/7               Desg FWD 19        128.9    P2p
Fa0/8               Desg FWD 19        128.10   P2p
Fa0/9               Desg FWD 19        128.11   P2p
Fa0/10              Desg FWD 19        128.12   P2p
Fa0/11              Root FWD 19        128.13   P2p
Fa0/12              Altn BLK 19        128.14   P2p
```

VLAN0020
```
  Spanning tree enabled protocol ieee
  Root ID    Priority    32788
             Address     000a.b8a9.d680
             Cost        19
             Port        13 (FastEthernet0/11)
             Hello Time   2 sec  Max Age 20 sec  Forward Delay 15 sec

  Bridge ID  Priority    32788  (priority 32768 sys-id-ext 20)
             Address     000a.b8a9.d780
             Hello Time   2 sec  Max Age 20 sec  Forward Delay 15 sec
             Aging Time 300
```

```
Interface           Role Sts Cost      Prio.Nbr Type
----------------    ---- --- --------- -------- ----------------------------
Fa0/7               Desg FWD 19        128.9    P2p
Fa0/8               Desg FWD 19        128.10   P2p
Fa0/9               Desg FWD 19        128.11   P2p
Fa0/10              Desg FWD 19        128.12   P2p
Fa0/11              Root FWD 19        128.13   P2p
```

```
Fa0/12              Altn BLK 19        128.14    P2p

<output omitted>

VLAN0090
  Spanning tree enabled protocol ieee
  Root ID    Priority    32858
             Address     000a.b8a9.d680
             Cost        19
             Port        13 (FastEthernet0/11)
             Hello Time   2 sec  Max Age 20 sec  Forward Delay 15 sec

  Bridge ID  Priority    32858  (priority 32768 sys-id-ext 90)
             Address     000a.b8a9.d780
             Hello Time   2 sec  Max Age 20 sec  Forward Delay 15 sec
             Aging Time 300

Interface        Role Sts Cost      Prio.Nbr Type
---------------- ---- --- --------- -------- -----------------------------
Fa0/7            Desg FWD 19        128.9    P2p
Fa0/8            Desg FWD 19        128.10   P2p
Fa0/9            Desg FWD 19        128.11   P2p
Fa0/10           Desg FWD 19        128.12   P2p
Fa0/11           Root FWD 19        128.13   P2p
Fa0/12           Altn BLK 19        128.14   P2p


VLAN0100
  Spanning tree enabled protocol ieee
  Root ID    Priority    32868
             Address     000a.b8a9.d680
             Cost        19
             Port        13 (FastEthernet0/11)
             Hello Time   2 sec  Max Age 20 sec  Forward Delay 15 sec

  Bridge ID  Priority    32868  (priority 32768 sys-id-ext 100)
             Address     000a.b8a9.d780
             Hello Time   2 sec  Max Age 20 sec  Forward Delay 15 sec
             Aging Time 300

Interface        Role Sts Cost      Prio.Nbr Type
---------------- ---- --- --------- -------- -----------------------------
Fa0/7            Desg FWD 19        128.9    P2p
Fa0/8            Desg FWD 19        128.10   P2p
Fa0/9            Desg FWD 19        128.11   P2p
Fa0/10           Desg FWD 19        128.12   P2p
Fa0/11           Root FWD 19        128.13   P2p
Fa0/12           Altn BLK 19        128.14   P2p
```

Spanning tree is running a separate spanning tree instance for each VLAN created, plus VLAN 1. This method assumes that each VLAN could be running on a differently shaped topology. However, in many networks, multiple VLANs follow the same physical topology, so multiple spanning-tree calculations for the same topologies can get redundant. MST lets you configure different spanning tree instances. Each instance can hold a group of VLANs and manages its own spanning tree calculation.

MST is convenient in that it is backward compatible with PVST and RPVST+. Two switches only run MST with each other if they are in the same MST region. An MST region is defined by switches having identical region names, revision numbers, and VLAN-to-instance assignments. If they differ by any single attribute, they are considered different MST regions and fall back to RPVST+.

Step 4: Configure MST globally.

a. To configure MST, first use the global configuration command **spanning-tree mode mst** on all four switches. The command is shown for DLS1 only.

```
DLS1(config)# spanning-tree mode mst
```

By default, all VLANs are assigned to instance 0, but can be moved around to different instances when MST is configured.

b. Issue the **show spanning-tree** command and observe that there is only one spanning tree (instance 0) coming up. Also notice that the mode is listed as MSTP.

```
DLS1# show spanning-tree


MST00
  Spanning tree enabled protocol mstp
  Root ID    Priority    32768
             Address     000a.b8a9.d680
             Cost        0
             Port        13 (FastEthernet0/11)
             Hello Time   2 sec  Max Age 20 sec  Forward Delay 15 sec

  Bridge ID  Priority    32768  (priority 32768 sys-id-ext 0)
             Address     000a.b8a9.d780
             Hello Time   2 sec  Max Age 20 sec  Forward Delay 15 sec


Interface        Role Sts Cost      Prio.Nbr Type
---------------- ---- --- --------- -------- --------------------------------
Fa0/7            Desg FWD 200000    128.9    P2p
Fa0/8            Desg BLK 200000    128.10   P2p
Fa0/9            Desg FWD 200000    128.11   P2p
Fa0/10           Desg FWD 200000    128.12   P2p
Fa0/11           Root FWD 200000    128.13   P2p
Fa0/12           Altn BLK 200000    128.14   P2p
```

c. If you use the **show spanning-tree mst configuration** command, you can see a switch's current MST configuration. Because you have not configured any MST region settings, the switch shows the default settings.

```
DLS1# show spanning-tree mst configuration
Name      []
Revision  0
Instance  Vlans mapped
--------  ----------------------------------------------------------------
0         1-4094
--------  ----------------------------------------------------------------
```

Step 5: Configure the MST region and instances.

Now that MST has been enabled, we can configure the MST region settings to group VLANs. We use the region name CISCO and a revision number of 1. We put VLANs 20 through 50 into instance 1, and 80 and 100 into instance 2. The rest of the VLANs remain in instance 0, the default.

a. To begin modifying the MST configuration, type the global configuration command **spanning-tree mst configuration**. Configuring MST is different from other switch configurations, because changes are not applied until you are finished (similar to the deprecated VLAN database mode), and you can abort changes if you wish.

Note: You must apply identical configurations on each switch for MST to work properly. The commands are shown for DLS1 only.

```
DLS1(config)# spanning-tree mst configuration
DLS1(config-mst)#
```

b. When you are in MST configuration mode, you can view the current configuration using the **show current** command. You do not need to leave configuration mode to execute this command. Notice that the output is identical to **show spanning-tree mst configuration**.

```
DLS1(config-mst)# show current
Current MST configuration
Name      []
Revision  0
Instance  Vlans mapped
--------  ----------------------------------------------------------------
0         1-4094
          ----------------------------------------------------------------
```

Change the region name by typing **name** *name*. Change the revision number by typing **revision** *number*.

```
DLS1(config-mst)# name CISCO
DLS1(config-mst)# revision 1
```

Note: The MST revision number is not like the configuration revision number used with VTP. It does not increment when changes are made. Along with the region name, the revision number identifies the MST domain and must be the same on all systems in the MST region.

c. The last configuration change you have to make is putting VLANs into instances. Use the command **instance** *number* **vlan** *vlan_range*. The instance number can be between 0 and 15. Remember that 0 is the default instance number.

```
DLS1(config-mst)# instance 1 vlan 20-50
DLS1(config-mst)# instance 2 vlan 80,100
```

d. You can verify the changes you are about to make with the **show pending** command. Remember that the changes that you just entered are not committed until you type **exit, end** or **Ctrl+C**. If you do not like the changes you made, you can leave the prompt without committing them by typing **abort**. In the output below, notice the difference between **show current** and **show pending**.

```
DLS1(config-mst)# show current
```

```
Current MST configuration
Name        []
Revision    0
Instance    Vlans mapped
--------    ------------------------------------------------------------
0           1-4094
            ------------------------------------------------------------

DLS1(config-mst)# show pending
Pending MST configuration
Name        [CISCO]
Revision    1
Instance    Vlans mapped
--------    ------------------------------------------------------------
0           1-19,51-79,81-99,101-4094
1           20-50
2           80,100
            ------------------------------------------------------------

DLS1(config-mst)# exit
```

e. If you enter the **show spanning-tree mst configuration** command, you can see that the current configuration reflects the changes you just committed. Remember to perform the same configuration on all four switches.

```
DLS1# show span mst configuration
Name        [CISCO]
Revision    1
Instance    Vlans mapped
--------    -----------------------------------------------------------
0           1-19,51-79,81-99,101-4094
1           20-50
2           80,100
            -----------------------------------------------------------
```

Why do the switches wait until you are finished making changes to MST to commit them, rather than changing MST as you enter commands (like most switch commands)?

_____

_____

_____

f. Verify that separate instances of spanning tree are running.

```
DLS1# show spanning-tree

MST0
  Spanning tree enabled protocol mstp
  Root ID    Priority    32768
```

```
                    Address         000a.b8a9.d680
                    Cost            0
                    Port            13 (FastEthernet0/11)
                    Hello Time    2 sec  Max Age 20 sec  Forward Delay 15 sec

       Bridge ID  Priority        32768  (priority 32768 sys-id-ext 0)
                    Address         000a.b8a9.d780
                    Hello Time    2 sec  Max Age 20 sec  Forward Delay 15 sec


   Interface          Role Sts Cost      Prio.Nbr Type
   ---------------- ---- --- --------- -------- -----------------------------
   Fa0/7              Desg FWD 200000    128.9    P2p
   Fa0/8              Desg FWD 200000    128.10   P2p
   Fa0/9              Desg FWD 200000    128.11   P2p
   Fa0/10             Desg FWD 200000    128.12   P2p
   Fa0/11             Root FWD 200000    128.13   P2p
   Fa0/12             Altn BLK 200000    128.14   P2p


MST1
   Spanning tree enabled protocol mstp
   Root ID    Priority        32769
                    Address         000a.b8a9.d680
                    Cost            200000
                    Port            13 (FastEthernet0/11)
                    Hello Time    2 sec  Max Age 20 sec  Forward Delay 15 sec

       Bridge ID  Priority        32769  (priority 32768 sys-id-ext 1)
                    Address         000a.b8a9.d780
                    Hello Time    2 sec  Max Age 20 sec  Forward Delay 15 sec


   Interface          Role Sts Cost      Prio.Nbr Type
   ---------------- ---- --- --------- -------- -----------------------------
   Fa0/7              Desg FWD 200000    128.9    P2p
   Fa0/8              Desg FWD 200000    128.10   P2p
   Fa0/9              Desg FWD 200000    128.11   P2p
   Fa0/10             Desg FWD 200000    128.12   P2p
   Fa0/11             Root FWD 200000    128.13   P2p
   Fa0/12             Altn BLK 200000    128.14   P2p


MST2
   Spanning tree enabled protocol mstp
   Root ID    Priority        32770
                    Address         000a.b8a9.d680
                    Cost            200000
                    Port            13 (FastEthernet0/11)
                    Hello Time    2 sec  Max Age 20 sec  Forward Delay 15 sec

       Bridge ID  Priority        32770  (priority 32768 sys-id-ext 2)
                    Address         000a.b8a9.d780
                    Hello Time    2 sec  Max Age 20 sec  Forward Delay 15 sec
```

```
Interface         Role Sts Cost      Prio.Nbr Type
----------------  ---- --- --------- -------- ----------------------------
Fa0/7             Desg FWD 200000    128.9    P2p
Fa0/8             Desg FWD 200000    128.10   P2p
Fa0/9             Desg FWD 200000    128.11   P2p
Fa0/10            Desg FWD 200000    128.12   P2p
Fa0/11            Root FWD 200000    128.13   P2p
Fa0/12            Altn BLK 200000    128.14   P2p
```

Challenge

You can modify per-instance MST spanning tree attributes the same way you can modify per-VLAN attributes. Make DLS1 the root of instance 1 and DLS2 the root of instance 2.

HINT: Use a question mark on the global configuration command **spanning-tree mst ?**.

Chapter 4 Implementing Inter-VLAN Routing

Lab 4-1, Inter-VLAN Routing with an External Router

Topology

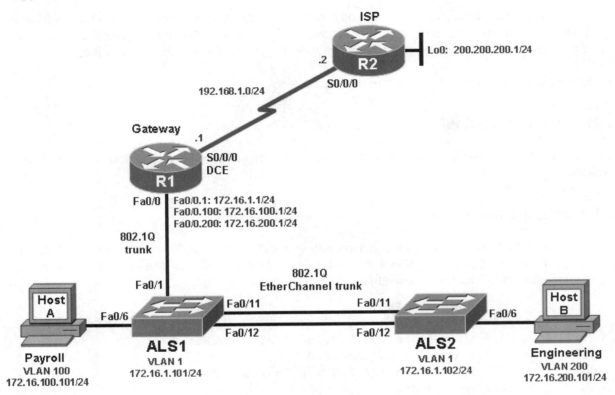

Objective

- Configure inter-VLAN routing using an external router, also known as a router on a stick.

Background

Inter-VLAN routing using an external router can be a cost-effective solution when it is necessary to segment a network into multiple broadcast domains. In this lab, you split an existing network into two separate VLANs on the access layer switches, and use an external router to route between the VLANs. An 802.1Q trunk connects the switch and the Fast Ethernet interface of the router for routing and management. Static routes are used between the gateway router and the ISP router. The switches are connected via an 802.1Q EtherChannel link.

Note: This lab uses Cisco 1841 routers with Cisco IOS Release 12.4(24)T1 and the Advanced IP Services image c1841-advipservicesk9-mz.124-24.T1.bin. The switches are Cisco WS-C2960-24TT-L with the Cisco IOS image c2960-lanbasek9-mz.122-46.SE.bin. You can use other routers (such as 2801 or 2811), switches (such as 2950), and Cisco IOS Software versions if they have comparable capabilities and features. Depending on the router or switch model and Cisco IOS Software version, the commands available and output produced might vary from what is shown in this lab.

Required Resources

- 2 routers (Cisco 1841 with Cisco IOS Release 12.4(24)T1 Advanced IP Services or comparable)
- 2 switches (Cisco 2960 with the Cisco IOS Release 12.2(46)SE C2960-LANBASEK9-M image or comparable)
- Serial and Ethernet cables

Step 1: Prepare the switches and routers for the lab.

a. Cable the network as shown in the topology diagram. On each switch, erase the startup configuration, delete the vlan.dat file, and reload the switches. Refer to Lab 1-1, "Clearing a Switch" and Lab 1-2, "Clearing a Switch Connected to a Larger Network" to prepare the switches for this lab.

b. Erase the startup configuration and reload the routers.

Step 2: Configure the hosts.

Configure PC hosts A and B with the IP address, subnet mask (/24), and default gateway shown in the topology.

Step 3: Configure the routers.

a. Configure the ISP router for communication with your gateway router. The static route used for the internal networks provides a path for the local network from the ISP. In addition, configure a loopback interface on the ISP router to simulate an external network.

```
Router(config)# hostname ISP
ISP(config)# interface Loopback0
ISP(config-if)# ip address 200.200.200.1 255.255.255.0
ISP(config-if)# interface Serial0/0/0
ISP(config-if)# ip address 192.168.1.2 255.255.255.0
ISP(config-if)# no shutdown
ISP(config-if)# exit
ISP(config)# ip route 172.16.0.0 255.255.0.0 192.168.1.1
```

b. Configure the Gateway router to communicate with the ISP router. Notice the use of a static default route. The default route tells the router to send any traffic with an unknown destination network to the ISP router.

```
Router(config)# hostname Gateway
Gateway(config)# interface Serial0/0/0
Gateway(config-if)# ip address 192.168.1.1 255.255.255.0
Gateway(config-if)# clockrate 64000
Gateway(config-if)# no shutdown
Gateway(config-if)# exit
Gateway(config)# ip route 0.0.0.0 0.0.0.0 192.168.1.2
```

c. Verify connectivity from the Gateway router using the **ping** command.

Was this ping successful?

Step 4: Configure the switches.

a. Configure the switch hostnames and IP addresses on the management VLAN according to the diagram. By default, VLAN 1 is used as the management VLAN. Create a default gateway on both access layer switches using the **ip default-gateway** *ip_address* command.

The following is a sample configuration for switch ALS1.

```
Switch(config)# hostname ALS1
ALS1(config)# interface vlan 1
ALS1(config-if)# ip address 172.16.1.101 255.255.255.0
ALS1(config-if)# no shutdown
ALS1(config-if)# exit
ALS1(config)# ip default-gateway 172.16.1.1
```

The following is a sample configuration for switch ALS2.

```
Switch(config)# hostname ALS2
ALS2(config)# interface vlan 1
ALS2(config-if)# ip address 172.16.1.102 255.255.255.0
ALS2(config-if)# no shutdown
ALS2(config-if)# exit
ALS2(config)# ip default-gateway 172.16.1.1
```

b. (Optional) Set an enable secret password and configure the vty lines for Telnet access to the switch.

```
ALS1(config)# enable secret cisco
ALS1(config)# line vty 0 15
ALS1(config-line)# password cisco
ALS1(config-line)# login
ALS1(config-line)# end

ALS2(config)# enable secret cisco
ALS2(config)# line vty 0 15
ALS2(config-line)# password cisco
ALS2(config-line)# login
ALS2(config-line)# end
```

c   By default, how many lines are available for Telnet on the access switches?

_____

Step 5: Confirm the VLANs.

a. Verify that the only existing VLANs are the built-in VLANs. Issue the **show vlan** command from privileged mode on both access layer switches.

```
ALS1# show vlan

VLAN Name                             Status    Ports
---- -------------------------------- --------- -------------------------------
1    default                          active    Fa0/1, Fa0/2, Fa0/3, Fa0/4
                                                Fa0/5, Fa0/6, Fa0/7, Fa0/8
                                                Fa0/9, Fa0/10, Fa0/11, Fa0/12
                                                Fa0/13, Fa0/14, Fa0/15, Fa0/16
```

```
                                          Fa0/17, Fa0/18, Fa0/19, Fa0/20
                                          Fa0/21, Fa0/22, Fa0/23, Fa0/24
                                          Gi0/1, Gi0/2
   1002 fddi-default                      act/unsup
   1003 token-ring-default                act/unsup
   1004 fddinet-default                   act/unsup
   1005 trnet-default                     act/unsup

   VLAN Type  SAID       MTU   Parent RingNo BridgeNo Stp  BrdgMode Trans1 Trans2
   ---- ----- ---------- ----- ------ ------ -------- ---- -------- ------ -----
   1    enet  100001     1500  -      -      -        -    -        0      0
   1002 fddi  101002     1500  -      -      -        -    -        0      0
   1003 tr    101003     1500  -      -      -        -    -        0      0
   1004 fdnet 101004     1500  -      -      -        ieee -        0      0
   1005 trnet 101005     1500  -      -      -        ibm  -        0      0

   Remote SPAN VLANs
   ------------------------------------------------------------------------


   Primary Secondary Type             Ports
   ------- --------- ---------------- ----------------------------------------
```

Which VLAN is the default management VLAN for Ethernet? What types of traffic are carried on this VLAN?

_____

_____

_____

Step 6: Configure trunk links and EtherChannel on switches.

a. Use the Fast Ethernet 0/11 and 0/12 ports of ALS1 and ALS2 to create an EtherChannel trunk between the switches.

```
ALS1# configure terminal
Enter configuration commands, one per line.  End with CNTL/Z.
ALS1(config)# interface range fastEthernet 0/11 - 12
ALS1(config-if-range)# switchport mode trunk
ALS1(config-if-range)# channel-group 1 mode desirable
ALS1(config-if-range)# end

ALS2# configure terminal
Enter configuration commands, one per line.  End with CNTL/Z.
ALS2(config)# interface range fastEthernet 0/11 - 12
ALS2(config-if-range)# switchport mode trunk
ALS2(config-if-range)# channel-group 1 mode desirable
ALS2(config-if-range)# end
```

b. Verify the EtherChannel configuration using the **show etherchannel** command.

```
ALS1# show etherchannel 1 summary
Flags:  D - down          P - in port-channel
        I - stand-alone  s - suspended
        H - Hot-standby (LACP only)
        R - Layer3        S - Layer2
        U - in use        f - failed to allocate aggregator
        u - unsuitable for bundling
        w - waiting to be aggregated
        d - default port


Number of channel-groups in use: 1
Number of aggregators:           1

Group  Port-channel  Protocol   Ports
------+-------------+----------+------------------------------------------
1      Po1(SU)       PAgP       Fa0/11(P)   Fa0/12(P)
```

Step 7: Configure VTP.

a. Set up the VTP domain for the access layer switches in global configuration mode. The default VTP mode is server for both switches. Configure ALS2 as a VTP client, and leave ALS1 as a server. Configure the VTP domain name and version on VTP server ALS1.

```
ALS2(config)# vtp mode client
Setting device to VTP CLIENT mode.

ALS1(config)# vtp domain SWLAB
Changing VTP domain name from NULL to SWLAB
%SW_VLAN-6-VTP_DOMAIN_NAME_CHG: VTP domain name changed to SWLAB.


ALS1(config)# vtp version 2
```

b. Use the **show vtp status** command to verify the ALS1 VTP configuration and that client ALS2 has learned the new VTP domain information from ALS1.

```
ALS1# show vtp status
VTP Version                    : running VTP2
Configuration Revision         : 1
Maximum VLANs supported locally : 255
Number of existing VLANs       : 5
VTP Operating Mode             : Server
VTP Domain Name                : SWLAB
VTP Pruning Mode               : Disabled
VTP V2 Mode                    : Enabled
VTP Traps Generation           : Disabled
MD5 digest                     : 0x6A 0x1A 0x90 0xA3 0x10 0xCE 0x86 0xFA
Configuration last modified by 172.16.1.101 at 2-28-10 00:36:24
Local updater ID is 172.16.1.101 on interface Vl1 (lowest numbered VLAN
interface found)

ALS2# show vtp status
VTP Version                    : running VTP2
Configuration Revision         : 1
Maximum VLANs supported locally : 255
```

```
Number of existing VLANs           : 5
VTP Operating Mode                 : Client
VTP Domain Name                    : SWLAB
VTP Pruning Mode                   : Disabled
VTP V2 Mode                        : Enabled
VTP Traps Generation               : Disabled
MD5 digest                         : 0x6A 0x1A 0x90 0xA3 0x10 0xCE 0x86 0xFA
Configuration last modified by 172.16.1.101 at 2-28-10 00:36:24
```

Step 8: Configure VLANs and switch access ports.

a. Configure the VLAN 100 named Payroll and VLAN 200 named Engineering on VTP server ALS1.

```
ALS1(config)# vlan 100
ALS1(config-vlan)# name Payroll
ALS1(config-vlan)# vlan 200
ALS1(config-vlan)# name Engineering
```

b. Use the **show vlan brief** command on ALS2 to verify that ALS2 has learned the new VLANs from ALS1.

```
ALS2# show vlan brief
```

```
VLAN Name                             Status    Ports
---- -------------------------------- --------- -------------------------------
1    default                          active    Fa0/1, Fa0/2, Fa0/3, Fa0/4
                                                Fa0/5, Fa0/6, Fa0/7, Fa0/8
                                                Fa0/9, Fa0/10, Fa0/13, Fa0/14
                                                Fa0/15, Fa0/16, Fa0/17, Fa0/18
                                                Fa0/19, Fa0/20, Fa0/21, Fa0/22
                                                Fa0/23, Fa0/24, Gi0/1, Gi0/2
100  Payroll                          active
200  Engineering                      active
1002 fddi-default                     act/unsup
1003 trcrf-default                    act/unsup
1004 fddinet-default                  act/unsup
1005 trbrf-default                    act/unsup
```

c. Configure the switch access ports for the hosts according to the diagram. Statically set the switch port mode to access, and use Spanning Tree PortFast on the interfaces. Assign the host attached to ALS1 Fast Ethernet 0/6 to VLAN 100, and the host attached to ALS2 Fast Ethernet 0/6 to VLAN 200.

```
ALS1(config)# interface fastEthernet 0/6
ALS1(config-if)# switchport mode access
ALS1(config-if)# switchport access vlan 100
ALS1(config-if)# spanning-tree portfast
%Warning: portfast should only be enabled on ports connected to a single
 host. Connecting hubs, concentrators, switches, bridges, etc... to this
 interface when portfast is enabled, can cause temporary bridging loops.
 Use with CAUTION

%Portfast has been configured on FastEthernet0/6 but will only
 have effect when the interface is in a non-trunking mode.

ALS2(config)# interface fastEthernet 0/6
ALS2(config-if)# switchport mode access
ALS2(config-if)# switchport access vlan 200
```

```
ALS2(config-if)# spanning-tree portfast
%Warning: portfast should only be enabled on ports connected to a single
 host. Connecting hubs, concentrators, switches, bridges, etc... to this
 interface when portfast is enabled, can cause temporary bridging loops.
 Use with CAUTION

%Portfast has been configured on FastEthernet0/6 but will only
 have effect when the interface is in a non-trunking mode.
```

d. Use the **show vlan brief** command to verify that Fa0/6 is in VLAN 100 on ALS1 and in VLAN 200 on ALS2.

```
ALS1# show vlan brief

VLAN Name                             Status    Ports
---- -------------------------------- --------- ------------------------------
1    default                          active    Fa0/1, Fa0/2, Fa0/3, Fa0/4
                                                Fa0/5, Fa0/7, Fa0/8, Fa0/9
                                                Fa0/10, Fa0/13, Fa0/14, Fa0/15
                                                Fa0/16, Fa0/17, Fa0/18, Fa0/19
                                                Fa0/20, Fa0/21, Fa0/22, Fa0/23
                                                Fa0/24, Gi0/1, Gi0/2
100  Payroll                          active    Fa0/6
200  Engineering                      active
1002 fddi-default                     act/unsup
1003 trcrf-default                    act/unsup
1004 fddinet-default                  act/unsup
1005 trbrf-default                    act/unsup

ALS2# show vlan brief

VLAN Name                             Status    Ports
---- -------------------------------- --------- ------------------------------
1    default                          active    Fa0/1, Fa0/2, Fa0/3, Fa0/4
                                                Fa0/5, Fa0/7, Fa0/8, Fa0/9
                                                Fa0/10, Fa0/13, Fa0/14, Fa0/15
                                                Fa0/16, Fa0/17, Fa0/18, Fa0/19
                                                Fa0/20, Fa0/21, Fa0/22, Fa0/23
                                                Fa0/24, Gi0/1, Gi0/2
100  Payroll                          active
200  Engineering                      active    Fa0/6
1002 fddi-default                     act/unsup
1003 trcrf-default                    act/unsup
1004 fddinet-default                  act/unsup
1005 trbrf-default                    act/unsup
```

Step 9: Configure ALS1 trunking to the Gateway router.

Configure switch ALS1 interface Fast Ethernet 0/1 for trunking with the Gateway router Fast Ethernet interface, according to the topology diagram.

```
ALS1(config)# interface fastEthernet 0/1
ALS1(config-if)# switchport mode trunk
ALS1(config-if)# end
```

Note: Optionally, you can apply the **spanning-tree portfast trunk** command to interface Fa0/1 of switch ALS1. This allows the link to the router to rapidly transition to the forwarding state despite being a trunk.

Step 10: Configure the Gateway router Fast Ethernet interface for VLAN trunking.

The native VLAN cannot be configured on a subinterface for Cisco IOS releases earlier than 12.1(3)T. The native VLAN IP address must be configured on the physical interface. Other VLAN traffic is configured on subinterfaces. Cisco IOS release 12.1(3)T and later support native VLAN configuration on a subinterface with the **encapsulation dot1q native** command. If a subinterface is configured using the **encapsulation dot1q native** command, the configuration on the physical interface is ignored. This technique is used in the lab configuration.

a. Create a subinterface for each VLAN. Enable each subinterface with the proper trunking protocol, and configure it for a particular VLAN with the **encapsulation** command. Assign an IP address to each subinterface, which hosts on the VLAN can use as their default gateway.

The following is a sample configuration for the Fast Ethernet 0/0 interface.

```
Gateway(config)# interface fastEthernet 0/0
Gateway(config-if)# no shut
```

The following is a sample configuration for the VLAN 1 subinterface.

```
Gateway(config)# interface fastEthernet 0/0.1
Gateway(config-subif)# description Management VLAN 1
Gateway(config-subif)# encapsulation dot1q 1 native
Gateway(config-subif)# ip address 172.16.1.1 255.255.255.0
```

Note: For enhanced switch security, it is considered best practice to use independent unused VLANs for native and management VLANs.

The following is a sample configuration for the VLAN 100 subinterface.

```
Gateway(config-subif)# interface fastEthernet 0/0.100
Gateway(config-subif)# description Payroll VLAN 100
Gateway(config-subif)# encapsulation dot1q 100
Gateway(config-subif)# ip address 172.16.100.1 255.255.255.0
```

The following is a sample configuration for the VLAN 200 subinterface.

```
Gateway(config-subif)# interface fastEthernet 0/0.200
Gateway(config-subif)# description Engineering VLAN 200
Gateway(config-subif)# encapsulation dot1q 200
Gateway(config-subif)# ip address 172.16.200.1 255.255.255.0
Gateway(config-subif)# end
```

b   Use the **show ip interface brief** command to verify the interface configuration and status.

```
Gateway# show ip interface brief
```

Interface	IP-Address	OK?	Method	Status	Protocol
FastEthernet0/0	unassigned	YES	unset	up	up
FastEthernet0/1.1	172.16.1.1	YES	manual	up	up
FastEthernet0/1.100	172.16.100.1	YES	manual	up	up
FastEthernet0/1.200	172.16.200.1	YES	manual	up	up
FastEthernet0/1	unassigned	YES	unset	administratively down	down
Serial0/0/0	192.168.1.1	YES	manual	up	up
Serial0/0/1	unassigned	YES	unset	administratively down	down

c. Use the **show interfaces description** command to verify the interface status and description assigned.

```
Gateway# show interfaces description
Interface                       Status          Protocol Description
Fa0/0                           up              up
Fa0/0.1                         up              up       Management VLAN 1
Fa0/0.100                       up              up       Payroll VLAN 100
Fa0/0.200                       up              up       Engineering VLAN 200
Fa0/1                           admin down      down
Se0/0/0                         up              up
Se0/0/1                         admin down      down
```

d. Use the **show vlans** command on the Gateway router.

```
Gateway# show vlans

Virtual LAN ID:  1 (IEEE 802.1Q Encapsulation)

    vLAN Trunk Interface:    FastEthernet0/1.1

 This is configured as native Vlan for the following interface(s) :
FastEthernet0/1

    Protocols Configured:    Address:              Received:         Transmitted:
          IP               172.16.1.1                198                    54
          Other                                        0                    29

    277 packets, 91551 bytes input
    83 packets, 15446 bytes output

Virtual LAN ID:  100 (IEEE 802.1Q Encapsulation)

    vLAN Trunk Interface:    FastEthernet0/1.100

    Protocols Configured:    Address:              Received:         Transmitted:
          IP               172.16.100.1                1                    25

    0 packets, 0 bytes input
    25 packets, 2350 bytes output

Virtual LAN ID:  200 (IEEE 802.1Q Encapsulation)

    vLAN Trunk Interface:    FastEthernet0/1.200

    Protocols Configured:    Address:              Received:         Transmitted:
          IP               172.16.200.1                1                    25

    0 packets, 0 bytes input
    25 packets, 2350 bytes output
```

e. Use the **show cdp neighbor detail** command on the Gateway router to verify that ALS1 is a neighbor. Telnet to the IP address given in the CDP information.

```
Gateway# show cdp neighbor detail
-------------------------
Device ID: ISP
```

```
Entry address(es):
   IP address: 192.168.1.2
Platform: Cisco 1841,  Capabilities: Router Switch IGMP
Interface: Serial0/0/0,  Port ID (outgoing port): Serial0/0/0
Holdtime : 174 sec

Version :
Cisco IOS Software, 1841 Software (C1841-ADVIPSERVICESK9-M), Version 12.4(24)
T1,
 RELEASE SOFTWARE (fc3)
Technical Support: http://www.cisco.com/techsupport
Copyright (c) 1986-2009 by Cisco Systems, Inc.
Compiled Fri 19-Jun-09 13:56 by prod_rel_team
advertisement version: 2
VTP Management Domain: ''
-------------------------
Device ID: ALS1
Entry address(es):
   IP address: 172.16.1.101
Platform: cisco WS-C2960-24TT-L,  Capabilities: Switch IGMP
Interface: FastEthernet0/0.1,  Port ID (outgoing port): FastEthernet0/1
Holdtime : 118 sec

Version :
Cisco IOS Software, C2960 Software (C2960-LANBASEK9-M), Version 12.2(46)SE,
RELE
ASE SOFTWARE (fc2)
Copyright (c) 1986-2008 by Cisco Systems, Inc.
Compiled Thu 21-Aug-08 15:59 by nachen

advertisement version: 2
Protocol Hello:  OUI=0x00000C, Protocol ID=0x0112; payload len=27,
value=0000000
0FFFFFFFF010221FF000000000000001D46350C80FF0000
VTP Management Domain: 'SWLAB'
Native VLAN: 1
Duplex: full
```

Was the Telnet successful?

Step 11: Verify inter-VLAN routing on the Gateway router and the host devices.

a. Ping to the 200.200.200.1 ISP loopback interface from either host. Was this ping successful?

b. Ping from Host A to Host B. Was this ping successful?

_____

_____

c. Telnet to the ALS2 VLAN 1 management IP address from the Engineering host. Was this Telnet successful?

_____

_____

If any of the tests failed, make the necessary corrections to the configurations for the router and switches.

Router Interface Summary Table

Router Interface Summary				
Router Model	Ethernet Interface #1	Ethernet Interface #2	Serial Interface #1	Serial Interface #2
1700	Fast Ethernet 0 (FA0)	Fast Ethernet 1 (FA1)	Serial 0 (S0)	Serial 1 (S1)
1800	Fast Ethernet 0/0 (FA0/0)	Fast Ethernet 0/1 (FA0/1)	Serial 0/0/0 (S0/0/0)	Serial 0/0/1 (S0/0/1)
2600	Fast Ethernet 0/0 (FA0/0)	Fast Ethernet 0/1 (FA0/1)	Serial 0/0 (S0/0)	Serial 0/1 (S0/1)
2800	Fast Ethernet 0/0 (FA0/0)	Fast Ethernet 0/1 (FA0/1)	Serial 0/0/0 (S0/0/0)	Serial 0/0/1 (S0/0/1)

Note: To find out how the router is configured, look at the interfaces to identify the type of router and how many interfaces the router has. Rather than list all combinations of configurations for each router class, this table includes identifiers for the possible combinations of Ethernet and serial interfaces in the device. The table does not include any other type of interface, even though a specific router might contain one. For example, for an ISDN BRI interface, the string in parenthesis is the legal abbreviation that can be used in Cisco IOS commands to represent the interface.

Lab 4-2, Inter-VLAN Routing with an Internal Route Processor and Monitoring CEF Functions

Topology

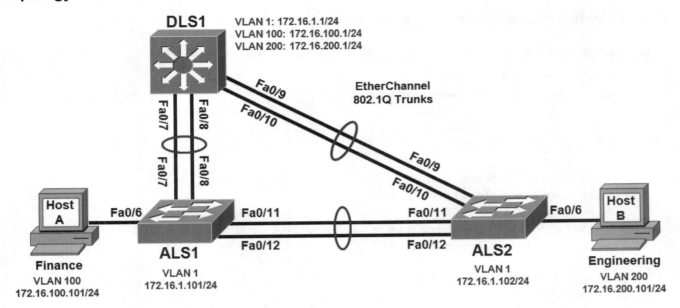

Objective

- Route between VLANs using a 3560 switch with an internal route processor using Cisco Express Forwarding (CEF).

Background

The current network equipment includes a 3560 distribution layer switch and two 2960 access layer switches. The network is segmented into three functional subnets using VLANs for better network management. The VLANs include Finance, Engineering, and a subnet for equipment management, which is the default management VLAN, VLAN 1. After VTP and trunking have been configured for the switches, switched virtual interfaces (SVI) are configured on the distribution layer switch to route between these VLANs, providing full connectivity to the internal network.

Note: This lab uses Cisco WS-C2960-24TT-L switches with the Cisco IOS image c2960-lanbasek9-mz.122-46.SE.bin and Catalyst 3560-24PS with the Cisco IOS image c3560-advipservicesk9-mz.122-46. SE.bin. You can use other switches (such as 2950 or 3550) and Cisco IOS Software versions if they have comparable capabilities and features. Depending on the switch model and Cisco IOS Software version, the commands available and output produced might vary from what is shown in this lab.

Required Resources

- 2 switches (Cisco 2960 with the Cisco IOS Release 12.2(46)SE C2960-LANBASEK9-M image or comparable)
- 1 switch (Cisco 3560 with the Cisco IOS Release 12.2(46)SE C3560-ADVIPSERVICESK9-mz image or comparable)
- Ethernet and console cables

Step 1: Prepare the switches for the lab.

Erase the startup configuration, delete the vlan.dat file, and reload the switches. Refer to Lab 1-1, "Clearing a Switch" and Lab 1-2, "Clearing a Switch Connected to a Larger Network" to prepare the switches for this lab. Cable the equipment as shown.

Step 2: Configure basic switch parameters.

a. Configure the hostname, password, and optionally, Telnet access on each switch.

```
Switch(config)# hostname ALS1
ALS1(config)# enable secret cisco
ALS1(config)# line vty 0 15
ALS1(config-line)# password cisco
ALS1(config-line)# login

Switch(config)# hostname ALS2
ALS2(config)# enable secret cisco
ALS2(config)# line vty 0 15
ALS2(config-line)# password cisco
ALS2(config-line)# login

Switch(config)# hostname DLS1
DLS1(config)# enable secret cisco
DLS1(config)# line vty 0 15
DLS1(config-line)#password cisco
DLS1(config-line)# login
```

b. Configure management IP addresses on VLAN 1 for all three switches according to the diagram.

```
ALS1(config)# interface vlan 1
ALS1(config-if)# ip address 172.16.1.101 255.255.255.0
ALS1(config-if)# no shutdown

ALS2(config)# interface vlan 1
ALS2(config-if)# ip address 172.16.1.102 255.255.255.0
ALS2(config-if)# no shutdown

DLS1(config)# interface vlan 1
DLS1(config-if)# ip address 172.16.1.1 255.255.255.0
DLS1(config-if)# no shutdown
```

c. Configure default gateways on the access layer switches. The distribution layer switch will not use a default gateway, because it acts as a Layer 3 device. The access layer switches act as Layer 2 devices and need a default gateway to send management VLAN traffic off of the local subnet.

```
ALS1(config)# ip default-gateway 172.16.1.1

ALS2(config)# ip default-gateway 172.16.1.1
```

Step 3: Configure trunks and EtherChannels between switches.

To distribute VLAN and VTP information between the switches, trunks are needed between the three switches. Configure these trunks according to the diagram. EtherChannel is used for these trunks. EtherChannel allows you to utilize both Fast Ethernet interfaces that are available between each device, thereby doubling the bandwidth.

a. Configure the trunks and EtherChannel from DLS1 to ALS1. The **switchport trunk encapsulation [isl |
    dot1q]** command is used because this switch also supports ISL encapsulation.

```
DLS1(config)# interface range fastEthernet 0/7 - 8
DLS1(config-if-range)# switchport trunk encapsulation dot1q
DLS1(config-if-range)# switchport mode trunk
DLS1(config-if-range)# channel-group 1 mode desirable
```

Creating a port-channel interface Port-channel 1

b. Configure the trunks and EtherChannel from DLS1 to ALS2.

```
DLS1(config)# interface range fastEthernet 0/9 - 10
DLS1(config-if-range)# switchport trunk encapsulation dot1q
DLS1(config-if-range)# switchport mode trunk
DLS1(config-if-range)# channel-group 2 mode desirable
```

Creating a port-channel interface Port-channel 2

c. Configure the trunks and EtherChannel between ALS1 and DLS1, and for the trunks and EtherChannel
    between ALS1 and ALS2.

```
ALS1(config)# interface range fastEthernet 0/11 - 12
ALS1(config-if-range)# switchport mode trunk
ALS1(config-if-range)# channel-group 1 mode desirable
```

Creating a port-channel interface Port-channel 1

```
ALS1(config-if-range)# exit
ALS1(config)# interface range fastEthernet 0/7 - 8
ALS1(config-if-range)# switchport mode trunk
ALS1(config-if-range)# channel-group 2 mode desirable
```

Creating a port-channel interface Port-channel 2

d. Configure the trunks and EtherChannel between ALS2 and DLS1, and for the trunks and EtherChannel
    between ALS2 and ALS1.

```
ALS2(config)# interface range fastEthernet 0/11 - 12
ALS2(config-if-range)# switchport mode trunk
ALS2(config-if-range)# channel-group 1 mode desirable
```

Creating a port-channel interface Port-channel 1

```
ALS2(config-if-range)# exit
ALS2(config)# interface range fastEthernet 0/9 - 10
ALS2(config-if-range)# switchport mode trunk
ALS2(config-if-range)# channel-group 2 mode desirable
```

Creating a port-channel interface Port-channel 2

e. Verify trunking between DLS1, ALS1, and ALS2 using the **show interface trunk** command on all
    switches.

```
DLS1# show interface trunk
```

Port	Mode	Encapsulation	Status	Native vlan
Po1	on	802.1q	trunking	1

```
Po2           on              802.1q           trunking       1

Port        Vlans allowed on trunk
Po1         1-4094
Po2         1-4094

Port        Vlans allowed and active in management domain
Po1         1
Po2         1

Port        Vlans in spanning tree forwarding state and not pruned
Po1         1
Po2         1
```

f.   Use the **show etherchannel summary** command on each switch to verify the EtherChannels.

The following is sample output from ALS1. Notice the two EtherChannels on the access layer switches.

```
ALS1# show etherchannel summary
Flags:  D - down         P - in port-channel
        I - stand-alone  s - suspended
        H - Hot-standby (LACP only)
        R - Layer3       S - Layer2
        U - in use       f - failed to allocate aggregator
        u - unsuitable for bundling
        w - waiting to be aggregated
        d - default port


Number of channel-groups in use: 2
Number of aggregators:           2

Group  Port-channel  Protocol   Ports
------+-------------+----------+-----------------------------------------------
1      Po1(SU)        PAgP       Fa0/11(P)    Fa0/12(P)
2      Po2(SU)        PAgP       Fa0/7(P)     Fa0/8(P)
```

On ALS1, which ports are used for channel group 2?

_____

Step 4: Configure VTP on ALS1 and ALS2.

a.   Change the VTP mode of ALS1 and ALS2 to client.

```
ALS1(config)# vtp mode client
Setting device to VTP CLIENT mode.


ALS2(config)# vtp mode client
Setting device to VTP CLIENT mode.
```

b.   Verify the VTP changes with the **show vtp status** command. The output on ALS2 is similar to that of

ALS1.

```
ALS2# show vtp status
VTP Version                    : running VTP1 (VTP2 capable)
Configuration Revision      : 0
Maximum VLANs supported locally : 255
Number of existing VLANs    : 5
VTP Operating Mode          : Client
VTP Domain Name             :
VTP Pruning Mode            : Disabled
VTP V2 Mode                 : Disabled
VTP Traps Generation        : Disabled
MD5 digest                  : 0xC8 0xAB 0x3C 0x3B 0xAB 0xDD 0x34 0xCF
Configuration last modified by 0.0.0.0 at 3-1-93 15:47:34
```

How many VLANs can be supported locally on the 2960 switch?

Step 5: Configure VTP on DLS1.

a. Create the VTP domain on DLS1 and create VLANs 100 and 200 for the domain.

```
DLS1(config)# vtp domain SWPOD
DLS1(config)# vtp version 2

DLS1(config)# vlan 100
DLS1(config-vlan)# name Finance
DLS1(config-vlan)# vlan 200
DLS1(config-vlan)# name Engineering
```

b. Verify VTP information throughout the domain using the **show vlan** and **show vtp status** commands.

How many existing VLANs are in the VTP domain?

Step 6: Configure ports.

Configure the host ports for the appropriate VLANs according to the diagram.

```
ALS1(config)# interface fastEthernet 0/6
ALS1(config-if)# switchport mode access
ALS1(config-if)# switchport access vlan 100

ALS2(config)# interface fastEthernet 0/6
ALS2(config-if)# switchport mode access
ALS2(config-if)# switchport access vlan 200
```

Ping from the host on VLAN 100 to the host on VLAN 200. Was the ping successful? Why do you think this is the case?

Ping from a host to the VLAN 1 management IP address of DLS1. Was the ping successful? Why do you think this is the case?

_____

_____

_____

Step 7: Configure VLAN interfaces and enable routing.

a. On DLS1, create the Layer 3 VLAN interfaces to route between VLANs using the **interface vlan** *vlan-id* command. These are known as SVIs. You do not need to set up VLAN 1, because this was done in Step 2.

```
DLS1(config)# interface vlan 100
DLS1(config-if)# ip add 172.16.100.1 255.255.255.0
DLS1(config-if)# no shut
DLS1(config-if)# interface vlan 200
DLS1(config-if)# ip address 172.16.200.1 255.255.255.0
DLS1(config-if)# no shutdown
```

b. The **ip routing** command is also needed to allow the switch to act as a Layer 3 device to route between these VLANs. Because the VLANs are all considered directly connected, a routing protocol is not needed at this time.

```
DLS1(config)# ip routing
```

c. Verify the configuration using the **show ip route** command on DLS1.

```
DLS1# show ip route
Codes: C - connected, S - static, R - RIP, M - mobile, B - BGP
       D - EIGRP, EX - EIGRP external, O - OSPF, IA - OSPF inter area
       N1 - OSPF NSSA external type 1, N2 - OSPF NSSA external type 2
       E1 - OSPF external type 1, E2 - OSPF external type 2, E - EGP
       i - IS-IS, su - IS-IS summary, L1 - IS-IS level-1, L2 - IS-IS level-2
       ia - IS-IS inter area, * - candidate default, U - per-user static route
       o - ODR, P - periodic downloaded static route

Gateway of last resort is not set

     172.16.0.0/24 is subnetted, 3 subnets
C       172.16.200.0 is directly connected, Vlan200
C       172.16.1.0 is directly connected, Vlan1
```

```
C          172.16.100.0 is directly connected, Vlan100
```

Step 8: Verify inter-VLAN routing by the internal route processor.

a. Ping from the Engineering host to the Finance host. Was the ping successful this time?

_____

b. Telnet from one of the hosts to the VLAN 1 IP address of DLS1. Can this switch be remotely accessed from this host?

_____

Step 9: Examine the CEF configuration.

CEF implements an advanced IP lookup and forwarding algorithm to deliver maximum Layer 3 switching performance. CEF is less CPU-intensive than route caching.

In dynamic networks, fast-switching cache entries are frequently invalidated because of routing changes. This can cause traffic to be process-switched using the routing table, instead of fast-switched using the route cache. CEF uses the Forwarding Information Base (FIB) lookup table to perform destination-based switching of IP packets.

CEF is enabled by default on the 3560 switch.

a. Use the **show ip cef** command to display the CEF FIB.

```
DLS1# show ip cef
Prefix               Next Hop           Interface
0.0.0.0/32           receive
172.16.1.0/24        attached           Vlan1
172.16.1.0/32        receive
172.16.1.1/32        receive
172.16.1.101/32      attached           Vlan1
172.16.1.102/32      attached           Vlan1
172.16.1.255/32      receive
172.16.100.0/24      attached           Vlan100
172.16.100.0/32      receive
172.16.100.1/32      receive
172.16.100.255/32    receive
172.16.200.0/24      attached           Vlan200
172.16.200.0/32      receive
172.16.200.1/32      receive
172.16.200.255/32    receive
224.0.0.0/4          drop
224.0.0.0/24         receive
255.255.255.255/32   receive
```

b. Use the **show ip interface** command to verify that CEF is enabled on an interface. The following output shows that CEF is enabled on VLAN 100.

```
DLS1# show ip interface vlan 100
Vlan100 is up, line protocol is up
   Internet address is 172.16.100.1/24
   Broadcast address is 255.255.255.255
   Address determined by setup command
   MTU is 1500 bytes
   Helper address is not set
   Directed broadcast forwarding is disabled
   Outgoing access list is not set
   Inbound  access list is not set
   Proxy ARP is enabled
   Local Proxy ARP is disabled
   Security level is default
   Split horizon is enabled
   ICMP redirects are always sent
   ICMP unreachables are always sent
   ICMP mask replies are never sent
   IP fast switching is enabled
   IP CEF switching is enabled
   IP CEF switching turbo vector
   IP multicast fast switching is disabled
   IP multicast distributed fast switching is disabled
   IP route-cache flags are Fast, CEF
   Router Discovery is disabled
   IP output packet accounting is disabled
   IP access violation accounting is disabled
   TCP/IP header compression is disabled
   RTP/IP header compression is disabled
   Probe proxy name replies are disabled
   Policy routing is disabled
   Network address translation is disabled
   WCCP Redirect outbound is disabled
   WCCP Redirect inbound is disabled
   WCCP Redirect exclude is disabled
   BGP Policy Mapping is disabled
```

c. Use the **show ip cef summary** command to display the CEF table summary.

```
DLS1# show ip cef summary
IPv4 CEF is enabled for distributed and running
VRF Default:
 18 prefixes (18/0 fwd/non-fwd)
 Table id 0, 0 resets
 Database epoch: 1 (18 entries at this epoch)
```

d. The **show ip cef detail** command shows CEF operation in detail for the switch.

```
DLS1# show ip cef detail
IPv4 CEF is enabled for distributed and running
VRF Default:
 18 prefixes (18/0 fwd/non-fwd)
 Table id 0, 0 resets
 Database epoch: 1 (18 entries at this epoch)
```

```
0.0.0.0/32, epoch 1, flags receive
  Special source: receive
  receive
172.16.1.0/24, epoch 1, flags attached, connected
  attached to Vlan1
172.16.1.0/32, epoch 1, flags receive
  receive
172.16.1.1/32, epoch 1, flags receive
  receive
172.16.1.101/32, epoch 1
  Adj source: IP adj out of Vlan1, addr 172.16.1.101
  attached to Vlan1
172.16.1.102/32, epoch 1
  Adj source: IP adj out of Vlan1, addr 172.16.1.102
  attached to Vlan1
172.16.1.255/32, epoch 1, flags receive
  receive
172.16.100.0/24, epoch 1, flags attached, connected
  attached to Vlan100
172.16.100.0/32, epoch 1, flags receive
  receive
172.16.100.1/32, epoch 1, flags receive
  receive
172.16.100.255/32, epoch 1, flags receive
  receive
172.16.200.0/24, epoch 1, flags attached, connected
  attached to Vlan200
172.16.200.0/32, epoch 1, flags receive
  receive
172.16.200.1/32, epoch 1, flags receive
  receive
172.16.200.255/32, epoch 1, flags receive
  receive
224.0.0.0/4, epoch 1
  Special source: drop
  drop
224.0.0.0/24, epoch 1, flags receive
  Special source: receive
  receive
255.255.255.255/32, epoch 1, flags receive
  Special source: receive
  Receive
```

Lab 4-3, VLANs, VTP, and Inter-VLAN Routing Case Study

Topology

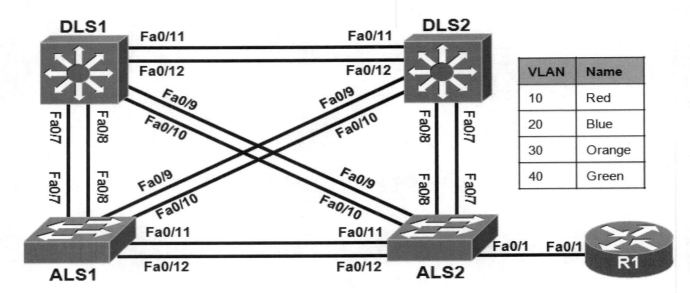

VLAN	Name
10	Red
20	Blue
30	Orange
40	Green

Objectives

- Plan and design the International Travel Agency switched network as shown in the diagram and described below.

- Implement the design on the switches and router.

- Verify that all configurations are operational and functioning according to the requirements.

Note: This lab uses Cisco 1841 routers with Cisco IOS Release 12.4(24)T1 and the Advanced IP Services image c1841-advipservicesk9-mz.124-24.T1.bin. The switches are Cisco WS-C2960-24TT-L with the Cisco IOS image c2960-lanbasek9-mz.122-46.SE.bin, and Catalyst 3560-24PS with the Cisco IOS image c3560-advipservicesk9-mz.122-46.SE.bin. You can use other routers (such as 2801 or 2811), switches (such as 2950 or 3550), and Cisco IOS Software versions if they have comparable capabilities and features. Depending on the router or switch model and Cisco IOS Software version, the commands available and output produced might vary from what is shown in this lab.

Required Resources

- 1 router (Cisco 1841 with Cisco IOS Release 12.4(24)T1 Advanced IP Services or comparable)

- 2 switches (Cisco 2960 with the Cisco IOS Release 12.2(46)SE C2960-LANBASEK9-M image or comparable)

- 2 switches (Cisco 3560 with the Cisco IOS Release 12.2(46)SE C3560-ADVIPSERVICESK9-mz image or comparable)

- Ethernet and console cables

Requirements

You will configure a group of switches and a router for the International Travel Agency. The network includes two distribution switches, DLS1 and DLS2, and two access layer switches, ALS1 and ALS2. External router R1 and DLS1 provide inter-VLAN routing. Design the addressing scheme using the address space 172.16.0.0/16 range. You can subnet it any way you want, although it is recommended to use /24 subnets for simplicity.

1. Disable the links between the access layer switches.

2. Place all switches in the VTP domain CISCO. Make DLS1 the VTP server and all other switches VTP clients.

3. On DLS1, create the VLANs shown in the VLAN table and assign the names given. For subnet planning, allocate a subnet for each VLAN.

4. Configure DLS1 as the primary spanning-tree root bridge for all VLANs. Configure DLS2 as the backup root bridge for all VLANs.

5. Configure Fa0/12 between DLS1 and DLS2 as a Layer 3 link and assign a subnet to it.

6. Create a loopback interface on DLS1 and assign a subnet to it.

7. Configure the Fa0/11 link between DLS1 and DLS2 as an ISL trunk.

8. Statically configure all inter-switch links as trunks.

9. Configure all other trunk links using 802.1Q.

10. Bind together the links from DLS1 to each access switch together in an EtherChannel.

11. Enable PortFast on all access ports.

12. Place Fa0/15 through Fa0/17 on ALS1 and ALS2 in VLAN 10. Place Fa0/18 and Fa0/19 on ALS1 and ALS2 in VLAN 20. Place Fa0/20 on ALS1 and ALS2 in VLAN 30.

13. Create an 802.1Q trunk link between R1 and ALS2. Allow only VLANs 10 and 40 to pass through the trunk.

14. Configure R1 subinterfaces for VLANs 10 and 40.

15. Create an SVI on DLS1 in VLANs 20, 30, and 40. Create an SVI on DLS2 in VLAN 10, an SVI on ALS1 in VLAN 30, and an SVI on ALS2 in VLAN 40.

16. Enable IP routing on DLS1. On R1 and DLS1, configure EIGRP for the whole major network (172.16.0.0/16) and disable automatic summarization.

Notes:

Router Interface Summary Table

Router Interface Summary				
Router Model	Ethernet Interface #1	Ethernet Interface #2	Serial Interface #1	Serial Interface #2
1700	Fast Ethernet 0 (Fa0)	Fast Ethernet 1 (Fa1)	Serial 0 (S0)	Serial 1 (S1)
1800	Fast Ethernet 0/0 (Fa0/0)	Fast Ethernet 0/1 (Fa0/1)	Serial 0/0/0 (S0/0/0)	Serial 0/0/1 (S0/0/1)
2600	Fast Ethernet 0/0 (Fa0/0)	Fast Ethernet 0/1 (Fa0/1)	Serial 0/0 (S0/0)	Serial 0/1 (S0/1)
2800	Fast Ethernet 0/0 (Fa0/0)	Fast Ethernet 0/1 (Fa0/1)	Serial 0/0/0 (S0/0/0)	Serial 0/0/1 (S0/0/1)

Note: To find out how the router is configured, look at the interfaces to identify the type of router and how many interfaces the router has. Rather than list all combinations of configurations for each router class, this table includes identifiers for the possible combinations of Ethernet and serial interfaces in the device. The table does not include any other type of interface, even though a specific router might contain one. For example, for an ISDN BRI interface, the string in parenthesis is the legal abbreviation that can be used in Cisco IOS commands to represent the interface.

Chapter 5 Implementing High Availability and Redundancy in a Campus Network

Lab 5-1, Hot Standby Router Protocol

Topology

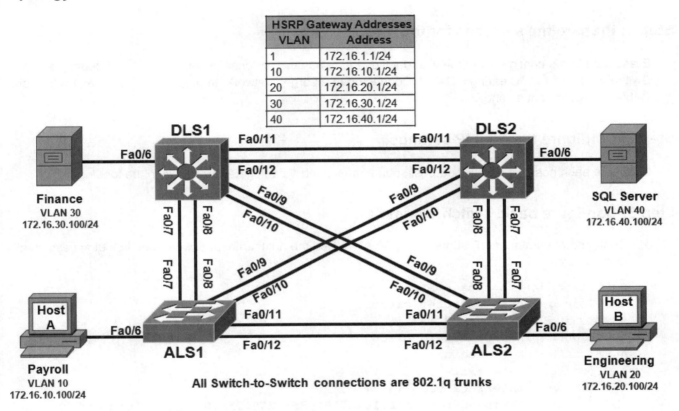

HSRP Gateway Addresses	
VLAN	**Address**
1	172.16.1.1/24
10	172.16.10.1/24
20	172.16.20.1/24
30	172.16.30.1/24
40	172.16.40.1/24

Objective

- Configure inter-VLAN routing with HSRP to provide redundant, fault-tolerant routing to the internal network.

Background

Hot Standby Router Protocol (HSRP) is a Cisco-proprietary redundancy protocol for establishing a fault-tolerant default gateway. It is described in RFC 2281. HSRP provides a transparent failover mechanism to the end stations on the network. This provides users at the access layer with uninterrupted service to the network if the primary gateway becomes inaccessible. The Virtual Router Redundancy Protocol (VRRP) is a standards-based alternative to HSRP and is defined in RFC 3768. The two technologies are similar but not compatible. This lab focuses on HSRP.

Note: This lab uses Cisco WS-C2960-24TT-L switches with the Cisco IOS image c2960-lanbasek9-mz.122-46.SE.bin, and Catalyst 3560-24PS with the Cisco IOS image c3560-advipservicesk9-mz.122-46. SE.bin. You can use other switches (such as 2950 or 3550) and Cisco IOS Software versions if they have comparable capabilities and features. Depending on the switch model and Cisco IOS Software version, the commands available and output produced might vary from what is shown in this lab.

Required Resources

- 2 switches (Cisco 2960 with the Cisco IOS Release 12.2(46)SE C2960-LANBASEK9-M image or comparable)
- 2 switches (Cisco 3560 with the Cisco IOS Release 12.2(46)SE C3560-ADVIPSERVICESK9-mz image or comparable)
- Ethernet and console cables

Step 1: Prepare the switches for the lab.

Erase the startup config, delete the vlan.dat file, and reload the switches. Refer to Lab 1-1, "Clearing a Switch" and Lab 1-2, "Clearing a Switch Connected to a Larger Network" to prepare the switches for this lab. Cable the equipment as shown.

Step 2: Configure the host IP settings.

Configure each host with the IP address, subnet mask, and default gateway shown in the topology.

Step 3: Configure basic switch parameters.

a. Configure management IP addresses in VLAN 1, and the hostname, password, and Telnet access on all four switches.

```
Switch(config)# hostname ALS1
ALS1(config)# enable secret cisco
ALS1(config)# line vty 0 15
ALS1(config-line)# password cisco
ALS1(config-line)# login
ALS1(config-line)# exit
ALS1(config)# interface vlan 1
ALS1(config-if)# ip address 172.16.1.101 255.255.255.0
ALS1(config-if)# no shutdown

Switch(config)# hostname ALS2
ALS2(config)# enable secret cisco
ALS2(config)# line vty 0 15
ALS2(config-line)# password cisco
ALS2(config-line)# login
ALS2(config-line)# exit
ALS2(config)# interface vlan 1
ALS2(config-if)# ip address 172.16.1.102 255.255.255.0
ALS2(config-if)# no shutdown

Switch(config)# hostname DLS1
DLS1(config)# enable secret cisco
DLS1(config)# line vty 0 15
DLS1(config-line)# password cisco
DLS1(config-line)# login
DLS1(config-line)# exit
```

```
DLS1(config)# interface vlan 1
DLS1(config-if)# ip address 172.16.1.3 255.255.255.0
DLS1(config-if)# no shutdown

Switch(config)# hostname DLS2
DLS2(config)# enable secret cisco
DLS2(config)# line vty 0 15
DLS2(config-line)# password cisco
DLS2(config-line)# login
DLS2(config-line)# exit
DLS2(config)# interface vlan 1
DLS2(config-if)# ip address 172.16.1.4 255.255.255.0
DLS2(config-if)# no shutdown
```

b. Configure default gateways on the access layer switches ALS1 and ALS2. The distribution layer switches will not use a default gateway because they act as Layer 3 devices. The access layer switches act as Layer 2 devices and need a default gateway to send management VLAN traffic off of the local subnet for the management VLAN.

```
ALS1(config)# ip default-gateway 172.16.1.1

ALS2(config)# ip default-gateway 172.16.1.1
```

Step 4: Configure trunks and EtherChannels between switches.

EtherChannel is used for the trunks because it allows you to utilize both Fast Ethernet interfaces that are available between each device, thereby doubling the bandwidth.

Note: It is good practice to shut down the interfaces on both sides of the link before a port channel is created and then reenable them after the port channel is configured.

a. Configure trunks and EtherChannels from DLS1 and DLS2 to the other three switches according to the diagram. The **switchport trunk encapsulation {isl | dot1q}** command is used because these switches also support ISL encapsulation.

```
DLS1(config)# interface range fastEthernet 0/7 - 8
DLS1(config-if-range)# switchport trunk encapsulation dot1q
DLS1(config-if-range)# switchport mode trunk
DLS1(config-if-range)# channel-group 1 mode desirable

Creating a port-channel interface Port-channel 1

DLS1(config-if-range)# interface range fastEthernet 0/9 - 10
DLS1(config-if-range)# switchport trunk encapsulation dot1q
DLS1(config-if-range)# switchport mode trunk
DLS1(config-if-range)# channel-group 2 mode desirable

Creating a port-channel interface Port-channel 2

DLS1(config-if-range)# interface range fastEthernet 0/11 - 12
DLS1(config-if-range)# switchport trunk encapsulation dot1q
DLS1(config-if-range)# switchport mode trunk
DLS1(config-if-range)# channel-group 3 mode desirable

Creating a port-channel interface Port-channel 3
```

```
DLS2(config)# interface range fastEthernet 0/7 - 8
DLS2(config-if-range)# switchport trunk encapsulation dot1q
DLS2(config-if-range)# switchport mode trunk
DLS2(config-if-range)# channel-group 1 mode desirable
```

```
Creating a port-channel interface Port-channel 1
```

```
DLS2(config-if-range)# interface range fastEthernet 0/9 - 10
DLS2(config-if-range)# switchport trunk encapsulation dot1q
DLS2(config-if-range)# switchport mode trunk
DLS2(config-if-range)# channel-group 2 mode desirable
```

```
Creating a port-channel interface Port-channel 2
```

```
DLS2(config-if-range)# interface range fastEthernet 0/11 - 12
DLS2(config-if-range)# switchport trunk encapsulation dot1q
DLS2(config-if-range)# switchport mode trunk
DLS2(config-if-range)# channel-group 3 mode desirable
```

```
Creating a port-channel interface Port-channel 3
```

b. Configure the trunks and EtherChannel from ALS1 and ALS2 to the other switches. Notice that no encapsulation type is needed because the 2960 supports only 802.1q trunks.

```
ALS1(config)# interface range fastEthernet 0/7 - 8
ALS1(config-if-range)# switchport mode trunk
ALS1(config-if-range)# channel-group 1 mode desirable
```

```
Creating a port-channel interface Port-channel 1
```

```
ALS1(config-if-range)# interface range fastEthernet 0/9 - 10
ALS1(config-if-range)# switchport mode trunk
ALS1(config-if-range)# channel-group 2 mode desirable
```

```
Creating a port-channel interface Port-channel 2
```

```
ALS1(config-if-range)# interface range fastEthernet 0/11 - 12
ALS1(config-if-range)# switchport mode trunk
ALS1(config-if-range)# channel-group 3 mode desirable
```

```
Creating a port-channel interface Port-channel 3
```

```
ALS2(config)# interface range fastEthernet 0/7 - 8
ALS2(config-if-range)# switchport mode trunk
ALS2(config-if-range)# channel-group 1 mode desirable
```

```
Creating a port-channel interface Port-channel 1
```

```
ALS2(config-if-range)# interface range fastEthernet 0/9 - 10
ALS2(config-if-range)# switchport mode trunk
ALS2(config-if-range)# channel-group 2 mode desirable
```

```
Creating a port-channel interface Port-channel 2
```

```
ALS2(config-if-range)# interface range fastEthernet 0/11 - 12
ALS2(config-if-range)# switchport mode trunk
ALS2(config-if-range)# channel-group 3 mode desirable
```

Creating a port-channel interface Port-channel 3

c. Verify trunking between DLS1, ALS1, and ALS2 using the **show interface trunk** command on all switches.

```
DLS1# show interface trunk

Port          Mode          Encapsulation  Status        Native vlan
Po1           on            802.1q         trunking      1
Po2           on            802.1q         trunking      1
Po3           on            802.1q         trunking      1


Port          Vlans allowed on trunk
Po1           1-4094
Po2           1-4094
Po3           1-4094


Port          Vlans allowed and active in management domain
Po1           1
Po2           1
Po3           1


Port          Vlans in spanning tree forwarding state and not pruned
Po1           1
Po2           1
Po3           1
```

d. Issue the **show etherchannel summary** command on each switch to verify the EtherChannels. In the following sample output from ALS1, notice the three EtherChannels on the access and distribution layer switches.

```
ALS1# show etherchannel summary
Flags:  D - down         P - in port-channel
        I - stand-alone  s - suspended
        H - Hot-standby (LACP only)
        R - Layer3       S - Layer2
        U - in use       f - failed to allocate aggregator
        u - unsuitable for bundling
        w - waiting to be aggregated
        d - default port


Number of channel-groups in use: 3
Number of aggregators:           3

Group Port-channel  Protocol    Ports
------+-------------+-----------+----------------------------------------------
1      Po1(SU)        PAgP       Fa0/7(P)    Fa0/8(P)
2      Po2(SU)        PAgP       Fa0/9(P)    Fa0/10(P)
3      Po3(SU)        PAgP       Fa0/11(P)   Fa0/12(P)
```

Which EtherChannel negotiation protocol is in use here?

_____

Step 5: Configure VTP on ALS1 and ALS2.

a. Change the VTP mode of ALS1 and ALS2 to client.

```
ALS1(config)# vtp mode client
Setting device to VTP CLIENT mode.

ALS2(config)# vtp mode client
Setting device to VTP CLIENT mode.
```

b. Verify the VTP changes with the **show vtp status** command.

```
ALS1# show vtp status
VTP Version                     : running VTP1 (VTP2 capable)
Configuration Revision          : 0
Maximum VLANs supported locally : 255
Number of existing VLANs        : 5
VTP Operating Mode              : Client
VTP Domain Name                 :
VTP Pruning Mode                : Disabled
VTP V2 Mode                     : Disabled
VTP Traps Generation            : Disabled
MD5 digest                      : 0xC8 0xAB 0x3C 0x3B 0xAB 0xDD 0x34 0xCF
Configuration last modified by 0.0.0.0 at 3-1-93 15:47:34
```

How many VLANs can be supported locally on the 2960 switch?

_____

Step 6: Configure VTP on DLS1.

a. Create the VTP domain on VTP server DLS1 and create VLANs 10, 20, 30, and 40 for the domain.

```
DLS1(config)# vtp domain SWPOD
DLS1(config)# vtp version 2

DLS1(config)# vlan 10
DLS1(config-vlan)# name Finance
DLS1(config-vlan)# vlan 20
DLS1(config-vlan)# name Engineering
DLS1(config-vlan)# vlan 30
DLS1(config-vlan)# name Server-Farm1
DLS1(config-vlan)# vlan 40
DLS1(config-vlan)# name Server-Farm2
```

b. Verify VTP information throughout the domain using the **show vlan** and **show vtp status** commands.

How many existing VLANs are in the VTP domain?

Step 7: Configure access ports.

a. Configure the host ports of all four switches. The following commands configure the switch port mode as access, place the port in the proper VLANs, and turn on spanning-tree PortFast for the ports.

```
DLS1(config)# interface fastEthernet 0/6
DLS1(config-if)# switchport mode access
DLS1(config-if)# switchport access vlan 30
DLS1(config-if)# spanning-tree portfast

DLS2(config)# interface fastEthernet 0/6
DLS2(config-if)# switchport mode access
DLS2(config-if)# switchport access vlan 40
DLS2(config-if)# spanning-tree portfast

ALS1(config)# interface fastEthernet 0/6
ALS1(config-if)# switchport mode access
ALS1(config-if)# switchport access vlan 10
ALS1(config-if)# spanning-tree portfast

ALS2(config)# interface fastEthernet 0/6
ALS2(config-if)# switchport mode access
ALS2(config-if)# switchport access vlan 20
ALS2(config-if)# spanning-tree portfast
```

b. Ping from the host on VLAN 10 to the host on VLAN 40. The ping should fail.

Are these results expected at this point? Why?

_____

_____

_____

Note: The **switchport host** command can be used to configure individual access ports. This command automatically activates access mode, PortFast, and removes all associations of the physical switch port with the port-channel interfaces (if there are any).

Step 8: Configure HSRP interfaces and enable routing.

HSRP provides redundancy in the network. The VLANs can be load-balanced by using the **standby** *group* **priority** *priority* command. The **ip routing** command is used on DLS1 and DLS2 to activate routing capabilities on these Layer 3 switches.

Each route processor can route between the various SVIs configured on its switch. In addition to the real IP address assigned to each distribution switch SVI, assign a third IP address in each subnet to be used as a virtual gateway address. HSRP negotiates and determines which switch accepts information forwarded to the virtual gateway IP address.

The **standby** command configures the IP address of the virtual gateway, sets the priority for each VLAN, and configures the router for preempt. Preemption allows the router with the higher priority to become the active router after a network failure has been resolved.

In the following configurations, the priority for VLANs 1, 10, and 20 is 150 on DLS1, making it the active router for those VLANs. VLANs 30 and 40 have a priority of 100 on DLS1, making DLS1 the standby router for these VLANs. DLS2 is configured to be the active router for VLANs 30 and 40 with a priority of 150, and the standby router for VLANs 1, 10, and 20 with a priority of 100.

```
DLS1(config)# ip routing

DLS1(config)# interface vlan 1
DLS1(config-if)# standby 1 ip 172.16.1.1
DLS1(config-if)# standby 1 preempt
DLS1(config-if)# standby 1 priority 150
DLS1(config-if)# exit

DLS1(config)# interface vlan 10
DLS1(config-if)# ip address 172.16.10.3 255.255.255.0
DLS1(config-if)# standby 1 ip 172.16.10.1
DLS1(config-if)# standby 1 preempt
DLS1(config-if)# standby 1 priority 150
DLS1(config-if)# exit

DLS1(config)# interface vlan 20
DLS1(config-if)# ip address 172.16.20.3 255.255.255.0
DLS1(config-if)# standby 1 ip 172.16.20.1
DLS1(config-if)# standby 1 preempt
DLS1(config-if)# standby 1 priority 150
DLS1(config-if)# exit

DLS1(config)# interface vlan 30
DLS1(config-if)# ip address 172.16.30.3 255.255.255.0
DLS1(config-if)# standby 1 ip 172.16.30.1
DLS1(config-if)# standby 1 preempt
DLS1(config-if)# standby 1 priority 100
DLS1(config-if)# exit

DLS1(config)# interface vlan 40
DLS1(config-if)# ip address 172.16.40.3 255.255.255.0
DLS1(config-if)# standby 1 ip 172.16.40.1
DLS1(config-if)# standby 1 preempt
DLS1(config-if)# standby 1 priority 100


DLS2(config)# ip routing

DLS2(config)# interface vlan 1
DLS2(config-if)# standby 1 ip 172.16.1.1
DLS2(config-if)# standby 1 preempt
DLS2(config-if)# standby 1 priority 100
```

```
DLS2(config-if)# exit

DLS2(config)# interface vlan 10
DLS2(config-if)# ip address 172.16.10.4 255.255.255.0
DLS2(config-if)# standby 1 ip 172.16.10.1
DLS2(config-if)# standby 1 preempt
DLS2(config-if)# standby 1 priority 100
DLS2(config-if)# exit

DLS2(config)# interface vlan 20
DLS2(config-if)# ip address 172.16.20.4 255.255.255.0
DLS2(config-if)# standby 1 ip 172.16.20.1
DLS2(config-if)# standby 1 preempt
DLS2(config-if)# standby 1 priority 100
DLS2(config-if)# exit

DLS2(config)# interface vlan 30
DLS2(config-if)# ip address 172.16.30.4 255.255.255.0
DLS2(config-if)# standby 1 ip 172.16.30.1
DLS2(config-if)# standby 1 preempt
DLS2(config-if)# standby 1 priority 150
DLS2(config-if)# exit

DLS2(config)# interface vlan 40
DLS2(config-if)# ip address 172.16.40.4 255.255.255.0
DLS2(config-if)# standby 1 ip 172.16.40.1
DLS2(config-if)# standby 1 preempt
DLS2(config-if)# standby 1 priority 150
```

Step 9: Verify the HSRP configuration.

a. Issue the **show standby** command on both DLS1 and DLS2.

```
DLS1# show standby
Vlan1 - Group 1
  State is Active
    5 state changes, last state change 00:02:48
  Virtual IP address is 172.16.1.1
  Active virtual MAC address is 0000.0c07.ac01
    Local virtual MAC address is 0000.0c07.ac01 (v1 default)
  Hello time 3 sec, hold time 10 sec
    Next hello sent in 2.228 secs
  Preemption enabled
  Active router is local
  Standby router is 172.16.1.4, priority 100 (expires in 7.207 sec)
  Priority 150 (configured 150)
  IP redundancy name is "hsrp-Vl1-1" (default)
Vlan10 - Group 1
  State is Active
    5 state changes, last state change 00:02:50
  Virtual IP address is 172.16.10.1
  Active virtual MAC address is 0000.0c07.ac01
    Local virtual MAC address is 0000.0c07.ac01 (v1 default)
  Hello time 3 sec, hold time 10 sec
```

```
      Next hello sent in 1.113 secs
   Preemption enabled
   Active router is local
   Standby router is 172.16.10.4, priority 100 (expires in 9.807 sec)
   Priority 150 (configured 150)
   IP redundancy name is "hsrp-Vl10-1" (default)
Vlan20 - Group 1
   State is Active
      5 state changes, last state change 00:02:55
   Virtual IP address is 172.16.20.1
   Active virtual MAC address is 0000.0c07.ac01
      Local virtual MAC address is 0000.0c07.ac01 (v1 default)
   Hello time 3 sec, hold time 10 sec
      Next hello sent in 1.884 secs
   Preemption enabled
   Active router is local
   Standby router is 172.16.20.4, priority 100 (expires in 9.220 sec)
   Priority 150 (configured 150)
   IP redundancy name is "hsrp-Vl20-1" (default)
Vlan30 - Group 1
   State is Standby
      4 state changes, last state change 00:02:45
   Virtual IP address is 172.16.30.1
   Active virtual MAC address is 0000.0c07.ac01
      Local virtual MAC address is 0000.0c07.ac01 (v1 default)
   Hello time 3 sec, hold time 10 sec
      Next hello sent in 2.413 secs
   Preemption enabled
   Active router is 172.16.30.4, priority 150 (expires in 8.415 sec)
   Standby router is local
   Priority 100 (default 100)
   IP redundancy name is "hsrp-Vl30-1" (default)
Vlan40 - Group 1
   State is Standby
      4 state changes, last state change 00:02:51
   Virtual IP address is 172.16.40.1
   Active virtual MAC address is 0000.0c07.ac01
      Local virtual MAC address is 0000.0c07.ac01 (v1 default)
   Hello time 3 sec, hold time 10 sec
      Next hello sent in 1.826 secs
   Preemption enabled
   Active router is 172.16.40.4, priority 150 (expires in 7.828 sec)
   Standby router is local
   Priority 100 (default 100)
   IP redundancy name is "hsrp-Vl40-1" (default)


DLS2# show standby
Vlan1 - Group 1
   State is Standby
      3 state changes, last state change 00:02:33
   Virtual IP address is 172.16.1.1
   Active virtual MAC address is 0000.0c07.ac01
      Local virtual MAC address is 0000.0c07.ac01 (v1 default)
```

```
Hello time 3 sec, hold time 10 sec
  Next hello sent in 2.950 secs
Preemption enabled
Active router is 172.16.1.3, priority 150 (expires in 8.960 sec)
Standby router is local
Priority 100 (default 100)
IP redundancy name is "hsrp-Vl1-1" (default)
Vlan10 - Group 1
  State is Standby
    3 state changes, last state change 00:02:34
Virtual IP address is 172.16.10.1
Active virtual MAC address is 0000.0c07.ac01
  Local virtual MAC address is 0000.0c07.ac01 (v1 default)
Hello time 3 sec, hold time 10 sec
  Next hello sent in 1.759 secs
Preemption enabled
Active router is 172.16.10.3, priority 150 (expires in 7.844 sec)
Standby router is local
Priority 100 (default 100)
IP redundancy name is "hsrp-Vl10-1" (default)
Vlan20 - Group 1
  State is Standby
    3 state changes, last state change 00:02:42
Virtual IP address is 172.16.20.1
Active virtual MAC address is 0000.0c07.ac01
  Local virtual MAC address is 0000.0c07.ac01 (v1 default)
Hello time 3 sec, hold time 10 sec
  Next hello sent in 2.790 secs
Preemption enabled
Active router is 172.16.20.3, priority 150 (expires in 8.289 sec)
Standby router is local
Priority 100 (default 100)
IP redundancy name is "hsrp-Vl20-1" (default)
Vlan30 - Group 1
  State is Active
    2 state changes, last state change 00:02:52
Virtual IP address is 172.16.30.1
Active virtual MAC address is 0000.0c07.ac01
  Local virtual MAC address is 0000.0c07.ac01 (v1 default)
Hello time 3 sec, hold time 10 sec
  Next hello sent in 1.549 secs
Preemption enabled
Active router is local
Standby router is 172.16.30.3, priority 100 (expires in 9.538 sec)
Priority 150 (configured 150)
IP redundancy name is "hsrp-Vl30-1" (default)
Vlan40 - Group 1
  State is Active
    2 state changes, last state change 00:02:58
Virtual IP address is 172.16.40.1
Active virtual MAC address is 0000.0c07.ac01
  Local virtual MAC address is 0000.0c07.ac01 (v1 default)
Hello time 3 sec, hold time 10 sec
```

```
      Next hello sent in 0.962 secs
   Preemption enabled
   Active router is local
   Standby router is 172.16.40.3, priority 100 (expires in 8.960 sec)
   Priority 150 (configured 150)
   IP redundancy name is "hsrp-Vl40-1" (default)
```

b.   Issue the **show standby brief** command on both DLS1 and DLS2.

DLS1# **show standby brief**

```
                     P indicates configured to preempt.
                     |
Interface   Grp  Pri P State   Active        Standby       Virtual IP
Vl1         1    150 P Active  local         172.16.1.4    172.16.1.1
Vl10        1    150 P Active  local         172.16.10.4   172.16.10.1
Vl20        1    150 P Active  local         172.16.20.4   172.16.20.1
Vl30        1    100 P Standby 172.16.30.4   local         172.16.30.1
Vl40        1    100 P Standby 172.16.40.4   local         172.16.40.1
```

DLS2# **show standby brief**

```
                     P indicates configured to preempt.
                     |
Interface   Grp  Pri P State   Active        Standby       Virtual IP
Vl1         1    100 P Standby 172.16.1.3    local         172.16.1.1
Vl10        1    100 P Standby 172.16.10.3   local         172.16.10.1
Vl20        1    100 P Standby 172.16.20.3   local         172.16.20.1
Vl30        1    150 P Active  local         172.16.30.3   172.16.30.1
Vl40        1    150 P Active  local         172.16.40.3   172.16.40.1
```

Which router is the active router for VLANs 1, 10, and 20? Which is the active router for 30 and 40?

_____

What is the default hello time for each VLAN? What is the default hold time?

_____

How is the active HSRP router selected?

_____

c.   Use the **show ip route** command to verify routing on both DLS1 and DLS2.

DLS1# **show ip route**
```
Codes: C - connected, S - static, R - RIP, M - mobile, B - BGP
       D - EIGRP, EX - EIGRP external, O - OSPF, IA - OSPF inter area
       N1 - OSPF NSSA external type 1, N2 - OSPF NSSA external type 2
       E1 - OSPF external type 1, E2 - OSPF external type 2, E - EGP
```

```
          i - IS-IS, su - IS-IS summary, L1 - IS-IS level-1, L2 - IS-IS level-2
          ia - IS-IS inter area, * - candidate default, U - per-user static route
          o - ODR, P - periodic downloaded static route

     Gateway of last resort is not set

          172.16.0.0/24 is subnetted, 5 subnets
     C        172.16.40.0 is directly connected, Vlan40
     C        172.16.30.0 is directly connected, Vlan30
     C        172.16.20.0 is directly connected, Vlan20
     C        172.16.10.0 is directly connected, Vlan10
     C        172.16.1.0 is directly connected, Vlan1
```

Step 10: Verify connectivity between VLANs.

Verify connectivity between VLANs using the **ping** command from the SQL Server (VLAN 40) to the other hosts and servers on the network.

The following is from the SQL Server (VLAN 40) to the Engineering host (VLAN 20):

```
C:\> ping 172.16.20.100

Pinging 172.16.20.100 with 32 bytes of data:

Reply from 172.16.20.100: bytes=32 time=2ms TTL=255
Reply from 172.16.20.100: bytes=32 time=2ms TTL=255
Reply from 172.16.20.100: bytes=32 time=2ms TTL=255
Reply from 172.16.20.100: bytes=32 time=2ms TTL=255

Ping statistics for 172.16.20.100:
    Packets: Sent = 4, Received = 4, Lost = 0 (0% loss),
Approximate round trip times in milli-seconds:
    Minimum = 2ms, Maximum = 2ms, Average = 2ms
```

Step 11: Verify HSRP functionally.

a. Verify HSRP by disconnecting the trunks to DLS2. You can simulate this using the **shutdown** command on those interfaces.

```
DLS2(config)# interface range fastEthernet 0/7 - 12
DLS2(config-if-range)# shutdown
```

Output to the console should reflect DLS1 becoming the active router for VLANs 30 and 40.

```
1w3d: %HSRP-6-STATECHANGE: Vlan30 Grp 1 state Standby -> Active
1w3d: %HSRP-6-STATECHANGE: Vlan40 Grp 1 state Standby -> Active
```

b. Verify that DLS1 is acting as the backup default gateway for VLANs 30 and 40 using the **show standby brief** command. DLS1 is now the active HSRP router for all VLANs and the standby router is unknown.

```
DLS1# show standby brief
                     P indicates configured to preempt.
                     |
Interface   Grp  Pri P State   Active      Standby      Virtual IP
Vl1         1    150 P Active  local       unknown      172.16.1.1
Vl10        1    150 P Active  local       unknown      172.16.10.1
Vl20        1    150 P Active  local       unknown      172.16.20.1
```

| V130 | 1 | 100 P Active | local | unknown | 172.16.30.1 |
| V140 | 1 | 100 P Active | local | unknown | 172.16.40.1 |

c. Repeat this process by bringing up the DLS2 trunks and shutting down the DLS1 interfaces. Use the **show standby brief** command to see the results.

Note: If both DLS1 and DLS2 have links to the Internet, failure of either switch will cause HSRP to redirect packets to the other switch. The functioning switch will take over as the default gateway to provide virtually uninterrupted connectivity for hosts at the access layer.

Lab 5-2, IP Service Level Agreements in a Campus Environment

Topology

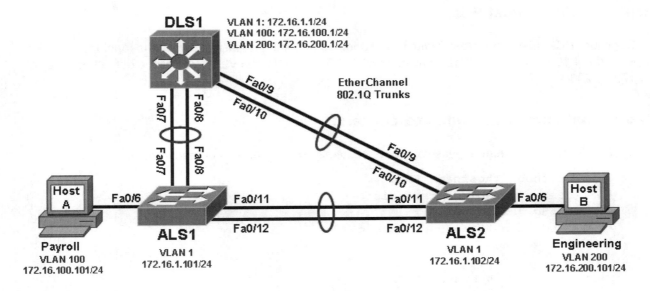

Objectives

- Configure trunking, VTP, and SVIs.
- Implement IP SLAs to monitor various network performance characteristics.

Background

Cisco IOS IP service level agreements (SLAs) allow users to monitor network performance between Cisco devices (switches or routers) or from a Cisco device to a remote IP device. Cisco IOS IP SLAs can be applied to VoIP and video applications as well as monitoring end-to-end IP network performance.

In this lab, you configure trunking, VTP, and SVIs. You configure IP SLA monitors to test ICMP echo network performance between DLS1 and each host. You also configure IP SLA monitors to test jitter between DLS1 and the access layer switches ALS1 and ALS2.

Note: This lab uses Cisco WS-C2960-24TT-L switches with the Cisco IOS image c2960-lanbasek9-mz.122-46.SE.bin, and Catalyst 3560-24PS with the Cisco IOS image c3560-advipservicesk9-mz.122-46. SE.bin. You can use other switches (such as 2950 or 3550) and Cisco IOS Software versions if they have comparable capabilities and features. Depending on the switch model and Cisco IOS Software version, the commands available and output produced might vary from what is shown in this lab.

Required Resources

- 2 switches (Cisco 2960 with the Cisco IOS Release 12.2(46)SE C2960-LANBASEK9-M image or comparable)
- 1 switch (Cisco 3560 with the Cisco IOS Release 12.2(46)SE C3560-ADVIPSERVICESK9-mz image or comparable)
- Ethernet and console cables

Step 1: Prepare the switches for the lab.

Erase the startup configuration, delete the vlan.dat file, and reload the switches. Refer to Lab 1-1 "Clearing a Switch" and Lab 1-2 "Clearing a Switch Connected to a Larger Network" to prepare the switches for this lab. Cable the equipment as shown.

Step 2: Configure host PCs.

Configure PCs Host A and Host B with the IP address and subnet mask shown in the topology. Host A is in VLAN 100 with a default gateway of 172.16.100.1. Host B is in VLAN 200 with a default gateway of 172.16.200.1.

Step 3: Configure basic switch parameters.

Configure the hostname, password, and, optionally, remote access on each switch.

```
Switch(config)# hostname ALS1
ALS1(config)# enable secret cisco
ALS1(config)# line vty 0 15
ALS1(config-line)# password cisco
ALS1(config-line)# login

Switch(config)# hostname ALS2
ALS2(config)# enable secret cisco
ALS2(config)# line vty 0 15
ALS2(config-line)# password cisco
ALS2(config-line)# login

Switch(config)# hostname DLS1
DLS1(config)# enable secret cisco
DLS1(config)# line vty 0 15
DLS1(config-line)#password cisco
DLS1(config-line)# login
```

Configure a management IP address on VLAN 1 for each of the three switches according to the diagram.

```
ALS1(config)# interface vlan 1
ALS1(config-if)# ip address 172.16.1.101 255.255.255.0
ALS1(config-if)# no shutdown

ALS2(config)# interface vlan 1
ALS2(config-if)# ip address 172.16.1.102 255.255.255.0
ALS2(config-if)# no shutdown

DLS1(config)# interface vlan 1
DLS1(config-if)# ip address 172.16.1.1 255.255.255.0
DLS1(config-if)# no shutdown
```

Configure default gateways on the access layer switches. The distribution layer switch will not use a default gateway because it acts as a Layer 3 device. The access layer switches act as Layer 2 devices and need a default gateway to send traffic off of the local subnet for the management VLAN.

```
ALS1(config)# ip default-gateway 172.16.1.1

ALS2(config)# ip default-gateway 172.16.1.1
```

Step 4: Configure trunks and EtherChannels between switches.

To distribute VLAN and VTP information, trunks are needed between the three switches. Configure these trunks according to the diagram. EtherChannel is used for these trunks.

Note: It is good practice to shut down the interfaces on both sides of the link before a port channel is created and then reenable them after the port channel is configured.

Configure the trunks and EtherChannel from DLS1 to ALS1.

```
DLS1(config)# interface range fastEthernet 0/7 - 8
DLS1(config-if-range)# switchport trunk encapsulation dot1q
DLS1(config-if-range)# switchport mode trunk
DLS1(config-if-range)# channel-group 1 mode desirable

Creating a port-channel interface Port-channel 1
```

Configure the trunks and EtherChannel from DLS1 to ALS2.

```
DLS1(config)# interface range fastEthernet 0/9 - 10
DLS1(config-if-range)# switchport trunk encapsulation dot1q
DLS1(config-if-range)# switchport mode trunk
DLS1(config-if-range)# channel-group 2 mode desirable

Creating a port-channel interface Port-channel 2
```

Configure the trunks and EtherChannel between ALS1 and DLS1 and between ALS1 and ALS2.

```
ALS1(config)# interface range fastEthernet 0/11 - 12
ALS1(config-if-range)# switchport mode trunk
ALS1(config-if-range)# channel-group 1 mode desirable

Creating a port-channel interface Port-channel 1

ALS1(config-if-range)# exit
ALS1(config)# interface range fastEthernet 0/7 - 8
ALS1(config-if-range)# switchport mode trunk
ALS1(config-if-range)# channel-group 2 mode desirable

Creating a port-channel interface Port-channel 2
```

Configure the trunks and EtherChannel between ALS2 and DLS1 and between ALS2 and ALS1.

```
ALS2(config)# interface range fastEthernet 0/11 - 12
ALS2(config-if-range)# switchport mode trunk
ALS2(config-if-range)# channel-group 1 mode desirable

Creating a port-channel interface Port-channel 1

ALS2(config-if-range)# exit
ALS2(config)# interface range fastEthernet 0/9 - 10
ALS2(config-if-range)# switchport mode trunk
ALS2(config-if-range)# channel-group 2 mode desirable

Creating a port-channel interface Port-channel 2
```

Step 5: Configure VTP on ALS1 and ALS2.

Change the VTP mode of ALS1 and ALS2 to client.

```
ALS1(config)# vtp mode client
Setting device to VTP CLIENT mode.

ALS2(config)# vtp mode client
Setting device to VTP CLIENT mode.
```

Step 6: Configure VTP on DLS1.

Create the VTP domain on DLS1, and create VLANs 100 and 200 for the domain.

```
DLS1(config)# vtp domain SWPOD
DLS1(config)# vtp version 2

DLS1(config)# vlan 100
DLS1(config-vlan)# name Finance
DLS1(config-vlan)# vlan 200
DLS1(config-vlan)# name Engineering
```

Step 7: Configure access ports.

Configure the host ports for the appropriate VLANs according to the diagram.

```
ALS1(config)# interface fastEthernet 0/6
ALS1(config-if)# switchport mode access
ALS1(config-if)# switchport access vlan 100

ALS2(config)# interface fastEthernet 0/6
ALS2(config-if)# switchport mode access
ALS2(config-if)# switchport access vlan 200
```

Step 8: Configure VLAN interfaces and enable routing.

On DLS1, create the SVIs for VLANs 100 and 200. Note that the corresponding Layer 2 VLANs must be configured for the Layer 3 SVIs to activate. This was done in Step 6.

```
DLS1(config)# interface vlan 100
DLS1(config-if)# ip address 172.16.100.1 255.255.255.0
DLS1(config-if)# interface vlan 200
DLS1(config-if)# ip address 172.16.200.1 255.255.255.0
```

The **ip routing** command is also needed to allow the DLS1 switch to act as a Layer 3 device to route between these VLANs. Because the VLANs are all considered directly connected, a routing protocol is not needed at this time. The default configuration on 3560 switches is **no ip routing**.

```
DLS1(config)# ip routing
```

Verify the configuration using the **show ip route** command on DLS1.

```
DLS1# show ip route
Codes: C - connected, S - static, R - RIP, M - mobile, B - BGP
       D - EIGRP, EX - EIGRP external, O - OSPF, IA - OSPF inter area
       N1 - OSPF NSSA external type 1, N2 - OSPF NSSA external type 2
       E1 - OSPF external type 1, E2 - OSPF external type 2, E - EGP
       i - IS-IS, su - IS-IS summary, L1 - IS-IS level-1, L2 - IS-IS level-2
```

```
       ia - IS-IS inter area, * - candidate default, U - per-user static route
       o - ODR, P - periodic downloaded static route

Gateway of last resort is not set

     172.16.0.0/24 is subnetted, 3 subnets
C        172.16.200.0 is directly connected, Vlan200
C        172.16.1.0 is directly connected, Vlan1
C        172.16.100.0 is directly connected, Vlan100
```

Run the following Tcl script on DLS1 to verify full connectivity. If these pings are not successful, troubleshoot.

Note: Tcl is only supported on DLS1.

```
DLS1# tclsh

foreach address {
172.16.1.1
172.16.1.101
172.16.1.102
172.16.100.1
172.16.200.1
172.16.100.101
172.16.200.101
} {
ping $address }
```

Step 9: Configure Cisco IOS IP SLA responders.

IP SLA responders are Cisco IOS devices that support the IP SLA control protocol. An IP SLA responder uses the Cisco IOS IP SLA Control Protocol for notification configuration and on which port to listen and respond. Some operations, such as ICMP echo, do not require a dedicated IP SLA responder.

Use the **ip sla responder** command on ALS1 and ALS2 to enable sending and receiving IP SLAs control packets.

Note: This command replaces the ip sla monitor responder command. All commands that used to begin with "ip sla monitor" now begin with "ip sla" (without "monitor").

```
ALS1(config)# ip sla responder

ALS2(config)# ip sla responder
```

Configure ALS1 and ALS2 as IP SLA responders for UDP jitter using the **ip sla responder udp-echo ipaddress** command. Specify the IP address of DLS1 VLAN 1 to act as the destination IP address for the reflected UDP traffic on both ALS1 and ALS2.

```
ALS1(config)# ip sla responder udp-echo ipaddress 172.16.1.1 port 5000

ALS2(config)# ip sla responder udp-echo ipaddress 172.16.1.1 port 5000
```

Step 10: Configure the Cisco IOS IP SLA source to measure network performance.

IP SLA uses generated traffic to measure network performance between two networking devices.

On DLS1, create an IP SLA operation and enter IP SLA configuration mode with the **ip sla** *operation-number* command.

```
DLS1(config)# ip sla 1
DLS1(config-ip-sla)#
```

Configure an IP SLA ICMP echo operation using the icmp-echo command in IP SLA configuration mode. The IP SLA ICMP echo operation does not require a dedicated Cisco IOS IP SLA responder (the destination device can be a non-Cisco device, such as a PC). By default, the ICMP operation repeats every 60 seconds. On DLS1, for ICMP echo operation 1, specify the IP address of Host A as the target. For ICMP echo operation 2, specify the IP address of Host B as the target.

```
DLS1(config-ip-sla)# icmp-echo 172.16.100.101
DLS1(config-ip-sla-echo)# exit

DLS1(config)# ip sla 2
DLS1(config-ip-sla)# icmp-echo 172.16.200.101
DLS1(config-ip-sla-echo)# exit
```

Jitter means inter-packet delay variance. UDP-based voice traffic associated with IP phone and PC softphone applications at the access layer require strict adherence to delay and jitter thresholds. To configure an IP SLA UDP jitter operation, use the udp-jitter command in IP SLA configuration mode. By default, the UDP jitter operation repeats every 60 seconds. For UDP jitter operation 3, specify the destination IP address of the ALS1 VLAN 1 interface as the target. For operation 4, specify the destination IP address of the ALS2 VLAN 1 interface as the target. The IP SLA communication port is 5000 for both operations.

```
DLS1(config)# ip sla 3
DLS1(config-ip-sla)# udp-jitter 172.16.1.101 5000
DLS1(config-ip-sla-jitter)# exit

DLS1(config)# ip sla 4
DLS1(config-ip-sla)# udp-jitter 172.16.1.102 5000
DLS1(config-ip-sla-jitter)# exit
```

Schedule the IP SLAs operations to run indefinitely beginning immediately using the ip sla schedule global configuration mode command.

```
DLS1(config)# ip sla schedule 1 life forever start-time now
DLS1(config)# ip sla schedule 2 life forever start-time now
DLS1(config)# ip sla schedule 3 life forever start-time now
DLS1(config)# ip sla schedule 4 life forever start-time now
```

Step 11: Monitor IP SLAs operations.

View the IP SLA configuration for IP SLA 1 on DLS1. The output for IP SLA 2 is similar.

```
DLS1# show ip sla configuration 1
IP SLAs, Infrastructure Engine-II.

Entry number: 1
Owner:
Tag:
Type of operation to perform: echo
Target address/Source address: 172.16.100.101/0.0.0.0

Type Of Service parameter: 0x0
Request size (ARR data portion): 28
```

```
Operation timeout (milliseconds): 5000
Verify data: No
Vrf Name:
Schedule:
    Operation frequency (seconds): 60
    Next Scheduled Start Time: Start Time already passed
    Group Scheduled : FALSE
    Randomly Scheduled : FALSE
    Life (seconds): Forever
    Entry Ageout (seconds): never
    Recurring (Starting Everyday): FALSE
    Status of entry (SNMP RowStatus): Active
Threshold (milliseconds): 5000
Distribution Statistics:
    Number of statistic hours kept: 2
    Number of statistic distribution buckets kept: 1
    Statistic distribution interval (milliseconds): 20
History Statistics:
    Number of history Lives kept: 0
    Number of history Buckets kept: 15
    History Filter Type: None
Enhanced History:
```

What type of operation is being performed with IP SLA 1?

_____

View the IP SLA configuration for IP SLA 3 on DLS1. The output for IP SLA 4 is similar.

DLS1# **show ip sla configuration 3**
```
IP SLAs, Infrastructure Engine-II.

Entry number: 3
Owner:
Tag:
Type of operation to perform: udp-jitter
Target address/Source address: 172.16.1.101/0.0.0.0
Target port/Source port: 5000/0
Type Of Service parameter: 0x0
Request size (ARR data portion): 32
Operation timeout (milliseconds): 5000
Packet Interval (milliseconds)/Number of packets: 20/10
Verify data: No
Vrf Name:
Control Packets: enabled
Schedule:
    Operation frequency (seconds): 60
    Next Scheduled Start Time: Start Time already passed
    Group Scheduled : FALSE
    Randomly Scheduled : FALSE
    Life (seconds): Forever
    Entry Ageout (seconds): never
```

```
      Recurring (Starting Everyday): FALSE
      Status of entry (SNMP RowStatus): Active
Threshold (milliseconds): 5000
Distribution Statistics:
    Number of statistic hours kept: 2
    Number of statistic distribution buckets kept: 1
    Statistic distribution interval (milliseconds): 20
Enhanced History:
```

What type of operation is being performed with IP SLA 3?

_____

Display global information about Cisco IOS IP SLAs on DLS1.

DLS1# **show ip sla application**

```
Version: 2.2.0 Round Trip Time MIB, Infrastructure Engine-II
Time of last change in whole IP SLAs: *13:16:30.493 UTC Fri Mar 5 2010
Estimated system max number of entries: 11928

Estimated number of configurable operations: 11924
Number of Entries configured  : 4
Number of active Entries       : 4
Number of pending Entries     : 0
Number of inactive Entries    : 0


Type of Operation to Perform: dhcp
Type of Operation to Perform: dns
Type of Operation to Perform: echo
Type of Operation to Perform: ftp
Type of Operation to Perform: http
Type of Operation to Perform: jitter
Type of Operation to Perform: pathEcho
Type of Operation to Perform: pathJitter
Type of Operation to Perform: tcpConnect
Type of Operation to Perform: udpEcho

IP SLAs low memory water mark: 16273927
```

Display information about Cisco IOS IP SLA responders on ALS1. The ALS2 output is similar.

ALS1# **show ip sla responder**
```
IP SLAs Responder is: Enabled
Number of control message received: 38 Number of errors: 0
Recent sources:
Recent error sources:

udpEcho Responder:
  IPv6/IP Address       Port
  172.16.1.1            5000
```

Display IP SLA statistics on DLS1 for IP SLA 1. The IP SLA 2 output is similar.

```
DLS1# show ip sla statistics 1

Round Trip Time (RTT) for        Index 1
        Latest RTT: 1 ms
Latest operation start time: *13:17:21.231 UTC Fri Mar 5 2010
Latest operation return code: OK
Number of successes: 15
Number of failures: 1
Operation time to live: Forever
```

From this output, you can see that the latest round-trip time (RTT) for SLA operation Index 1 (icmp-echo) is 1 millisecond (ms). The number of packets sent successfully from DLS1 to PC Host A was 15, and there was one failure.

Display IP SLA statistics on DLS1 for IP SLA 3. The IP SLA 4 output is similar.

```
DLS1# show ip sla statistics 3

Round Trip Time (RTT) for        Index 3
        Latest RTT: 3 ms
Latest operation start time: *13:19:45.322 UTC Fri Mar 5 2010
Latest operation return code: OK
RTT Values
        Number Of RTT: 10
        RTT Min/Avg/Max: 2/3/5 ms
Latency one-way time milliseconds
        Number of Latency one-way Samples: 0
        Source to Destination Latency one way Min/Avg/Max: 0/0/0 ms
        Destination to Source Latency one way Min/Avg/Max: 0/0/0 ms
Jitter time milliseconds
        Number of SD Jitter Samples: 9
        Number of DS Jitter Samples: 9
        Source to Destination Jitter Min/Avg/Max: 0/1/2 ms
        Destination to Source Jitter Min/Avg/Max: 0/1/1 ms
Packet Loss Values
        Loss Source to Destination: 0        Loss Destination to Source: 0
        Out Of Sequence: 0       Tail Drop: 0    Packet Late Arrival: 0
Voice Score Values
        Calculated Planning Impairment Factor (ICPIF): 0
        Mean Opinion Score (MOS): 0
Number of successes: 14
Number of failures: 0
Operation time to live: Forever
```

From this output, you can see that the latest RTT for SLA operation Index 3 (udp-jitter) is 3 ms. Jitter time from source to destination and from destination to source is averaging 1 ms, which is acceptable for voice applications. The number of packets sent successfully from DLS1 to ALS1 was 14, and there were no failures.

Disable interface VLAN 1 on ALS1 using the **shutdown** command.

```
ALS1(config)# interface vlan 1
ALS1(config-if)# shutdown
```

Allow a few minutes to pass and then issue the **show ip sla statistics 3** command on DLS1. The output should look similar to the following.

```
DLS1# show ip sla statistics 3

Round Trip Time (RTT) for        Index 3
        Latest RTT: NoConnection/Busy/Timeout
Latest operation start time: *13:19:45.322 UTC Fri Mar 5 2010
Latest operation return code: Timeout
RTT Values
        Number Of RTT: 0
        RTT Min/Avg/Max: 0/0/0 ms
Latency one-way time milliseconds
        Number of Latency one-way Samples: 0
        Source to Destination Latency one way Min/Avg/Max: 0/0/0 ms
        Destination to Source Latency one way Min/Avg/Max: 0/0/0 ms
Jitter time milliseconds
        Number of SD Jitter Samples: 0
        Number of DS Jitter Samples: 0
        Source to Destination Jitter Min/Avg/Max: 0/0/0 ms
        Destination to Source Jitter Min/Avg/Max: 0/0/0 ms
Packet Loss Values
        Loss Source to Destination: 0        Loss Destination to Source: 0
        Out Of Sequence: 0        Tail Drop: 0        Packet Late Arrival: 0
Voice Score Values
        Calculated Planning Impairment Factor (ICPIF): 0
        Mean Opinion Score (MOS): 0
Number of successes: 14
Number of failures: 2
Operation time to live: Forever
```

If there is a connectivity problem between IP SLA source DLS1 and responder ALS1 or ALS2, the communication to the responder will be lost and statistics will cease to be collected, except for the number of failed tests.

Note: The IP SLA itself is an additional task that must be performed by the switch CPU. A large number of intensive SLAs could create a significant burden on the CPU, possibly interfering with other switch functions and having detrimental impact on the overall device performance. Therefore, you should carefully evaluate the benefits of running IP SLAs. The CPU load should be monitored after the SLAs are deployed to verify that they do not stress the device's CPU above safe limits.

Chapter 6 Securing the Campus Infrastructure

Lab 6-1, Securing Layer 2 Switches

Topology

HSRP Gateway Addresses	
VLAN	**IP Address**
1	172.16.1.1/24
100	172.16.100.1/24
200	172.16.200.1/24

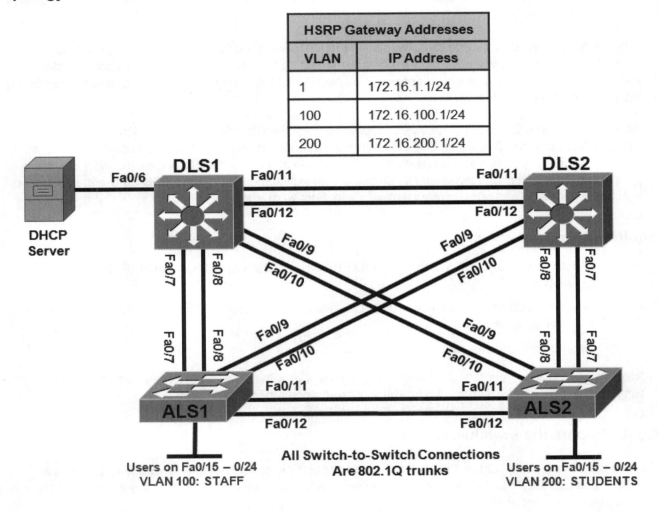

All Switch-to-Switch Connections
Are 802.1Q trunks

Users on Fa0/15 – 0/24
VLAN 100: STAFF

Users on Fa0/15 – 0/24
VLAN 200: STUDENTS

Objectives

- Secure the Layer 2 network against MAC flood attacks.

- Prevent DHCP spoofing attacks.

- Prevent unauthorized access to the network using AAA and 802.1X.

Background

A fellow network engineer that you have known and trusted for many years has invited you to lunch this week. At lunch, he brings up the subject of network security and how two of his former co-workers had been arrested for using different Layer 2 attack techniques to gather data from other users in the office for their own personal gain in their careers and finances. The story shocks you because you have always known your friend to be very cautious with security on his network. His story makes you realize that your business network has been cautious with external threats, Layer 3–7 security, firewalls at the borders, and so on, but insufficient at Layer 2 security and protection inside the local network.

When you get back to the office, you meet with your boss to discuss your concerns. After reviewing the company's security policies, you begin to work on a Layer 2 security policy.

First, you establish which network threats you are concerned about and then put together an action plan to mitigate these threats. While researching these threats, you learn about other potential threats to Layer 2 switches that might not be malicious but could threaten network stability. You decide to include these threats in the policies as well.

Other security measures need to be put in place to further secure the network, but you begin with configuring the switches against a few specific types of attacks, including MAC flood attacks, DHCP spoofing attacks, and unauthorized access to the local network. You plan to test the configurations in a lab environment before placing them into production.

Note: This lab uses Cisco WS-C2960-24TT-L switches with the Cisco IOS image c2960-lanbasek9-mz.122-46.SE.bin, and Catalyst 3560-24PS with the Cisco IOS image c3560-advipservicesk9-mz.122-46.SE.bin. You can use other switches (such as 2950 or 3550) and Cisco IOS Software versions if they have comparable capabilities and features. Depending on the switch model and Cisco IOS Software version, the commands available and output produced might vary from what is shown in this lab.

Required Resources

- 2 switches (Cisco 2960 with the Cisco IOS Release 12.2(46)SE C2960-LANBASEK9-M image or comparable)

- 2 switches (Cisco 3560 with the Cisco IOS Release 12.2(46)SE C3560-ADVIPSERVICESK9-mz image or comparable)

- Ethernet and console cables

Note: Be sure to save your final device configurations to use with the next lab. Because the VLAN and VTP commands do not display in the configs, you must re-enter them in the next lab.

Step 1: Prepare the switches for the lab.

Erase the startup config, delete the vlan.dat file, and reload the switches. Refer to Lab 1-1, "Clearing a Switch" and Lab 1-2, "Clearing a Switch Connected to a Larger Network" to prepare the switches for this lab. Cable the equipment as shown.

Step 2: Configure the basic switch parameters and trunking.

a.   Configure the management IP addresses in VLAN 1. Configure the hostname, password, and Telnet access on all four switches. HSRP will be used later in the lab, so set up the IP addressing for VLAN 1 on DLS1 and DLS2. Because 172.16.1.1 will be the virtual default gateway for VLAN 1, use .3 and .4 for the IP addresses on DLS1 and DLS2, respectively.

b.   Configure a default gateway on the access layer switches. The distribution layer switches are Layer 3 devices and do not need default gateways.

c.   Configure 802.1q trunking between the switches according to the diagram. On the 2960 switches, only dot1q is supported, therefore the **switchport trunk encapsulation** command is unavailable.

```
Switch(config)# hostname ALS1
ALS1(config)# enable secret class
ALS1(config)# line vty 0 15
ALS1(config-line)# password cisco
ALS1(config-line)# login
ALS1(config-line)# exit
ALS1(config)# interface vlan 1
ALS1(config-if)# ip address 172.16.1.101 255.255.255.0
ALS1(config-if)# no shutdown
ALS1(config-if)# exit
ALS1(config)# ip default-gateway 172.16.1.1
ALS1(config)# interface range fastethernet 0/7 - 12
ALS1(config-if-range)# switchport mode trunk

Switch(config)# hostname ALS2
ALS2(config)# enable secret class
ALS2(config)# line vty 0 15
ALS2(config-line)# password cisco
ALS2(config-line)# login
ALS2(config-line)# exit
ALS2(config)# interface vlan 1
ALS2(config-if)# ip address 172.16.1.102 255.255.255.0
ALS2(config-if)# no shutdown
ALS2(config-if)# exit
ALS2(config)# ip default-gateway 172.16.1.1
ALS2(config)# interface range fastethernet 0/7 - 12
ALS2(config-if-range)# switchport mode trunk

Switch(config)# hostname DLS1
DLS1(config)# enable secret class
DLS1(config)# line vty 0 15
DLS1(config-line)# password cisco
DLS1(config-line)# login
DLS1(config-line)# exit
DLS1(config)# interface vlan 1
DLS1(config-if)# ip address 172.16.1.3 255.255.255.0
DLS1(config-if)# no shutdown
DLS1(config-if)# exit
DLS1(config)# interface range fastethernet 0/7 - 12
DLS1(config-if-range)# switchport trunk encapsulation dot1q
DLS1(config-if-range)# switchport mode trunk

Switch(config)# hostname DLS2
DLS2(config)# enable secret class
DLS2(config)# line vty 0 15
DLS2(config-line)# password cisco
DLS2(config-line)# login
DLS2(config-line)# exit
DLS2(config)# interface vlan 1
DLS2(config-if)# ip address 172.16.1.4 255.255.255.0
DLS2(config-if)# no shutdown
DLS2(config-if)# exit
DLS2(config)# interface range fastethernet 0/7 - 12
```

```
DLS2(config-if-range)# switchport trunk encapsulation dot1q
DLS2(config-if-range)# switchport mode trunk
```

d. Verify trunking and spanning-tree operations using the **show interfaces trunk** and **show spanning-tree** commands.

Which switch is the root bridge?

_____

_____

For ALS1 and ALS2, which trunks have a role of designated (Desg), Alternate (Altn), and Root?

_____

_____

Is trunk negotiation being used here? Which mode are the trunks in?

_____

_____

Step 3: Configure VTP on ALS1 and ALS2.

Set up the VLANs according to the diagram. Two VLANs are in use at this time: one for students, and one for faculty and staff. These VLANs will be created on DLS1, which is set up as a VTP server. DLS2 also remains in its default VTP mode and acts as a server as well. ALS1 and ALS2 are configured as VTP clients.

The user access ports for these VLANs also need to be configured on ALS1 and ALS2. Set up these ports as static access ports and activate spanning-tree PortFast. Configure these ports according to the diagram.

a. Configure ALS1 for the VTP client changes.

```
ALS1(config)# vtp mode client
Setting device to VTP CLIENT mode.
ALS1(config)# interface range fa0/15 - 24
ALS1(config-if-range)# switchport mode access
ALS1(config-if-range)# switchport access vlan 100
ALS1(config-if-range)# spanning-tree portfast

%Warning: portfast should only be enabled on ports connected to a single
 host. Connecting hubs, concentrators, switches, bridges, etc... to this
 interface when portfast is enabled, can cause temporary bridging loops.
 Use with CAUTION

%Portfast will be configured in 10 interfaces due to the range command
 but will only have effect when the interfaces are in a non-trunking mode.
```

b. Configure ALS2 for the VTP client changes.

```
ALS2(config)# vtp mode client
Setting device to VTP CLIENT mode.
ALS2(config)# interface range fa0/15 - 24
ALS2(config-if-range)# switchport mode access
ALS2(config-if-range)# switchport access vlan 200
ALS2(config-if-range)# spanning-tree portfast

%Warning: portfast should only be enabled on ports connected to a single
 host. Connecting hubs, concentrators, switches, bridges, etc... to this
 interface when portfast is enabled, can cause temporary bridging loops.
 Use with CAUTION

%Portfast will be configured in 10 interfaces due to the range command
 but will only have effect when the interfaces are in a non-trunking mode.
```

Step 4: Configure IP routing, the VLANs, VLAN SVIs, and HSRP on DLS1 and DLS2.

HSRP is a requirement for the network, and VLANs 100 and 200 are configured to use HSRP to provide redundancy at Layer 3. Use the **priority** command to make DLS1 the active router for VLANs 1 and 100, and DLS2 the active router for VLAN 200.

a. Configure VTP, VLANs, and IP routing on DLS1.

```
DLS1(config)# vtp domain SWPOD
DLS1(config)# vtp version 2
DLS1(config)# vlan 100
DLS1(config-vlan)# name Staff
DLS1(config-vlan)# vlan 200
DLS1(config-vlan)# name Student
DLS1(config-vlan)# exit

DLS1(config)# ip routing
```

b. Configure switch virtual interfaces (SVIs) and HSRP on DLS1.

```
DLS1(config)# interface vlan 1
DLS1(config-if)# standby 1 ip 172.16.1.1
DLS1(config-if)# standby 1 preempt
DLS1(config-if)# standby 1 priority 150

DLS1(config-if)# interface vlan 100
DLS1(config-if)# ip add 172.16.100.3 255.255.255.0
DLS1(config-if)# standby 1 ip 172.16.100.1
DLS1(config-if)# standby 1 preempt
DLS1(config-if)# standby 1 priority 150

DLS1(config-if)# interface vlan 200
DLS1(config-if)# ip add 172.16.200.3 255.255.255.0
DLS1(config-if)# standby 1 ip 172.16.200.1
DLS1(config-if)# standby 1 preempt
DLS1(config-if)# standby 1 priority 100
```

c. Configure IP routing, VLAN SVIs, and HSRP on DLS2.

```
DLS2(config)# ip routing
DLS2(config)# interface vlan 1
```

```
DLS2(config-if)# standby 1 ip 172.16.1.1
DLS2(config-if)# standby 1 preempt
DLS2(config-if)# standby 1 priority 100
DLS2(config-if)# interface vlan 100
DLS2(config-if)# ip add 172.16.100.4 255.255.255.0
DLS2(config-if)# standby 1 ip 172.16.100.1
DLS2(config-if)# standby 1 preempt
DLS2(config-if)# standby 1 priority 100

DLS2(config-if)# interface vlan 200
DLS2(config-if)# ip add 172.16.200.4 255.255.255.0
DLS2(config-if)# standby 1 ip 172.16.200.1
DLS2(config-if)# standby 1 preempt
DLS2(config-if)# standby 1 priority 150
```

d. Verify your configurations using the **show vlan brief**, **show vtp status**, **show standby brief**, and **show ip route** commands. Output from DLS1 is shown here.

```
DLS1# show vlan brief

VLAN Name                             Status     Ports
---- -------------------------------- ---------  ------------------------------
--
1    default                          active     Fa0/1, Fa0/2, Fa0/3, Fa0/4
                                                 Fa0/5, Fa0/6, Fa0/13, Fa0/14
                                                 Fa0/15, Fa0/16, Fa0/17, Fa0/18
                                                 Fa0/19, Fa0/20, Fa0/21, Fa0/22
                                                 Fa0/23, Fa0/24, Gi0/1, Gi0/2

100  Staff                            active
200  Student                          active
1002 fddi-default                     act/unsup
1003 token-ring-default               act/unsup
1004 fddinet-default                  act/unsup
1005 trnet-default                    act/unsup
```

How many VLANs are active in the VTP domain?

```
DLS1# show vtp status
VTP Version                      : running VTP2
Configuration Revision           : 2
Maximum VLANs supported locally  : 1005
Number of existing VLANs         : 7
VTP Operating Mode               : Server
VTP Domain Name                  : SWPOD
VTP Pruning Mode                 : Disabled
VTP V2 Mode                      : Enabled
VTP Traps Generation             : Disabled
MD5 digest                       : 0x1A 0x33 0x4D 0xA1 0x18 0xE6 0xBE 0xBA
Configuration last modified by 172.16.1.3 at 3-1-93 00:41:51
```

```
Local updater ID is 172.16.1.3 on interface Vl1 (lowest numbered VLAN
interface
found)
```

DLS1# **show standby brief**

```
                    P indicates configured to preempt.
                    |
Interface   Grp  Pri P State   Active           Standby         Virtual IP
Vl1         1    150 P Active  local            172.16.1.4      172.16.1.1
Vl100       1    150 P Active  local            172.16.100.4    172.16.100.1
Vl200       1    100 P Standby 172.16.200.4     local           172.16.200.1
```

What is the active router for VLANs 1 and 100? What is the active router for VLAN 200?

_____

_____

DLS1# **show ip route**
```
Codes: C - connected, S - static, R - RIP, M - mobile, B - BGP
       D - EIGRP, EX - EIGRP external, O - OSPF, IA - OSPF inter area
       N1 - OSPF NSSA external type 1, N2 - OSPF NSSA external type 2
       E1 - OSPF external type 1, E2 - OSPF external type 2
       i - IS-IS, su - IS-IS summary, L1 - IS-IS level-1, L2 - IS-IS level-2
       ia - IS-IS inter area, * - candidate default, U - per-user static route
       o - ODR, P - periodic downloaded static route

Gateway of last resort is not set

     172.16.0.0/24 is subnetted, 3 subnets
C       172.16.1.0 is directly connected, Vlan1
C       172.16.100.0 is directly connected, Vlan100
C       172.16.200.0 is directly connected, Vlan200
```

What would be the effect on virtual interface VLAN 100 if VLAN 100 had not been created?

_____

Step 5: Specify verification methods and mitigation techniques for attack types.

Complete the following table with the appropriate verification methods and mitigation approaches for the attack types specified in the left column.

Attack Type	Verification	Mitigation
MAC address spoofing or flooding		
DHCP spoofing		
Unauthorized LAN access		

Step 6: Configure port security.

To protect against MAC flooding or spoofing attacks, configure port security on the VLAN 100 and 200 access ports. Because the two VLANs serve different purposes—one for staff and one for students—configure the ports to meet the different requirements.

The student VLAN must allow MAC addresses assigned to a port to change, because most of the students use laptops and move around within the network. Set up port security so that only one MAC address is allowed on a port at a given time. This type of configuration does not work on ports that need to service IP phones with PCs attached. In this case, there would be two allowed MAC addresses. To enable security on a port, you must first issue the **switchport port-security** command by itself.

The staff MAC addresses do not change often, because the staff uses desktop workstations provided by the IT department. In this case, you can configure the staff VLAN so that the MAC address learned on a port is added to the configuration on the switch as if the MAC address were configured using the **switchport port-security mac-address** command. This feature, which is called sticky learning, is available on some switch platforms. It combines the features of dynamically learned and statically configured addresses. The staff ports also allow for a maximum of two MAC addresses to be dynamically learned per port.

a. Enter the configuration for the student access ports on ALS2. To enable basic port security, issue the **switchport port-security** command.

    Note: By default, issuing the **switchport port-security** command by itself sets the maximum number of MAC addresses to 1, and the violation mode to shutdown. It is not necessary to specify the maximum number of addresses, unless it is greater than 1.

    ```
    ALS2(config)# interface range fastethernet 0/15 - 24
    ALS2(config-if-range)# switchport port-security
    ```

b. Verify the configuration for ALS2 using the **show port-security** *interface* command.

    ```
    ALS2# show port-security interface fa0/15
    Port Security              : Enabled
    Port Status                : Secure-down
    Violation Mode             : Shutdown
    Aging Time                 : 0 mins
    Aging Type                 : Absolute
    SecureStatic Address Aging : Disabled
    Maximum MAC Addresses      : 1
    Total MAC Addresses        : 0
    Configured MAC Addresses   : 0
    ```

```
Sticky MAC Addresses       : 0
Last Source Address:Vlan   : 0000.0000.0000:0
Security Violation Count   : 0
```

c. Enter the configuration of the staff ports on ALS1. First, enable port security with the **switchport port-security** command. Use the **switchport port-security maximum** *#_of_MAC_addresses* command to change the maximum number of MAC addresses to 2, and use the **switchport port-security mac-address sticky** command to allow the two addresses to be learned dynamically.

```
ALS1(config)# interface range fastethernet 0/15 - 24
ALS1(config-if-range)# switchport port-security
ALS1(config-if-range)# switchport port-security maximum 2
ALS1(config-if-range)# switchport port-security mac-address sticky
```

This time two MAC addresses are allowed. Both will be dynamically learned and then added to the running configuration.

d. Verify the configuration using the **show port-security** *interface* command.

```
ALS1# show port-security int fa0/15
Port Security               : Enabled
Port Status                 : Secure-down
Violation Mode              : Shutdown
Aging Time                  : 0 mins
Aging Type                  : Absolute
SecureStatic Address Aging  : Disabled
Maximum MAC Addresses       : 2
Total MAC Addresses         : 0
Configured MAC Addresses    : 0
Sticky MAC Addresses        : 0
Last Source Address:Vlan    : 0000.0000.0000:0
Security Violation Count    : 0
```

Step 7: Configure DHCP snooping.

DHCP spoofing is a type of attack primarily used to assign IP addressing and configuration information by an unauthorized device. This can lead to a denial of service or traffic interception. The attacker replies to a DHCP request, claiming to have valid gateway and DNS information. A valid DHCP server might also reply to the request, but if the attacker's reply reaches the requestor first, the invalid information from the attacker is used.

To help protect the network from such an attack, you can use DHCP snooping. DHCP snooping is a Cisco Catalyst feature that determines which switch ports are allowed to respond to DHCP requests. Ports are identified as trusted or untrusted. Trusted ports permit all DHCP messages, while untrusted ports permit (ingress) DHCP requests only. Trusted ports can host a DHCP server or can be an uplink toward a DHCP server. If a rogue device on an untrusted port attempts to send a DHCP response packet into the network, the port is disabled. From a DHCP snooping perspective, untrusted access ports should not send any DHCP server responses, such as a DHCPOFFER, DHCPACK, or DHCPNAK.

a. Enable DLS1 and DLS2 to trust DHCP relay information from ALS1 and ALS2 so that the DHCP server can respond to the ALS1 and ALS2 trusted port requests. This is accomplished using the **ip dhcp relay information trust-all** command.

```
DLS1(config)# ip dhcp relay information trust-all
```

```
DLS2(config)# ip dhcp relay information trust-all
```

Note: It is not necessary to enable DHCP snooping on the distribution layer switches, although this would allow DLS1 and DLS2 to trust ALS1 and ALS2 as relay agents.

b. Configure ALS1 and ALS2 to trust DHCP information on the trunk ports only, and limit the rate that requests are received on the access ports.

Configuring DHCP snooping on the access layer switches involves the following process:

- Turn snooping on globally using the **ip dhcp snooping** command.

- Configure the trusted interfaces with the **ip dhcp snooping trust** command. By default, all ports are considered untrusted unless statically configured to be trusted.

- Configure a DHCP request rate limit on the user access ports to limit the number of DHCP requests that are allowed per second. This is configured using the **ip dhcp snooping limit rate** *rate_in_pps*. This command prevents DHCP starvation attacks by limiting the rate of the DHCP requests on untrusted ports.

- Configure the VLANs that will use DHCP snooping. In this scenario, DHCP snooping will be used on both the student and staff VLANs.

```
ALS1(config)# ip dhcp snooping
ALS1(config)# interface range fastethernet 0/7 - 12
ALS1(config-if-range)# ip dhcp snooping trust
ALS1(config-if-range)# exit
ALS1(config)# interface range fastethernet 0/15 - 24
ALS1(config-if-range)# ip dhcp snooping limit rate 20
ALS1(config-if-range)# exit
ALS1(config)# ip dhcp snooping vlan 100,200

ALS2(config)# ip dhcp snooping
ALS2(config)# interface range fastethernet 0/7 - 12
ALS2(config-if-range)# ip dhcp snooping trust
ALS2(config-if-range)# exit
ALS2(config)# interface range fastethernet 0/15 - 24
ALS2(config-if-range)# ip dhcp snooping limit rate 20
ALS2(config-if-range)# exit
ALS2(config)# ip dhcp snooping vlan 100,200
```

c. Verify the configurations on ALS1 and ALS2 using the **show ip dhcp snooping** command.

```
ALS2# show ip dhcp snooping
Switch DHCP snooping is enabled
DHCP snooping is configured on following VLANs:
100,200
DHCP snooping is operational on following VLANs:
100,200
DHCP snooping is configured on the following L3 Interfaces:

Insertion of option 82 is enabled
   circuit-id format: vlan-mod-port
    remote-id format: MAC
Option 82 on untrusted port is not allowed
Verification of hwaddr field is enabled
Verification of giaddr field is enabled
DHCP snooping trust/rate is configured on the following Interfaces:
```

Interface	Trusted	Rate limit (pps)
FastEthernet0/7	yes	unlimited
FastEthernet0/8	yes	unlimited
FastEthernet0/9	yes	unlimited
FastEthernet0/10	yes	unlimited
FastEthernet0/11	yes	unlimited
FastEthernet0/12	yes	unlimited
FastEthernet0/15	no	20
FastEthernet0/16	no	20
FastEthernet0/17	no	20
FastEthernet0/18	no	20
FastEthernet0/19	no	20
FastEthernet0/20	no	20
FastEthernet0/21	no	20
FastEthernet0/22	no	20
FastEthernet0/23	no	20
FastEthernet0/24	no	20

Will DHCP replies be allowed on access ports assigned to VLAN 200?

_____

_____

How many DHCP packets will be allowed on Fast Ethernet 0/16 per second?

_____

Step 8: Configure AAA.

The authentication portion of AAA requires a user to be identified before being allowed access to the network. Authentication is configured by defining a list of methods for authentication and applying that list to specific interfaces. If lists are not defined, a default list is used.

For this network, it has been decided that AAA using 802.1X will be used to control user access for the staff VLAN using a local list of usernames and passwords. When a radius server is added to the network, all user ports, including the student VLAN, will also be added to the configuration.

The IEEE 802.1X standard defines a port-based access control and authentication protocol that restricts unauthorized workstations from connecting to a LAN through publicly accessible switch ports. The authentication server authenticates each workstation that is connected to a switch port before making any services that are offered by the switch or the LAN available.

Until the workstation is authenticated, 802.1X access control allows only Extensible Authentication Protocol over LAN (EAPOL) traffic through the port to which the workstation is connected. After authentication succeeds, normal traffic can pass through the port.

a. Enter the configuration for ALS1.

Use the **aaa new-model** command to turn on AAA authentication on ALS1. The **aaa authentication dot1x default local** command tells the switch to use a local database of usernames and passwords to authenticate the users. Users are assigned to the database using the username *username* password *password* command. The **dot1x system-auth-control** command activates global support for 802.1X authentication.

The Fast Ethernet interfaces used for VLAN 100 staff access are configured using the dot1x port-control auto command. The auto keyword allows the switch port to begin in the unauthorized state, and allows the negotiation between the client and server to authenticate the user. Once authenticated, the user is allowed access to the network resources.

```
ALS1(config)# username janedoe password 0 cisco
ALS1(config)# username johndoe password 0 cisco
ALS1(config)# username joesmith password 0 cisco
ALS1(config)# aaa new-model
ALS1(config)# aaa authentication dot1x default local
ALS1(config)# dot1x system-auth-control
ALS1(config)# int range fa 0/15 - 24
ALS1(config-if-range)# dot1x port-control auto
```

Note: For switches running Cisco IOS version 12.2(50)SE or later, the **dot1x port-control auto** command is replaced with the following interface-level commands:

```
authentication port-control auto
dot1x pae authenticator
```

b. Verify the AAA configuration using the **show dot1x interface** command.

```
ALS1#show dot1x interface fa0/15
Dot1x Info for FastEthernet0/15
------------------------------------
PAE                     = AUTHENTICATOR
PortControl             = AUTO
ControlDirection        = Both
HostMode                = SINGLE_HOST
Violation Mode          = PROTECT
ReAuthentication        = Disabled
QuietPeriod             = 60
ServerTimeout           = 0
SuppTimeout             = 30
ReAuthPeriod            = 3600 (Locally configured)
ReAuthMax               = 2
MaxReq                  = 2
TxPeriod                = 30
RateLimitPeriod         = 0
```

If a user with a username frankadams attempts to connect to the staff VLAN access ports, will the user be allowed access? Will the user be allowed access to the student VLAN ports?

_____

_____

_____

Note: Save your final device configurations for use with the next lab.

How will the configuration need to be changed when a radius server is added to the network?

_____

_____

_____

_____

_____

_____

_____

_____

_____

Lab 6-2, Securing Spanning Tree Protocol

Topology

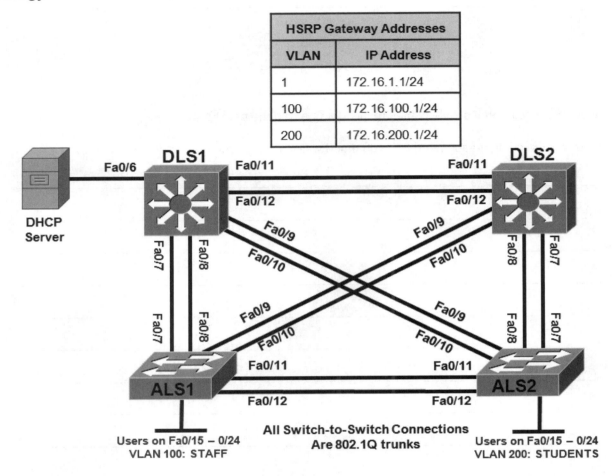

HSRP Gateway Addresses	
VLAN	**IP Address**
1	172.16.1.1/24
100	172.16.100.1/24
200	172.16.200.1/24

All Switch-to-Switch Connections Are 802.1Q trunks

Users on Fa0/15 – 0/24
VLAN 100: STAFF

Users on Fa0/15 – 0/24
VLAN 200: STUDENTS

Objectives

- Secure the Layer 2 spanning-tree topology with BPDU guard.
- Protect the primary and secondary root bridge with root guard.
- Protect switch ports from unidirectional links with UDLD.

Background

This lab is a continuation of Lab 6-1 and uses the network configuration set up in that lab.

In this lab, you will secure the network against possible spanning-tree disruptions, such as rogue access point additions and the loss of stability to the root bridge by the addition of switches to the network. The improper addition of switches to the network can be either malicious or accidental. In either case, the network can be secured against such a disruption.

Note: This lab uses Cisco WS-C2960-24TT-L switches with the Cisco IOS image c2960-lanbasek9-mz.122-46.SE.bin, and Catalyst 3560-24PS switches with the Cisco IOS image c3560-advipservicesk9-mz.122-46.SE.bin. You can use other switches (such as 2950 or 3550) and Cisco IOS Software versions if they have comparable capabilities and features. Depending on the switch model and Cisco IOS Software version, the commands available and output produced might vary from what is shown in this lab.

Required Resources

- 2 switches (Cisco 2960 with the Cisco IOS Release 12.2(46)SE C2960-LANBASEK9-M image or comparable)

- 2 switches (Cisco 3560 with the Cisco IOS Release 12.2(46)SE C3560-ADVIPSERVICESK9-mz image or comparable)

- Ethernet and console cables

Note: Be sure to save your final device configurations to use with the next lab.

Step 1: Load or verify the configurations from Lab 6-1.

a. Verify that the configurations from Lab 6-1 are loaded on the devices by issuing the **show vtp status** command. The output should show that the current VTP domain is SWPOD, and VLANs 100 and 200 should be represented in the number of existing VLANs. The output from switch ALS2 is shown as an example. If the switches are not configured properly, erase the startup config, delete the vlan.dat file, and load the configurations saved at the end of lab 6-1.

Note: If you are loading the configurations from Lab 6-1, they do not include VLAN and VTP commands. You must first configure ALS1 and ALS2 as VTP clients and then create VLANs 100 (staff) and 200 (student) and the VTP domain name on DLS1. Refer to Lab 6-1 for assistance.

```
ALS1# show vtp status
VTP Version                    : running VTP2
Configuration Revision         : 4
Maximum VLANs supported locally : 255
Number of existing VLANs       : 7
VTP Operating Mode             : Client
VTP Domain Name                : SWPOD
VTP Pruning Mode               : Disabled
VTP V2 Mode                    : Enabled
VTP Traps Generation           : Disabled
MD5 digest                     : 0x18 0x59 0xE2 0xE0 0x28 0xF3 0xE7 0xD1
Configuration last modified by 172.16.1.3 at 3-12-93 19:46:16
```

How many VLANs exist in the network? How many of these are defaults?

_____

b. Issue the **show vlan brief** command on DLS1. The student and staff VLANs should be listed in the output of this command.

```
DLS1# show vlan brief

VLAN Name                             Status    Ports
---- -------------------------------- --------- -------------------------------
1    default                          active    Fa0/1, Fa0/2, Fa0/3, Fa0/4
                                                Fa0/5, Fa0/6, Fa0/13, Fa0/14
                                                Fa0/15, Fa0/16, Fa0/17, Fa0/18
                                                Fa0/19, Fa0/20, Fa0/21, Fa0/22
```

                                                      Fa0/23, Fa0/24, Gi0/1, Gi0/2

100	staff	active
200	student	active
1002	fddi-default	act/unsup
1003	token-ring-default	act/unsup
1004	fddinet-default	act/unsup
1005	trnet-default	act/unsup

Which ports are not listed for VLAN 1? Why is this?

_____

_____

c. Issue the **show interfaces trunk** command on DLS2. If trunking was configured properly in Lab 6-1, interfaces Fast Ethernet 0/7–0/12 should be in trunking mode on all switches.

DLS2# **show interfaces trunk**

Port	Mode	Encapsulation	Status	Native vlan
Fa0/7	on	802.1q	trunking	1
Fa0/8	on	802.1q	trunking	1
Fa0/9	on	802.1q	trunking	1
Fa0/10	on	802.1q	trunking	1
Fa0/11	on	802.1q	trunking	1
Fa0/12	on	802.1q	trunking	1

Port	Vlans allowed on trunk
Fa0/7	1-4094
Fa0/8	1-4094
Fa0/9	1-4094
Fa0/10	1-4094
Fa0/11	1-4094
Fa0/12	1-4094

Port	Vlans allowed and active in management domain
Fa0/7	1,100,200
Fa0/8	1,100,200
Fa0/9	1,100,200
Fa0/10	1,100,200
Fa0/11	1,100,200

Port	Vlans allowed and active in management domain
Fa0/12	1,100,200

Port	Vlans in spanning tree forwarding state and not pruned
Fa0/7	1,100,200
Fa0/8	1,100,200
Fa0/9	1,100,200
Fa0/10	1,100,200
Fa0/11	1,100,200
Fa0/12	1,100,200

Are any VLANs being pruned from these trunks? How can you tell?

_____

_____

_____

d. Issue the **show spanning-tree vlan 1** command on DLS2. The results from this command might vary, and DLS2 might not be the root in your topology. In the following output, this bridge is currently the root of the spanning tree.

```
DLS2# show spanning-tree vlan 1

VLAN0001
  Spanning tree enabled protocol ieee
  Root ID    Priority    32769
             Address     000a.b8a9.d680
             This bridge is the root
             Hello Time   2 sec  Max Age 20 sec  Forward Delay 15 sec

  Bridge ID  Priority    32769  (priority 32768 sys-id-ext 1)
             Address     000a.b8a9.d680
             Hello Time   2 sec  Max Age 20 sec  Forward Delay 15 sec
             Aging Time 300

Interface        Role Sts Cost      Prio.Nbr Type
---------------- ---- --- --------- -------- --------------------------------
Fa0/7            Desg FWD 19        128.9    P2p
Fa0/8            Desg FWD 19        128.10   P2p
Fa0/9            Desg FWD 19        128.11   P2p
Fa0/10           Desg FWD 19        128.12   P2p
Fa0/11           Desg FWD 19        128.13   P2p
Fa0/12           Desg FWD 19        128.14   P2p
```

Where is the spanning-tree root in your lab network? Is this root bridge optimal for your network?

_____

_____

What is the priority of the current root bridge?

_____

Step 2: Configure the primary and secondary root bridges for the VLANs.

In most cases, you must manually configure the spanning-tree root to ensure optimized paths throughout the Layer 2 network. This topic is covered in Module 3. For this scenario, DLS1 acts as the root for VLANs 1 and 100 and performs the secondary function for VLAN 200. In addition, DLS2 is the primary root bridge for VLAN 200 and secondary bridge for VLANs 1 and 100.

a. Configure STP priority for the primary and secondary roots using the **spanning-tree vlan** *vlan ID* **root {primary | secondary}** command.

```
DLS1(config)# spanning-tree vlan 1,100 root primary
DLS1(config)# spanning-tree vlan 200 root secondary

DLS2(config)# spanning-tree vlan 1,100 root secondary
DLS2(config)# spanning-tree vlan 200 root primary
```

b. Verify the configuration on both DLS1 and DLS2 using the **show spanning-tree** command.

```
DLS2# show spanning-tree


VLAN0001
  Spanning tree enabled protocol ieee
  Root ID    Priority    24577
             Address     000a.b8a9.d780
             Cost        19
             Port        13 (FastEthernet0/11)
             Hello Time   2 sec  Max Age 20 sec  Forward Delay 15 sec

  Bridge ID  Priority    28673  (priority 28672 sys-id-ext 1)
             Address     000a.b8a9.d680
             Hello Time   2 sec  Max Age 20 sec  Forward Delay 15 sec
             Aging Time 300


Interface        Role Sts Cost      Prio.Nbr Type
---------------- ---- --- --------- -------- --------------------------------
Fa0/7            Desg FWD 19        128.9    P2p
Fa0/8            Desg FWD 19        128.10   P2p
Fa0/9            Desg FWD 19        128.11   P2p
Fa0/10           Desg FWD 19        128.12   P2p
Fa0/11           Root FWD 19        128.13   P2p
Fa0/12           Altn BLK 19        128.14   P2p


VLAN0100
  Spanning tree enabled protocol ieee
  Root ID    Priority    24676
             Address     000a.b8a9.d780
             Cost        19
             Port        13 (FastEthernet0/11)
             Hello Time   2 sec  Max Age 20 sec  Forward Delay 15 sec

  Bridge ID  Priority    28772  (priority 28672 sys-id-ext 100)
             Address     000a.b8a9.d680
             Hello Time   2 sec  Max Age 20 sec  Forward Delay 15 sec
             Aging Time 300
```

```
Interface          Role Sts Cost      Prio.Nbr Type
---------------    ---- --- --------- -------- -------------------------------
Fa0/7              Desg FWD 19        128.9    P2p
Fa0/8              Desg FWD 19        128.10   P2p
Fa0/9              Desg FWD 19        128.11   P2p
Fa0/10             Desg FWD 19        128.12   P2p
Fa0/11             Root FWD 19        128.13   P2p
Fa0/12             Altn BLK 19        128.14   P2p


VLAN0200
   Spanning tree enabled protocol ieee
   Root ID    Priority    24776
              Address     000a.b8a9.d680
              This bridge is the root
              Hello Time   2 sec  Max Age 20 sec  Forward Delay 15 sec

   Bridge ID  Priority    24776  (priority 24576 sys-id-ext 200)
              Address     000a.b8a9.d680
              Hello Time   2 sec  Max Age 20 sec  Forward Delay 15 sec
              Aging Time 300

Interface          Role Sts Cost      Prio.Nbr Type
---------------    ---- --- --------- -------- -------------------------------
Fa0/7              Desg FWD 19        128.9    P2p
Fa0/8              Desg FWD 19        128.10   P2p
Fa0/9              Desg FWD 19        128.11   P2p
Fa0/10             Desg FWD 19        128.12   P2p
Fa0/11             Desg FWD 19        128.13   P2p
Fa0/12             Desg FWD 19        128.14   P2p
```

According to the output, what is the root for VLAN 100? For VLAN 200?

_____

Step 3: Configure root guard.

To maintain an efficient STP topology, the root bridge must remain predictable. If a foreign or rogue switch is maliciously or accidentally added to the network, the STP topology could be changed if the new switch has a lower BID than the current root bridge. Root guard helps prevent this by putting a port that hears these BPDUs in the root-inconsistent state. Data cannot be sent or received over the port while it is in this state, but the switch can listen to BPDUs received on the port to detect a new root advertising itself.

Root guard is enabled on a per-port basis with the **spanning-tree guard root** command. You should use root guard on switch ports where you would never expect to find the root bridge for a VLAN.

a. In the topology diagram, Fast Ethernet ports 0/13 and 0/14 on each switch are not being used as trunk or access ports. It is possible that a switch could be accidentally or maliciously added to those ports. Configure root guard on these ports to ensure that if a switch is added, it is not allowed to take over as root.

```
DLS1(config)# interface range fastEthernet 0/13 - 14
DLS1(config-if-range)# spanning-tree guard root
```

b. Configure root guard on the same ports for DLS2, ALS1, and ALS2.

What will happen if a switch is connected to Fa0/13 via a crossover cable?

_____

_____

Step 4: Demonstrate root guard functionality.

Verify your configuration to make sure that root guard was not accidentally configured on a port that should hear root advertisements, such as a port on ALS2 that is connected to the root bridge.

a. Use the **show spanning-tree vlan 1** command on ALS2 to look for a root port. In the following example, Fa0/9 is a root port for VLAN 1 on ALS2.

```
ALS2# show spanning-tree vlan 1

VLAN0001
  Spanning tree enabled protocol ieee
  Root ID    Priority    24577
             Address     000a.b8a9.d780
             Cost        19
             Port        11 (FastEthernet0/9)
             Hello Time   2 sec  Max Age 20 sec  Forward Delay 15 sec

  Bridge ID  Priority    32769  (priority 32768 sys-id-ext 1)
             Address     0019.068d.6980
             Hello Time   2 sec  Max Age 20 sec  Forward Delay 15 sec
             Aging Time 300

Interface        Role Sts Cost      Prio.Nbr Type
---------------- ---- --- --------- -------- --------------------------------
Fa0/5            Desg FWD 19        128.7    P2p
Fa0/7            Altn BLK 19        128.9    P2p
Fa0/8            Altn BLK 19        128.10   P2p
Fa0/9            Root FWD 19        128.11   P2p
Fa0/10           Altn BLK 19        128.12   P2p
```

b. Configure root guard on the root port that you found. Note that this configuration is for teaching purposes only. This would *not* be done in a production network.

```
ALS2(config)# interface FastEthernet 0/9
ALS2(config-if)# spanning-tree guard root
```

Notice that as soon as you issue this command, you receive a message that root guard has been enabled and that the port is now in the blocking state for the specific VLANs configured. This port has been transitioned to this state because it receives a BPDU that claims to be the root.

```
1w4d: %SPANTREE-2-ROOTGUARD_CONFIG_CHANGE: Root guard enabled on port
FastEthernet0/9.
1w4d: %SPANTREE-2-ROOTGUARD_BLOCK: Root guard blocking port FastEthernet0/9 on
```

`VLAN0001.`

c. Verify which ports are in this inconsistent state with the **show spanning-tree inconsistentports** command.

```
ALS2# show spanning-tree inconsistentports

Name                    Interface              Inconsistency
--------------------    --------------------   ------------------
VLAN0001                FastEthernet0/9        Root Inconsistent
VLAN0100                FastEthernet0/9        Root Inconsistent
VLAN0200                FastEthernet0/9        Root Inconsistent

Number of inconsistent ports (segments) in the system : 3
```

d. Because this configuration is not intended for normal operation, remove it using the **no spanning-tree guard root** command.

```
ALS2(config)# interface FastEthernet 0/9
ALS2(config-if)# no spanning-tree guard root
```

When the configuration is removed, a message indicates that the port is being unblocked.

```
1w4d: %SPANTREE-2-ROOTGUARD_CONFIG_CHANGE: Root guard disabled on port
FastEthernet0/9.
1w4d: %SPANTREE-2-ROOTGUARD_UNBLOCK: Root guard unblocking port
FastEthernet0/9 on VLAN0001.
```

Step 5: Configure BPDU guard.

Because PortFast is enabled on all user access ports on ALS1 and ALS2, BPDUs are not expected to be heard on these ports. Any BPDUs that are heard could result in a disruption of the STP topology, so you should protect these ports from any type of accidental or malicious behavior which leads to BPDUs arriving at the port. If a rogue access point or switch is placed on these ports, BPDUs would most likely be heard.

BPDU guard protects ports from this type of situation by placing the interface in the error-disable state. The BPDU guard feature provides a secure response to invalid configurations because the network administrator must manually put the interface back in service.

a. To enable BPDU guard on PortFast-enabled ports, use the **spanning-tree portfast bpduguard default** global configuration command.

```
ALS1(config)# spanning-tree portfast bpduguard default
```

```
ALS2(config)# spanning-tree portfast bpduguard default
```

b. Verify your configuration using the **show spanning-tree summary** command.

```
ALS2# show spanning-tree summary
Switch is in pvst mode
Root bridge for: none
Extended system ID            is enabled
Portfast Default              is disabled
PortFast BPDU Guard Default   is enabled
Portfast BPDU Filter Default  is disabled
Loopguard Default             is disabled
EtherChannel misconfig guard  is enabled
UplinkFast                    is disabled
```

```
BackboneFast                    is disabled
Configured Pathcost method used is short
```

Name	Blocking	Listening	Learning	Forwarding	STP Active
VLAN0001	5	0	0	2	7
VLAN0100	5	0	0	1	6
VLAN0200	5	0	0	1	6
3 vlans	15	0	0	4	19

Which action will be taken if a wireless access point sending BPDUs is connected to Fa0/15 on ALS1?

_____

_____

Step 6: Enable broadcast storm control on trunk ports.

If a basic unmanaged switch is connected to an access port, a broadcast storm can result, which can lead to network failure. Implementing broadcast storm protection on trunk interfaces can help prevent this.

a. Enable storm control for broadcasts on Fast Ethernet ports 0/7 and 0/8 on ALS1 with a 50 percent rising suppression level using the **storm-control broadcast** command. ALS1 trunk ports Fa0/7 and Fa0/8 are shown here as an example.

```
ALS1(config)# interface FastEthernet 0/7
ALS1(config-if)# storm-control broadcast level 50
ALS1(config-if)# interface FastEthernet 0/8
ALS1(config-if)# storm-control broadcast level 50
```

b. Verify the configuration of interface Fa0/7 with the **show running-config** command.

```
ALS1# show running-config interface fastEthernet 0/7
Building configuration...

Current configuration : 155 bytes
!
interface FastEthernet0/7
 switchport mode trunk
 storm-control broadcast level 50.00
 ip dhcp snooping trust
end
```

Step 7: Configure UDLD.

A unidirectional link occurs when traffic is transmitted between neighbors in one direction only. Unidirectional links can cause spanning-tree topology loops. UDLD allows devices to detect when a unidirectional link exists and shut down the affected interface.

You can configure UDLD on a per-port basis or globally for all fiber-optic gigabit interfaces. The **aggressive** keyword places the port in the error-disable state when a violation occurs on the port.

```
DLS1(config)# udld ?
  aggressive   Enable UDLD protocol in aggressive mode on fiber ports except
               where locally configured
  enable       Enable UDLD protocol on fiber ports except where locally
               configured
```

b. Enable UDLD protection on Fast Ethernet ports 1–24 on all switches using the **udld port aggressive** command. Configure UDLD globally for all fiber-optic gigabit interfaces for future use using the **udld enable** command.

Note: This lab assumes the existence of fiber-optic gigabit ports, although this might not be the case with your lab equipment.

```
DLS1(config)# interface range FastEthernet 0/1 - 24
DLS1(config-if-range)# udld port aggressive
DLS1(config-if-range)# exit
DLS1(config)# udld enable

DLS2(config)# interface range FastEthernet 0/1 - 24
DLS2(config-if-range)# udld port aggressive
DLS2(config-if-range)# exit
DLS2(config)# udld enable

ALS1(config)# interface range FastEthernet 0/1 - 24
ALS1(config-if-range)# udld port aggressive
ALS1(config-if-range)# exit
ALS1(config)# udld enable

ALS2(config)# interface range FastEthernet 0/1 - 24
ALS2(config-if-range)# udld port aggressive
ALS2(config-if-range)# exit
ALS2(config)# udld enable
```

c. Verify your configuration using the **show udld** *interface-id* command.

```
ALS2# show udld Fa0/15

Interface Fa0/15
---
Port enable administrative configuration setting: Enabled / in aggressive mode
Port enable operational state: Enabled / in aggressive mode
Current bidirectional state: Unknown
Current operational state: Link down
Message interval: 7
Time out interval: 5
No neighbor cache information stored
```

What is the operation state of this interface?

_____

Note: Although not configured in this lab, loop guard can be configured as an alternative or in addition to UDLD. The functionality overlaps, partly in the sense that both protect against STP failures caused by unidirectional links. Based on the various design considerations, you can choose UDLD or the loop guard feature or both. In regards to STP, the most noticeable difference between the two features is the absence of protection in UDLD against STP failures caused by problems in software. As a result, the designated switch does not send BPDUs. However, this type of failure is (by an order of magnitude) more rare than failures caused by unidirectional links. In return, UDLD might be more flexible in the case of unidirectional links on EtherChannel. In this case, UDLD disables only failed links, and the channel should remain functional with the links that remain. In such a failure, loop guard puts it into loop-inconsistent state to block the whole channel.

Note: Save your final device configurations for use with the next lab.

Lab 6-3, Securing VLANs with Private VLANs, RACLs, and VACLs

Topology

HSRP Gateway Addresses		
VLAN		**IP Address**
1	Management	172.16.1.1/24
100	Staff	172.16.100.1/24
150	Server-farm	172.16.150.1/24
200	Student	172.16.200.1/24

PVLAN	Purpose
150	Primary
151	Isolated
152	Community

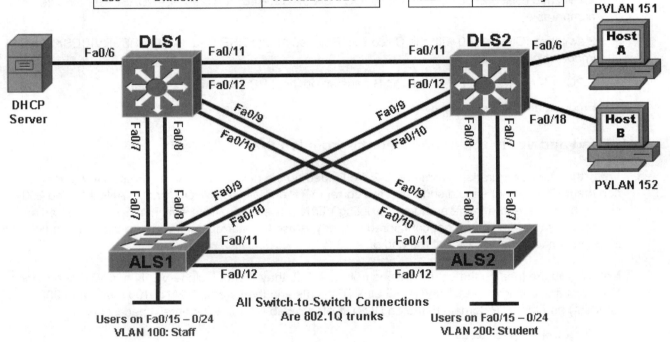

Objectives

- Secure the server farm using private VLANs.
- Secure the staff VLAN from the student VLAN.
- Secure the staff VLAN when temporary staff personnel are used.

Background

In this lab, you will configure the network to protect the VLANs using router ACLs, VLAN ACLs, and private VLANs. First, you will secure the new server farm by using private VLANs so that broadcasts on one server VLAN are not heard by the other server VLAN. Service providers use private VLANs to separate different customers' traffic while utilizing the same parent VLAN for all server traffic. The private VLANs provide traffic isolation between devices, even though they might exist on the same VLAN.

You will then secure the staff VLAN from the student VLAN by using a RACL, which prevents traffic from the student VLAN from reaching the staff VLAN. This allows the student traffic to utilize the network and Internet services while keeping the students from accessing any of the staff resources.

Lastly, you will configure a VACL that allows a host on the staff network to be set up to use the VLAN for access but keeps the host isolated from the rest of the staff machines. This machine is used by temporary staff employees.

Note: This lab uses Cisco WS-C2960-24TT-L switches with the Cisco IOS image c2960-lanbasek9-mz.122-46.SE.bin, and Catalyst 3560-24PS switches with the Cisco IOS image c3560-advipservicesk9-mz.122-46.SE.bin. You can use other switches (such as 2950 or 3550) and Cisco IOS Software versions if they have comparable capabilities and features. Depending on the switch model and Cisco IOS Software version, the commands available and output produced might vary from what is shown in this lab.

Required Resources

- 2 switches (Cisco 2960 with the Cisco IOS Release 12.2(46)SE C2960-LANBASEK9-M image or comparable)
- 2 switches (Cisco 3560 with the Cisco IOS Release 12.2(46)SE C3560- ADVIPSERVICESK9-mz image or comparable)
- 2 PCs (Windows OS) PC-A and PC-B (plus an optional PC for testing, if available)
- Ethernet and console cables

Step 1: Load and verify the configurations from lab 6-2.

a. Verify that the configurations from Lab 6-2 are loaded on the devices by issuing the **show vtp status** command. The output should show that the current VTP domain is SWPOD, and VLANs 100 and 200 should be represented in the number of existing VLANs. The output from switch ALS1 is shown as an example. If the switches are not configured properly, erase the startup config, delete the vlan.dat file, and load the configurations saved at the end of lab 6-2.

    Note: If you are loading the configurations from Lab 6-2, they do not include VLAN and VTP commands. You must first configure ALS1 and ALS2 as VTP clients and then create VLANs 100 (staff) and 200 (student) and the VTP domain name on DLS1. Refer to Lab 6-1 for assistance if necessary.

    ```
    ALS1# show vtp status
    VTP Version                       : running VTP2
    Configuration Revision        : 4
    Maximum VLANs supported locally : 255
    Number of existing VLANs          : 7
    VTP Operating Mode                : Client
    VTP Domain Name                   : SWPOD
    VTP Pruning Mode              : Disabled
    VTP V2 Mode                   : Enabled
    VTP Traps Generation          : Disabled
    MD5 digest                    : 0x18 0x59 0xE2 0xE0 0x28 0xF3 0xE7 0xD1
    Configuration last modified by 172.16.1.3 at 3-12-93 19:46:16
    ```

    Will VLAN information be stored in NVRAM when this device is rebooted? Explain.

    _____

b. Issue the **show vlan** command on DLS1. The student and staff VLANs should be listed in the output of this command.

```
DLS1# show vlan brief

VLAN Name                             Status    Ports
---- -------------------------------- --------- ------------------------------
1    default                          active    Fa0/1, Fa0/2, Fa0/3, Fa0/4
                                                Fa0/5, Fa0/6, Fa0/13, Fa0/14
                                                Fa0/15, Fa0/16, Fa0/17, Fa0/18
                                                Fa0/19, Fa0/20, Fa0/21, Fa0/22
                                                Fa0/23, Fa0/24
                                                Gi0/1, Gi0/2
100  staff                            active
200  student                          active
1002 fddi-default                     act/unsup
1003 token-ring-default               act/unsup
1004 fddinet-default                  act/unsup
1005 trnet-default                    act/unsup
```

How many of these VLANs are present by default?

_____

c. Issue the **show interfaces trunk** command on each switch. If trunking was configured properly in Labs 6-1 and 6-2, Fast Ethernet 0/7–0/12 should be in trunking mode on all switches.

```
DLS1# show interfaces trunk

Port       Mode        Encapsulation  Status       Native vlan
Fa0/7      on          802.1q         trunking     1
Fa0/8      on          802.1q         trunking     1
Fa0/9      on          802.1q         trunking     1
Fa0/10     on          802.1q         trunking     1
Fa0/11     on          802.1q         trunking     1
Fa0/12     on          802.1q         trunking     1

Port       Vlans allowed on trunk
Fa0/7      1-4094
Fa0/8      1-4094
Fa0/9      1-4094
Fa0/10     1-4094
Fa0/11     1-4094
Fa0/12     1-4094

Port       Vlans allowed and active in management domain
Fa0/7      1,100,200
Fa0/8      1,100,200
Fa0/9      1,100,200
Fa0/10     1,100,200
Fa0/11     1,100,200

Port       Vlans allowed and active in management domain
Fa0/12     1,100,200
```

```
Port            Vlans in spanning tree forwarding state and not pruned
Fa0/7           1,100,200
Fa0/8           1,100,200
Fa0/9           1,100,200
Fa0/10          1,100,200
Fa0/11          1,100,200
Fa0/12          1,100,200
```

What is the native VLAN for these trunk ports?

_____

Note: You can change the native VLAN to something other than VLAN 1 on trunk ports using the **switchport trunk native vlan** *vlan-id* command in interface configuration mode. Changing the native VLAN for trunk ports to an unused VLAN can help prevent VLAN hopping attacks. The unused VLAN (for example, VLAN 999) must exist on each switch and be specified on the trunked switch ports.

d. Issue the **show standby brief** command on DLS2.

DLS2# **show standby brief**

```
Interface    Grp Prio P State    Active         Standby        Virtual IP
Vl1          1   100  P Standby  172.16.1.3     local          172.16.1.1
Vl100        1   100  P Standby  172.16.100.3   local          172.16.100.1
Vl200        1   150  P Active   local          172.16.200.3   172.16.200.1
```

For which VLANs is DLS2 the active router?

_____

What is the priority of the current root bridge for VLAN 200?

_____

Step 2: Configure private VLANs.

Within the server farm VLAN, all servers should be allowed access to the router or gateway but not be able to listen to each other's broadcast traffic. Private VLANs solve this problem. When you use a private VLAN, the primary VLAN (normal VLAN) can be logically associated with unidirectional, or secondary, VLANs. Servers or hosts in the secondary VLANs can communicate with the primary VLAN but not with another secondary VLAN. You can define the secondary VLANs as either isolated or community.

Stations attached to a port in a secondary VLAN can communicate with trunk ports and promiscuous ports associated with the appropriate primary VLAN. A host on an isolated secondary VLAN can communicate with the primary VLAN (for example, the default gateway SVI), but not hosts in any other secondary VLAN. In addition, the host associated with the isolated port cannot communicate with any other device on the same isolated secondary VLAN. It is essentially isolated from everything except the primary VLAN.

Hosts on ports in a community VLAN cannot communicate with hosts in other secondary VLANs. However, hosts on ports in this type of private VLAN can communicate with hosts on other ports within the community. This lets you have workgroups within an organization while keeping them isolated from each other.

a. The first step is to configure the switches for the primary VLAN. Based on the topology diagram, VLAN 150 will be used for the new server farm. On VTP server DLS1, add VLAN 150, name the VLAN **server-farm** and exit vlan config mode.

```
DLS1(config)# vlan 150
DLS1(config-vlan)# name server-farm
DLS1(config-vlan)# exit
```

b. Add HSRP information for the new VLAN on DLS1 and DLS2. Make DLS2 the primary router, and make DLS1 the standby router.

```
DLS1(config)# interface vlan 150
DLS1(config-if)# ip address 172.16.150.3 255.255.255.0
DLS1(config-if)# standby 1 ip 172.16.150.1
DLS1(config-if)# standby 1 priority 100
DLS1(config-if)# standby 1 preempt

DLS2(config)# interface vlan 150
DLS2(config-if)# ip add 172.16.150.4 255.255.255.0
DLS2(config-if)# standby 1 ip 172.16.150.1
DLS2(config-if)# standby 1 priority 150
DLS2(config-if)# standby 1 preempt
```

c. Verify the HSRP configuration for VLAN 150 using the **show standby vlan 150 brief** command on DLS2.

```
DLS2# show standby vlan 150 brief

                     P indicates configured to preempt.
                     |
Interface   Grp Prio P State    Active       Standby        Virtual IP
Vl150        1   150 P Active   local        172.16.150.3   172.16.150.1
```

The command output shows that DLS2 is the active router for VLAN 150.

d. Set up the primary and secondary private VLAN (PVLAN) information on DLS1 and DLS2. Configure both switches in transparent mode for VTP using the **vtp mode transparent** global configuration command.

Note: To define PVLANs on DLS1 and DLS2, it is necessary for the switch VTP mode to be set to transparent.

```
DLS1(config)# vtp mode transparent
Setting device to VTP TRANSPARENT mode.

DLS2(config)# vtp mode transparent
Setting device to VTP TRANSPARENT mode.
```

e. Configure DLS1 and DLS2 to contain the new PVLANs. Secondary PVLAN 151 is an isolated VLAN used for Fast Ethernet port 0/6, while secondary PVLAN 152 is used as a community PVLAN for Fast Ethernet ports 0/18–0/20. Configure these new PVLANs in global configuration mode. You also need to associate these secondary VLANs with primary VLAN 150.

```
DLS1(config)# vlan 151
DLS1(config-vlan)# private-vlan isolated
```

```
DLS1(config-vlan)# exit
DLS1(config)# vlan 152
DLS1(config-vlan)# private-vlan community
DLS1(config-vlan)# exit
DLS1(config)# vlan 150
DLS1(config-vlan)# private-vlan primary
DLS1(config-vlan)# private-vlan association 151,152

DLS2(config)# vlan 151
DLS2(config-vlan)# private-vlan isolated
DLS2(config-vlan)# exit
DLS2(config)# vlan 152
DLS2(config-vlan)# private-vlan community
DLS2(config-vlan)# exit
DLS2(config)# vlan 150
DLS2(config-vlan)# private-vlan primary
DLS2(config-vlan)# private-vlan association 151,152
```

f.   The **private-vlan mapping** interface configuration command permits PVLAN traffic to be switched through Layer 3. Configure this command for interface VLAN 150 on DLS1 and DLS2.

```
DLS1(config)# interface vlan 150
DLS1(config-if)# private-vlan mapping 151-152
DLS1(config-if)# end

DLS2(config)# interface vlan 150
DLS2(config-if)# private-vlan mapping 151-152
DLS2(config-if)# end
```

g.   Verify the creation of the secondary PVLANs and their association with the primary VLAN using the **show vlan private-vlan** command. Note that no ports are currently associated with these VLANs. This is expected behavior.

```
DLS2# show vlan private-vlan

Primary Secondary Type              Ports
------- --------- ----------------- -----------------------------------------
150     151       isolated
150     152       community
```

Will hosts assigned to ports on private VLAN 151 be able to communicate directly with each other?

h.   On DLS2, configure the Fast Ethernet ports that are associated with the server farm private VLANs. Fast Ethernet port 0/6 is used for the secondary isolated PVLAN 151, and ports 0/18–0/20 are used for the secondary community VLAN 152. The **switchport mode private-vlan host** command sets the mode on the interface and the switchport private-vlan host-association *primary-vlan-id secondary-vlan-id* command assigns the appropriate VLANs to the interface. The following commands configure the PVLANs on DLS2.

```
DLS2(config)# interface fastethernet 0/6
DLS2(config-if)# switchport mode private-vlan host
```

```
DLS2(config-if)# switchport private-vlan host-association 150 151
DLS2(config-if)# exit
DLS2(config)# interface range fa0/18 - 20
DLS2(config-if-range)# switchport mode private-vlan host
DLS2(config-if-range)# switchport private-vlan host-association 150 152
```

As servers are added to Fast Ethernet 0/18–20, will these servers be allowed to hear broadcasts from each other? Explain.

_____

_____

i. Use the **show vlan private-vlan** command and note that the ports configured are currently associated with these VLANs.

```
DLS2# show vlan private-vlan

Primary Secondary Type              Ports
------- --------- ----------------- ------------------------------------------
150     151       isolated          Fa0/6
150     152       community         Fa0/18, Fa0/19, Fa0/20
```

j. Configure host PC-A on DLS2 port Fa0/6 with an IP address in VLAN 150 (for example: 172.16.150.6/24). Use the VLAN 150 HSRP address (172.16.150.1) as the default gateway. This PC represents a server in isolated PVLAN 151.

k. (optional) If you have two additional PCs, attach one to DLS2 port Fa0/18 and the other to port Fa0/19 in the community PVLAN 152. Configure each host with an IP address in VLAN 150 (for example: 172.16.150.18/24 and 172.16.150.19/24). Use the VLAN 150 HSRP address (172.16.150.1) as the default gateway.

l. From PC-A in isolated PVLAN 151 on DLS2 ping the primary VLAN 150 default gateway HSRP virtual IP address 172.16.150.1 and other IP addresses in the network, including PC-B if connected to DLS2 port Fa0/18 in PVLAN 152. Which pings should succeed and which should fail?

_____

_____

_____

_____

_____

Step 3: Configure RACLs between VLANs.

Configure router access control lists (RACLs) to separate the student and staff VLANs. The staff VLAN (100) can access the student VLAN (200), but the student VLAN does not have access to the staff VLAN for security purposes.

a. To deny the student subnet, use an extended IP access list on DLS1 and DLS2, and assign the access list to the appropriate VLAN interfaces using the **ip access-group** *acl-num* {**in** | **out**} command.

```
DLS1(config)# access-list 100 permit tcp 172.16.200.0 0.0.0.255 172.16.100.0
0.0.0.255 established
DLS1(config)# access-list 100 permit icmp 172.16.200.0 0.0.0.255 172.16.100.0
0.0.0.255 echo-reply
DLS1(config)# access-list 100 deny ip 172.16.200.0 0.0.0.255 172.16.100.0
0.0.0.255
DLS1(config)# access-list 100 permit ip any any
DLS1(config)# interface vlan 100
DLS1(config-if)# ip access-group 100 in
DLS1(config)# interface vlan 200
DLS1(config-if)# ip access-group 100 in

DLS2(config)# access-list 100 permit tcp 172.16.200.0 0.0.0.255 172.16.100.0
0.0.0.255 established
DLS2(config)# access-list 100 permit icmp 172.16.200.0 0.0.0.255 172.16.100.0
0.0.0.255 echo-reply
DLS(config)# access-list 100 deny ip 172.16.200.0 0.0.0.255 172.16.100.0
0.0.0.255
DLS2(config)# access-list 100 permit ip any any
DLS2(config)# interface vlan 100
DLS2(config-if)# ip access-group 100 in
DLS2(config)# interface vlan 200
DLS2(config-if)# ip access-group 100 in
```

b. Check the configuration using the **show ip access-list** and **show ip interface vlan** *vlan-id* commands.

```
DLS1# show access-lists
Extended IP access list 100
    10 permit tcp 172.16.200.0 0.0.0.255 172.16.100.0 0.0.0.255 established
    20 permit icmp 172.16.200.0 0.0.0.255 172.16.100.0 0.0.0.255 echo-reply
    30 deny ip 172.16.200.0 0.0.0.255 172.16.100.0 0.0.0.255
    40 permit ip any any

DLS1# show ip interface vlan 100
Vlan100 is up, line protocol is up
  Internet address is 172.16.100.3/24
  Broadcast address is 255.255.255.255
  Address determined by non-volatile memory
  MTU is 1500 bytes
  Helper address is not set
  Directed broadcast forwarding is disabled
  Multicast reserved groups joined: 224.0.0.2
  Outgoing access list is not set
  Inbound  access list is 100
<output omitted>
```

c. After the access list has been applied verify the configuration in one of the following ways. Option 1 using real hosts is preferred.

Option 1: Connect host PC-A to ALS1 port Fa0/15 in staff VLAN 100 and assign it IP address 172.16.100.15/24 with default gateway 172.16.100.1. Connect host PC-B to ALS2 port Fa0/15 in student VLAN 200 and assign it IP address 172.16.200.15/24 with default gateway 172.16.200.1. Ping the staff host from the student host. This ping should fail. Then ping the student host from the staff host. This ping should succeed.

Option 2: On ALS1 set up a simulated host in VLAN 100 and one in VLAN 200 by creating a VLAN 100 and 200 interface on the switch. Give the VLAN 100 interface an IP address in VLAN 100. Give the VLAN 200 interface an IP address in VLAN 200. The following is a sample configuration on ALS1.

```
ALS1(config)# int vlan 100
ALS1(config-if)# ip address 172.16.100.100 255.255.255.0

ALS1(config)# int vlan 200
ALS1(config-if)# ip address 172.16.200.200 255.255.255.0
```

d. Ping the interface of the gateway for the staff VLAN (172.16.100.1) with a source of staff VLAN 100 (172.16.100.100) and then ping with a source of student VLAN 200. The pings from the student VLAN should fail.

```
ALS1# ping 172.16.100.1 source vl100

Type escape sequence to abort.
Sending 5, 100-byte ICMP Echos to 172.16.100.1, timeout is 2 seconds:
Packet sent with a source address of 172.16.100.100
!!!!!
Success rate is 100 percent (5/5), round-trip min/avg/max = 1/205/1007 ms

ALS1# ping 172.16.100.1 source vl200

Type escape sequence to abort.
Sending 5, 100-byte ICMP Echos to 172.16.100.1, timeout is 2 seconds:
Packet sent with a source address of 172.16.200.200
.U.U.
Success rate is 0 percent (0/5)
```

What does a U signify in the output of the ping command?

_____

_____

_____

_____

Step 4: Configure VACLs.

Configure the network so that the temporary staff host cannot access the rest of the staff VLAN, yet still be able to use the default gateway of the staff subnet to connect to the rest of the network and the ISP. You can accomplish this task by using a VLAN ACL (VACL).

Because the temporary staff PC is located on DLS1 Fast Ethernet 0/3, the VACL must be placed on DLS1.

a. Configure an access list on DLS1 called temp-host using the **ip access-list extended** *name* command. This list defines the traffic between the host and the rest of the network. Then define the traffic using the **permit ip host** *ip-address subnet wildcard-mask* command.

```
DLS1(config)# ip access-list extended temp-host
DLS1(config-ext-nacl)# permit ip host 172.16.100.150 172.16.100.0 0.0.0.255
```

b. The VACL is defined using a VLAN access map. Access maps are evaluated in a numbered sequence. To set up an access map, use the **vlan access-map** *map-name seq#* command. The following configuration defines an access map named block-temp, which uses the **match** statement to match the traffic defined in the access list and denies that traffic. You also need to add a line to the access map that allows all other traffic. If this line is not added, an implicit deny catches all other traffic and deniesDLS1(config)# **vlan access-map block-temp 10**

```
DLS1(config-access-map)# match ip address temp-host
DLS1(config-access-map)# action drop
DLS1(config-access-map)# vlan access-map block-temp 20
DLS1(config-access-map)# action forward
DLS1(config-access-map)# exit
```

c. Define which VLANs the access map should be applied to using the **vlan filter** *map-name* **vlan-list** *vlan-ID* command.

```
DLS1(config)# vlan filter block-temp vlan-list 100
```

d. Verify the VACL configuration using the **show vlan access-map** command on DLS1.

```
DLS1# show vlan access-map
Vlan access-map "block-temp"  10
  Match clauses:
    ip  address: temp-host
  Action:
    drop
Vlan access-map "block-temp"  20
  Match clauses:
  Action:
    forward
```

e. (Optional) If possible, connect a PC to the Fast Ethernet 0/3 port of DLS1 and assign the host an IP address of 172.16.100.150/24. Configure the Fast Ethernet 0/3 port as an access port in VLAN 100. Try to ping to another staff host. The ping should not be successful.

Chapter 7 Preparing the Campus Infrastructure for Advanced Services

Lab 7-1, Configuring Switches for IP Telephony Support

Topology

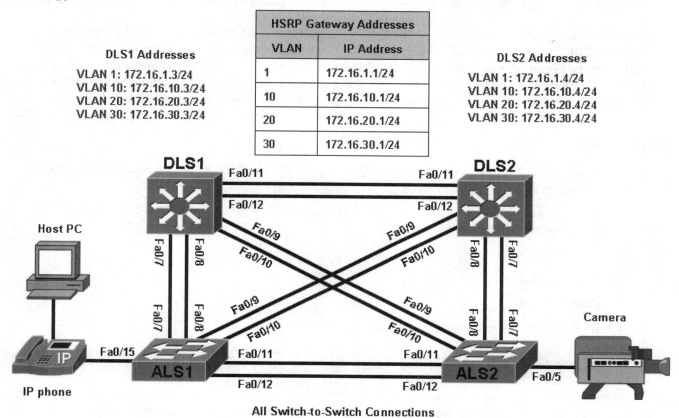

Objectives

- Configure auto QoS to support IP phones.
- Configure CoS override for data frames.
- Configure the distribution layer to trust access layer QoS measures.
- Manually configure CoS for devices that cannot specify CoS (camera).
- Configure HSRP for voice and data VLANs to ensure redundancy.
- Configure 802.1Q trunks and EtherChannels for Layer 2 redundancy and load balancing.

Background

IP phones have been deployed throughout the network. Each phone is connected to an access port on a 2960 Cisco switch. Each user PC is connected to the network using the IP phone internal switch so that the phones can be deployed without additional wiring.

Note: The access layer switches depicted in the topology are assumed to support PoE for the IP phones. However, the switches used in this lab do not support PoE. This will not affect the commands used in this lab.

In this lab, you configure the quality of service (QoS) on the access and distribution layer switches so that they trust the class of service (CoS) mapping provided by the IP phone through Cisco Discovery Protocol (CDP). To ensure redundancy for the phones and user end stations, you will use Hot Standby Router Protocol (HSRP) on the distribution layer switches.

A camera for video is also deployed on the network, which requires that its access port on the 2960 be manually configured. It is not necessary to have an IP phone or camera to successfully complete the lab. The focus is on the configuration of access and distribution layer switches to support QoS for these devices.

Note: This lab uses Cisco WS-C2960-24TT-L switches with the Cisco IOS image c2960-lanbasek9-mz.122-46.SE.bin, and Catalyst 3560-24PS with the Cisco IOS image c3560-advipservicesk9-mz.122-46.SE.bin. You can use other switches (such as a 2950 or 3550) and Cisco IOS Software versions if they have comparable capabilities and features. Depending on the switch model and Cisco IOS Software version, the commands available and output produced might vary from what is shown in this lab.

Required Resources

- 2 switches (Cisco 2960 with the Cisco IOS Release 12.2(46)SE C2960-LANBASEK9-M image or comparable)
- 2 switches (Cisco 3560 with the Cisco IOS Release 12.2(46)SE C3560-ADVIPSERVICESK9-mz image or comparable)
- Host PC (optional)
- IP phone (optional)
- Camera (optional)
- Ethernet and console cables

Step 1: Prepare the switches for the lab.

Erase the startup configuration, delete the vlan.dat file, and reload the switches. Refer to Lab 1-1, "Clearing a Switch" and Lab 1-2, "Clearing a Switch Connected to a Larger Network" to prepare the switches for this lab. Cable the equipment as shown.

Step 2: Configure basic switch parameters.

Configure the management IP addresses in VLAN 1, and the hostname, password, and Telnet access on all four switches. Also configure a default gateway on the access layer switches. The distribution layer switches act as Layer 3 devices and do not need default gateways.

```
Switch(config)# hostname ALS1
ALS1(config)# enable secret class
ALS1(config)# line vty 0 15
ALS1(config-line)# password cisco
ALS1(config-line)# login
ALS1(config-line)# exit
ALS1(config)# interface vlan 1
ALS1(config-if)# ip address 172.16.1.101 255.255.255.0
ALS1(config-if)# no shutdown
ALS1(config-if)# exit
```

```
ALS1(config)# ip default-gateway 172.16.1.1

Switch(config)# hostname ALS2
ALS2(config)# enable secret class
ALS2(config)# line vty 0 15
ALS2(config-line)# password cisco
ALS2(config-line)# login
ALS2(config-line)# exit
ALS2(config)# interface vlan 1
ALS2(config-if)# ip address 172.16.1.102 255.255.255.0
ALS2(config-if)# no shutdown
ALS2(config-if)# exit
ALS2(config)# ip default-gateway 172.16.1.1

Switch(config)# hostname DLS1
DLS1(config)# enable secret class
DLS1(config)# line vty 0 15
DLS1(config-line)# password cisco
DLS1(config-line)# login
DLS1(config-line)# exit
DLS1(config)# interface vlan 1
DLS1(config-if)# ip address 172.16.1.3 255.255.255.0
DLS1(config-if)# no shutdown

Switch(config)# hostname DLS2
DLS2(config)# enable secret class
DLS2(config)# line vty 0 15
DLS2(config-line)# password cisco
DLS2(config-line)# login
DLS2(config-line)# exit
DLS2(config)# interface vlan 1
DLS2(config-if)# ip address 172.16.1.4 255.255.255.0
DLS2(config-if)# no shutdown
```

Step 3: Configure the trunks and EtherChannels.

Configure the trunks according to the diagram, and configure EtherChannels between the switches. Using EtherChannel for the trunks provides Layer 2 load balancing over redundant trunks.

a. The following is a sample configuration for the trunks and EtherChannel from DLS1 to the other three switches. Notice that the 3560 switch needs the **switchport trunk encapsulation {dot1q | isl}** command, because this switch also supports ISL encapsulation.

```
DLS1(config)# interface range fastEthernet 0/7 - 8
DLS1(config-if-range)# switchport trunk encapsulation dot1q
DLS1(config-if-range)# switchport mode trunk
DLS1(config-if-range)# channel-group 1 mode active

Creating a port-channel interface Port-channel 1

DLS1(config-if-range)# interface range fastEthernet 0/9 - 10
DLS1(config-if-range)# switchport trunk encapsulation dot1q
DLS1(config-if-range)# switchport mode trunk
DLS1(config-if-range)# channel-group 2 mode active
```

Creating a port-channel interface Port-channel 2

```
DLS1(config-if-range)# interface range fastEthernet 0/11 - 12
DLS1(config-if-range)# switchport trunk encapsulation dot1q
DLS1(config-if-range)# switchport mode trunk
DLS1(config-if-range)# channel-group 3 mode active
```

Creating a port-channel interface Port-channel 3

b. The following is a sample configuration for the trunks and EtherChannels from DLS2 to the other three switches.

```
DLS2(config)# interface range fastEthernet 0/7 - 8
DLS2(config-if-range)# switchport trunk encapsulation dot1q
DLS2(config-if-range)# switchport mode trunk
DLS2(config-if-range)# channel-group 1 mode active
```

Creating a port-channel interface Port-channel 1

```
DLS2(config-if-range)# interface range fastEthernet 0/9 - 10
DLS2(config-if-range)# switchport trunk encapsulation dot1q
DLS2(config-if-range)# switchport mode trunk
DLS2(config-if-range)# channel-group 2 mode active
```

Creating a port-channel interface Port-channel 2

```
DLS2(config-if-range)# interface range fastEthernet 0/11 - 12
DLS2(config-if-range)# switchport trunk encapsulation dot1q
DLS2(config-if-range)# switchport mode trunk
DLS2(config-if-range)# channel-group 3 mode active
```

Creating a port-channel interface Port-channel 3

c. The following is a sample configuration for the trunks and EtherChannel from ALS1 and ALS2 to the other switches.

```
ALS1(config)# interface range fastEthernet 0/7 - 8
ALS1(config-if-range)# switchport mode trunk
ALS1(config-if-range)# channel-group 1 mode active
```

Creating a port-channel interface Port-channel 1

```
ALS1(config-if-range)# interface range fastEthernet 0/9 - 10
ALS1(config-if-range)# switchport mode trunk
ALS1(config-if-range)# channel-group 2 mode active
```

Creating a port-channel interface Port-channel 2

```
ALS1(config-if-range)# interface range fastEthernet 0/11 - 12
ALS1(config-if-range)# switchport mode trunk
ALS1(config-if-range)# channel-group 3 mode active
```

Creating a port-channel interface Port-channel 3

```
ALS2(config)# interface range fastEthernet 0/7 - 8
ALS2(config-if-range)# switchport mode trunk
ALS2(config-if-range)# channel-group 1 mode active

Creating a port-channel interface Port-channel 1

ALS2(config-if-range)# interface range fastEthernet 0/9 - 10
ALS2(config-if-range)# switchport mode trunk
ALS2(config-if-range)# channel-group 2 mode active

Creating a port-channel interface Port-channel 2

ALS2(config-if-range)# interface range fastEthernet 0/11 - 12
ALS2(config-if-range)# switchport mode trunk
ALS2(config-if-range)# channel-group 3 mode active

Creating a port-channel interface Port-channel 3
```

d. Use the **show interfaces trunk** command on all switches to verify the trunks.

Which VLANs are currently allowed on the newly created trunks?

_____

e. Use the **show etherchannel summary** command on each switch to verify the EtherChannels.

Which EtherChannel negotiation protocol is in use here?

_____

Step 4: Configure VTP on ALS1 and ALS2.

a. Change the VTP mode of ALS1 and ALS2 to client.

```
ALS1(config)# vtp mode client
Setting device to VTP CLIENT mode.

ALS2(config)# vtp mode client
```

b. Verify the VTP changes with the **show vtp status** command.

How many VLANs can be supported locally on the 2960 switch?

_____

Step 5: Configure VTP and the VLANs on DLS1.

a. Create the VTP domain on DLS1, and create VLANs 10, 20, and 30 for the computer data, voice, and video VLANs in the domain.

```
DLS1(config)# vtp domain SWPOD
DLS1(config)# vtp version 2
DLS1(config)# vlan 10
DLS1(config-vlan)# name CP-DATA
DLS1(config-vlan)# exit
DLS1(config)# vlan 20
DLS1(config-vlan)# name VOICE
DLS1(config-vlan)# exit
DLS1(config)# vlan 30
DLS1(config-vlan)# name VIDEO
```

b. Verify the VTP information throughout the domain using the **show vlan** and **show vtp status** commands.

How many existing VLANs are in the VTP domain?

_____

Step 6: Configure IP routing, VLAN SVIs, and HSRP on DLS1 and DLS2.

a. Configure HSRP between the VLANs to provide redundancy in the network. To achieve some load balancing, use the **standby** [*group*] **priority** command. Use the **ip routing** command on DLS1 and DLS2 to activate routing capabilities on the switch.

Each route processor will have its own IP address on each switched virtual interface (SVI) and also be assigned an HSRP virtual IP address for each VLAN. Devices connected to VLANs 10, 20, and 30 use the gateway IP address for the VLANs.

The **standby** command is also used to configure the IP address of the virtual gateway and configure the router for preemption. The **preempt** option allows for the active router with the higher priority to take over again after a network failure has been resolved.

Notice in the following configurations that the priority for VLANs 1 and 10 has been configured for 150 on DLS1, making DLS1 the active router for those VLANs. VLANs 20 and 30 have been configured for a priority of 100 on DLS1, making DLS1 the standby router for these VLANs. Reverse priorities have been configured on the VLANs on DLS2. DLS2 is the active router for VLANs 20 and 30, and the standby router for VLANs 1 and 10.

HSRP Configuration for DLS1

```
DLS1(config)# ip routing
DLS1(config)# interface vlan 1
DLS1(config-if)# standby 1 ip 172.16.1.1
DLS1(config-if)# standby 1 preempt
DLS1(config-if)# standby 1 priority 150
DLS1(config-if)# exit
DLS1(config)# interface vlan 10
DLS1(config-if)# ip address 172.16.10.3 255.255.255.0
DLS1(config-if)# standby 1 ip 172.16.10.1
DLS1(config-if)# standby 1 preempt
DLS1(config-if)# standby 1 priority 150
DLS1(config-if)# exit
```

```
DLS1(config)# interface vlan 20
DLS1(config-if)# ip address 172.16.20.3 255.255.255.0
DLS1(config-if)# standby 1 ip 172.16.20.1
DLS1(config-if)# standby 1 preempt
DLS1(config-if)# standby 1 priority 100
DLS1(config-if)# exit
DLS1(config)# interface vlan 30
DLS1(config-if)# ip address 172.16.30.3 255.255.255.0
DLS1(config-if)# standby 1 ip 172.16.30.1
DLS1(config-if)# standby 1 preempt
DLS1(config-if)# standby 1 priority 100
```

HSRP Configuration for DLS2

```
DLS2(config)# ip routing
DLS2(config)# interface vlan 1
DLS2(config-if)# standby 1 ip 172.16.1.1
DLS2(config-if)# standby 1 preempt
DLS2(config-if)# standby 1 priority 100
DLS2(config-if)# exit
DLS2(config)# interface vlan 10
DLS2(config-if)# ip address 172.16.10.4 255.255.255.0
DLS2(config-if)# standby 1 ip 172.16.10.1
DLS2(config-if)# standby 1 preempt
DLS2(config-if)# standby 1 priority 100
DLS2(config-if)# exit
DLS2(config)# interface vlan 20
DLS2(config-if)# ip address 172.16.20.4 255.255.255.0
DLS2(config-if)# standby 1 ip 172.16.20.1
DLS2(config-if)# standby 1 preempt
DLS2(config-if)# standby 1 priority 150
DLS2(config-if)# exit
DLS2(config)# interface vlan 30
DLS2(config-if)# ip address 172.16.30.4 255.255.255.0
DLS2(config-if)# standby 1 ip 172.16.30.1
DLS2(config-if)# standby 1 preempt
DLS2(config-if)# standby 1 priority 150
```

b.   Enter the **show standby brief** command on both DLS1 and DLS2.

Which router is the active router for VLANs 1 and 10? Which is the active router for VLAN 20?

_____

_____

_____

How is the active HSRP router selected?

_____

_____

_____

_____

c. Enter the **show standby** command on both DLS1 and DLS2.

What is the default hello time for each VLAN? What is the default hold time?

_____

d. Verify routing using the **show ip route** command. The following is sample output from DLS1.

```
DLS1# show ip route
Codes: C - connected, S - static, R - RIP, M - mobile, B - BGP
       D - EIGRP, EX - EIGRP external, O - OSPF, IA - OSPF inter area
       N1 - OSPF NSSA external type 1, N2 - OSPF NSSA external type 2
       E1 - OSPF external type 1, E2 - OSPF external type 2, E - EGP
       i - IS-IS, su - IS-IS summary, L1 - IS-IS level-1, L2 - IS-IS level-2
       ia - IS-IS inter area, * - candidate default, U - per-user static route
       o - ODR, P - periodic downloaded static route

Gateway of last resort is not set

     172.16.0.0/24 is subnetted, 4 subnets
C       172.16.20.0 is directly connected, Vlan20
C       172.16.30.0 is directly connected, Vlan30
C       172.16.1.0 is directly connected, Vlan1
C       172.16.10.0 is directly connected, Vlan10
```

Step 7: Configure access ports to trust IP phone CoS.

The access layer switches will be the QoS trust boundaries for the network. Data coming in on the switch ports will either have the CoS trusted or altered based on the information received on the ports.

Configure Fast Ethernet access ports 15 to 24 to trust the CoS for recognized IP phones on the network. The CoS of a Cisco IP phone is 5 by default. Any port that has a device other than a Cisco phone will not trust the CoS that is advertised. This configuration is accomplished by using the Cisco auto QoS features offered on these switches. Using a single command at the interface level, you can implement both trust boundaries and QoS features. Information obtained through CDP is used to determine when an IP phone is attached to the access port.

The following configuration also sets the voice VLAN on the interface with the **switchport voice vlan** _vlan-number_ command.

Configure Fast Ethernet ports 15 through 24 on ALS1 and ALS2 using the **interface range** command.

```
ALS1(config)# interface range fastEthernet 0/15 - 24
ALS1(config-if-range)# switchport mode access
ALS1(config-if-range)# switchport access vlan 10
ALS1(config-if-range)# switchport voice vlan 20
ALS1(config-if-range)# auto qos voip cisco-phone

ALS2(config)# interface range fastEthernet 0/15 - 24
ALS2(config-if-range)# switchport mode access
ALS2(config-if-range)# switchport access vlan 10
ALS2(config-if-range)# switchport voice vlan 20
ALS2(config-if-range)# auto qos voip cisco-phone
```

Note: Configuring auto QoS on an interface automatically adds global **mls qos srr-queue**, **class-map** and **policy-map** commands to the running configuration. A number of interface-specific command are also added, including **spanning-tree portfast**.

Step 8: Verify the access layer auto QoS configuration.

Verify the auto QoS configuration at the access layer using the **show mls qos interface** *interface-type interface-number* and **show run** commands.

```
ALS1# show mls qos interface fastEthernet 0/15
FastEthernet0/15
Attached policy-map for Ingress: AutoQoS-Police-CiscoPhone
trust state: not trusted
trust mode: trust cos
trust enabled flag: dis
COS override: dis
default COS: 0
DSCP Mutation Map: Default DSCP Mutation Map
Trust device: cisco-phone
qos mode: port-based

ALS1# show run interface fastEthernet 0/15
interface FastEthernet0/15
 switchport access vlan 10
 switchport voice vlan 20
 srr-queue bandwidth share 10 10 60 20
 priority-queue out
 mls qos trust device cisco-phone
 mls qos trust cos
 auto qos voip cisco-phone
 spanning-tree portfast
 service-policy input AutoQoS-Police-CiscoPhone
```

What is the default CoS for a PC connected to these interfaces?

_____

_____

Step 9: Configure the distribution layer switches to trust access layer CoS.

Configure the distribution layer switches to trust the CoS information in the Layer 2 frames being sent from the access layer. Because the trust boundary is at the access layer, frames being sent from this layer should be trusted into the distribution layer for optimal QoS.

```
DLS1(config)# mls qos
DLS1(config)# interface range fastEthernet 0/7 - 12
DLS1(config-if-range)# auto qos voip trust

DLS2(config)# mls qos
DLS2(config)# interface range fastEthernet 0/7 - 12
DLS2(config-if-range)# auto qos voip trust
```

Step 10: Verify the distribution layer auto QoS configuration.

a. Verify auto QoS at the distribution layer on DLS1 and DLS2 using the **show auto qos interface** command.

```
DLS1# show auto qos interface
FastEthernet0/7
auto qos voip trust

FastEthernet0/8
auto qos voip trust

FastEthernet0/9
auto qos voip trust

FastEthernet0/10
auto qos voip trust

FastEthernet0/11
auto qos voip trust

FastEthernet0/12
auto qos voip trust
```

b   Use the **show mls qos interface fastEthernet** *interface ID* command on DLS1 to verify QoS on the trunk interfaces.

```
DLS1# show mls qos interface fastEthernet 0/7
FastEthernet0/7
trust state: trust cos
trust mode: trust cos
trust enabled flag: ena
COS override: dis
default COS: 0
DSCP Mutation Map: Default DSCP Mutation Map
Trust device: none
qos mode: port-based
```

Step 11: Manually assign access layer CoS for the camera.

A camera needs to be moved from its current location in the network and connected to FastEthernet0/5 of

ALS2.

Video traffic must have priority treatment within the network, because it has different requirements than data or voice traffic. The priority of the video traffic will be configured to be lower than the priority of the voice traffic.

a. Because the camera is not capable of setting its own CoS, assign a CoS of 3 to ensure that the video traffic is identified by other switches and routers within the network.

```
ALS2(config)# interface fastEthernet 0/5
ALS2(config-if)# switchport mode access
ALS2(config-if)# switchport access vlan 30
ALS2(config-if)# mls qos trust cos
ALS2(config-if)# mls qos cos 3
```

b. Verify the configuration using the **show mls qos interface** command on ALS2.

```
ALS2# show mls qos interface fastEthernet 0/5
FastEthernet0/5
trust state: trust cos
trust mode: trust cos
trust enabled flag: ena
COS override: dis
default COS: 3
DSCP Mutation Map: Default DSCP Mutation Map
Trust device: none
qos mode: port-based
```

Lab 7-2, Configuring a WLAN Controller

Topology

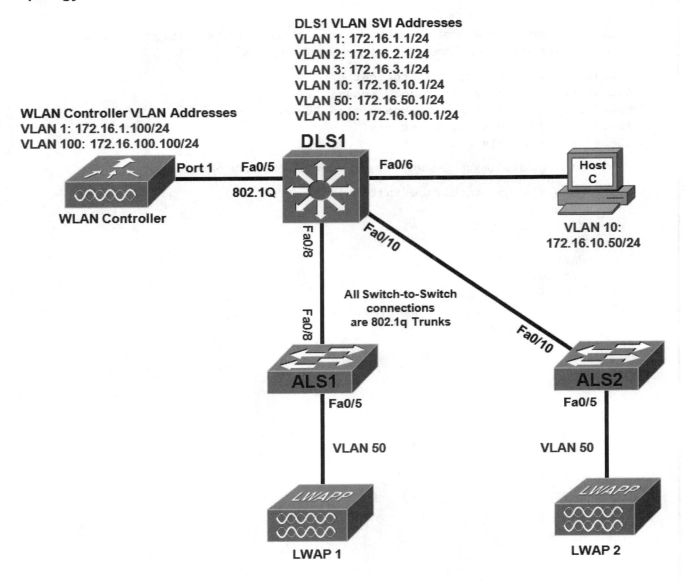

DLS1 VLAN SVI Addresses
VLAN 1: 172.16.1.1/24
VLAN 2: 172.16.2.1/24
VLAN 3: 172.16.3.1/24
VLAN 10: 172.16.10.1/24
VLAN 50: 172.16.50.1/24
VLAN 100: 172.16.100.1/24

WLAN Controller VLAN Addresses
VLAN 1: 172.16.1.100/24
VLAN 100: 172.16.100.100/24

Objectives

- Implement campus network infrastructure to support wireless.
- Configure a WLAN controller (optional).

Background

In this lab, you will configure the network infrastructure (Layer 2 and Layer 3 switches) to prepare for a wireless solution involving a wireless LAN (WLAN) controller and two lightweight wireless access points (LWAPs). The WLAN controller and LWAPs are optional and might not be present in your topology. If that is the case, read through those portions of the lab that deal with their configuration to become familiar with the process and commands.

Note: This lab uses Cisco WS-C2960-24TT-L switches with the Cisco IOS image c2960-lanbasek9-

mz.122-46.SE.bin, and Catalyst 3560-24PS with the Cisco IOS image c3560-advipservicesk9-mz.122-46. SE.bin. You can use other switches (such as a 2950 or 3550) and Cisco IOS Software versions if they have comparable capabilities and features. Depending on the switch model and Cisco IOS Software version, the commands available and output produced might vary from what is shown in this lab.

Required Resources

- 2 switches (Cisco 2960 with the Cisco IOS Release 12.2(46)SE C2960-LANBASEK9-M image or comparable)
- 1 switch (Cisco 3560 with the Cisco IOS Release 12.2(46)SE C3560-advipservicesk9-mz image or comparable)
- 1 WLAN controller (optional, however configuration instructions are provided)
- 2 LWAPs (optional)
- Console and Ethernet cables

Step 1: Prepare the switches for the lab.

a. Erase the startup-config file, delete the vlan.dat file, and reload each switch to clear the previous configurations.

b. Configure the switch hostnames as shown in the topology.

c. (Optional) To reset the WLAN controller, use the **clear controller** command followed by the **reset system** command.

Step 2: Configure VLANs, trunks, and VTP.

VLAN 1 – Management VLAN for the WLC.

VLAN 2 and VLAN 3 – For hosts in the WLANs.

VLAN 10 – The management computer Host C is in this VLAN.

VLAN 50 – The LWAPs are in this VLAN.

VLAN 100 – The AP-manager interface of the WLAN controller is in this VLAN.

a. Configure DLS1 as a VTP server, and ALS1 and ALS2 as clients in the VTP domain CISCO. Configure the switch-to-switch links shown in the diagram as 802.1Q trunks. Add VLANs 2, 3, 10, 50, and 100 to DLS1.

```
DLS1(config)# vtp mode server
DLS1(config)# vtp domain CISCO
DLS1(config)# vtp version 2
DLS1(config)# vlan 2,3,10,50,100
DLS1(config-vlan)# interface fastEthernet 0/8
DLS1(config-if)# switchport trunk encapsulation dot1q
DLS1(config-if)# switchport mode trunk
DLS1(config-if)# interface fastEthernet 0/10
DLS1(config-if)# switchport trunk encapsulation dot1q
DLS1(config-if)# switchport mode trunk
```

```
ALS1(config)# vtp mode client
ALS1(config)# interface fastEthernet 0/8
ALS1(config-if)# switchport mode trunk

ALS2(config)# vtp mode client
ALS2(config)# interface fastEthernet 0/10
ALS2(config-if)# switchport mode trunk
```

b. Verify that VTP traffic has passed between the switches by comparing the non-zero VTP configuration revision using the **show vtp status** command.

```
DLS1# show vtp status
VTP Version                         : running VTP2
Configuration Revision         : 1
Maximum VLANs supported locally : 1005
Number of existing VLANs       : 10
VTP Operating Mode             : Server
VTP Domain Name                : CISCO
VTP Pruning Mode               : Disabled
VTP V2 Mode                    : Enabled
VTP Traps Generation           : Disabled
MD5 digest                     : 0xE3 0x5B 0x2E 0x20 0x27 0xF9 0xF1 0x1B
Configuration last modified by 0.0.0.0 at 3-2-10 00:49:40
Local updater ID is 0.0.0.0 (no valid interface found)


ALS1# show vtp status
VTP Version                         : running VTP2
Configuration Revision         : 1
Maximum VLANs supported locally : 255
Number of existing VLANs       : 10
VTP Operating Mode             : Client
VTP Domain Name                : CISCO
VTP Pruning Mode               : Disabled
VTP V2 Mode                    : Enabled
VTP Traps Generation           : Disabled
MD5 digest                     : 0xE3 0x5B 0x2E 0x20 0x27 0xF9 0xF1 0x1B
Configuration last modified by 0.0.0.0 at 3-2-10 00:49:40


ALS2# show vtp status
VTP Version                         : running VTP2
Configuration Revision         : 1
Maximum VLANs supported locally : 255
Number of existing VLANs       : 10
VTP Operating Mode             : Client
VTP Domain Name                : CISCO
VTP Pruning Mode               : Disabled
VTP V2 Mode                    : Enabled
VTP Traps Generation           : Disabled
MD5 digest                     : 0xE3 0x5B 0x2E 0x20 0x27 0xF9 0xF1 0x1B
Configuration last modified by 0.0.0.0 at 3-2-10 00:49:40
```

Step 3: Configure SVIs.

Configure all the switch virtual interfaces (SVIs) shown in the diagram for DLS1.

```
DLS1(config)# interface vlan 1
DLS1(config-if)# ip address 172.16.1.1 255.255.255.0
DLS1(config-if)# no shutdown
DLS1(config-if)# interface vlan 2
DLS1(config-if)# ip address 172.16.2.1 255.255.255.0
DLS1(config-if)# interface vlan 3
DLS1(config-if)# ip address 172.16.3.1 255.255.255.0
DLS1(config-if)# interface vlan 10
DLS1(config-if)# ip address 172.16.10.1 255.255.255.0
DLS1(config-if)# interface vlan 50
DLS1(config-if)# ip address 172.16.50.1 255.255.255.0
DLS1(config-if)# interface vlan 100
DLS1(config-if)# ip address 172.16.100.1 255.255.255.0
```

Step 4: Configure DHCP.

DHCP gives out dynamic IP addresses on a subnet to network devices or hosts rather than statically setting the addresses. This is useful when dealing with LWAPs, which usually do not have an initial configuration. The WLAN controller that the LWAP associates with defines the configuration. A lightweight access point can dynamically receive an IP address and then communicate over IP with the WLAN controller. In this scenario, you also use DHCP to assign IP addresses to hosts that connect to the WLANs.

a. Configure DLS1 to exclude the first 150 addresses from each subnet from DHCP to avoid conflicts with static IP addresses using the **ip dhcp excluded-address** *low-address* [*high-address*] global configuration command.

```
DLS1(config)# ip dhcp excluded-address 172.16.1.1 172.16.1.150
DLS1(config)# ip dhcp excluded-address 172.16.2.1 172.16.2.150
DLS1(config)# ip dhcp excluded-address 172.16.3.1 172.16.3.150
DLS1(config)# ip dhcp excluded-address 172.16.10.1 172.16.10.150
DLS1(config)# ip dhcp excluded-address 172.16.50.1 172.16.50.150
DLS1(config)# ip dhcp excluded-address 172.16.100.1 172.16.100.150
```

b. To advertise on different subnets, create DHCP pools with the **ip dhcp pool** *name* command. After a pool is configured for a subnet, the Cisco IOS DHCP server processes requests on that subnet, because it is enabled by default. From the DHCP pool prompt, set the network and mask to use with the **network** *address* /*mask* command. Set a default gateway with the **default-router** *address* command.

VLAN 50 also uses the **option** command, which allows you to specify a DHCP option. In this case, option 43 is specified (a vendor-specific option), which gives the LWAPs the IP address of the WLAN controller AP Manager interface. It is specified in a hexadecimal TLV (type, length, value) format. This configuration uses **f104ac106464**, which is made up of the following:

*   f1 is the hardcoded type of option.

*   04 represents the length of the value (an IP address is 4 octets).

*   ac106464 is the hexadecimal representation of 172.16.100.100, which is going to be the AP manager address of the WLAN controller.

DHCP option 60 specifies the identifier that access points will use in DHCP.

Note: This lab uses Cisco Aironet 1240 series access points. If you are using a different access point series, see www.cisco.com/en/US/docs/wireless/access_point/1500/installation/guide/1500_axg.html.

```
DLS1(config)# ip dhcp pool pool1
DLS1(dhcp-config)# network 172.16.1.0 /24
```

```
DLS1(dhcp-config)# default-router 172.16.1.1

DLS1(dhcp-config)# ip dhcp pool pool2
DLS1(dhcp-config)# network 172.16.2.0 /24
DLS1(dhcp-config)# default-router 172.16.2.1

DLS1(dhcp-config)# ip dhcp pool pool3
DLS1(dhcp-config)# network 172.16.3.0 /24
DLS1(dhcp-config)# default-router 172.16.3.1

DLS1(dhcp-config)# ip dhcp pool pool10
DLS1(dhcp-config)# network 172.16.10.0 /24
DLS1(dhcp-config)# default-router 172.16.10.1

DLS1(dhcp-config)# ip dhcp pool pool50
DLS1(dhcp-config)# network 172.16.50.0 /24
DLS1(dhcp-config)# default-router 172.16.50.1
DLS1(dhcp-config)# option 43 hex f104ac106464
DLS1(dhcp-config)# option 60 ascii "Cisco AP c1240"

DLS1(dhcp-config)# ip dhcp pool pool100
DLS1(dhcp-config)# network 172.16.100.0 /24
DLS1(dhcp-config)# default-router 172.16.100.1
```

Step 5: Configure infrastructure wireless support.

On ALS1 and ALS2, configure the switch port of each access point with the **spanning-tree portfast** command so that the access point receives an IP address from DHCP immediately, thereby avoiding spanning-tree delays. All control and data traffic between the controller and the access points passes over this VLAN to this interface. Configure the ports going to the access points to be in VLAN 50. DLS1 will route the traffic between the VLANs. Configure the interface on DLS1 that connects to the WLAN controller as an 802.1Q trunk.

```
DLS1(config)# interface fastEthernet 0/5
DLS1(config-if)# switchport trunk encapsulation dot1q
DLS1(config-if)# switchport mode trunk

ALS1(config)# interface fastEthernet 0/5
ALS1(config-if)# switchport mode access
ALS1(config-if)# switchport access vlan 50
ALS1(config-if)# spanning-tree portfast

ALS2(config)# interface fastEthernet 0/5
ALS2(config-if)# switchport mode access
ALS2(config-if)# switchport access vlan 50
ALS2(config-if)# spanning-tree portfast
```

Step 6: Configure the switch port for the management host.

a. Host C is attached to DLS1 and is running Microsoft Windows. Configure the switch port to which the host is attached to be in VLAN 10 and enable PortFast.

```
DLS1(config)# interface fastEthernet 0/6
DLS1(config-if)# switchport mode access
DLS1(config-if)# switchport access vlan 10
```

```
DLS1(config-if)# spanning-tree portfast
```

b. Configure the host with an IP address in VLAN 10, which will (optionally) be used to access the HTTP web interface of the WLAN controller. Configure the IP address 172.16.10.50/24 with the default gateway 172.16.10.1.

c. From Host C, ping the DLS1 VLAN 10 interface. You should receive responses. If you do not, troubleshoot, verifying the VLAN of the switch port, and the IP address and subnet mask on each device on VLAN 10.

```
C:\> ping 172.16.10.1

Pinging 172.16.10.1 with 32 bytes of data:

Reply from 172.16.10.1: bytes=32 time=1ms TTL=255
Reply from 172.16.10.1: bytes=32 time<1ms TTL=255
Reply from 172.16.10.1: bytes=32 time<1ms TTL=255
Reply from 172.16.10.1: bytes=32 time<1ms TTL=255

Ping statistics for 172.16.10.1:
    Packets: Sent = 4, Received = 4, Lost = 0 (0% loss),
Approximate round trip times in milli-seconds:
    Minimum = 0ms, Maximum = 1ms, Average = 0ms
```

Step 7: Enable IP routing on DLS1.

a. Enabling IP routing on DLS1 lets DLS1 route between all subnets shown in the diagram. DLS1 can effectively route between all the VLANs configured because it has an SVI in each subnet.

```
DLS1(config)# ip routing
```

b. Each IP subnet is shown in the output of the **show ip route** command issued on DLS1.

```
DLS1# show ip route
Codes: C - connected, S - static, R - RIP, M - mobile, B - BGP
       D - EIGRP, EX - EIGRP external, O - OSPF, IA - OSPF inter area
       N1 - OSPF NSSA external type 1, N2 - OSPF NSSA external type 2
       E1 - OSPF external type 1, E2 - OSPF external type 2
       i - IS-IS, su - IS-IS summary, L1 - IS-IS level-1, L2 - IS-IS level-2
       ia - IS-IS inter area, * - candidate default, U - per-user static route
       o - ODR, P - periodic downloaded static route

Gateway of last resort is not set

     172.16.0.0/24 is subnetted, 6 subnets
C       172.16.50.0 is directly connected, Vlan50
C       172.16.10.0 is directly connected, Vlan10
C       172.16.1.0 is directly connected, Vlan1
C       172.16.2.0 is directly connected, Vlan2
C       172.16.3.0 is directly connected, Vlan3
C       172.16.100.0 is directly connected, Vlan100
```

Step 8: (Optional) Configure initial settings on the WLAN controller.

When you restart the WLAN controller, a configuration wizard prompts you to enter basic configuration attributes. You have entered the wizard interface when you see "Welcome to the Cisco Wizard Configuration

Tool." Pressing Enter at a prompt accepts the default for a configuration option. The default is in square brackets. If there is more than one choice in square brackets, the default is the option in capital letters.

a.   The first prompt asks for a hostname. Use the default. Use **cisco** as both the username and password.

```
Welcome to the Cisco Wizard Configuration Tool
Use the '-' character to backup
System Name [Cisco_49:43:c0]:
Enter Administrative User Name (24 characters max): cisco
Enter Administrative Password (24 characters max): cisco
```

b.   Enter the management interface information. The management interface communicates with the management workstation in VLAN 1. The interface number is 1, because this is the port trunked from the controller to the switch. The VLAN number is 0 for untagged. It is untagged because VLAN 1 is the native 802.1Q VLAN and is, therefore, sent untagged through 802.1Q trunks.

```
Management Interface IP Address: 172.16.1.100
Management Interface Netmask: 255.255.255.0
Management Interface Default Router: 172.16.1.1
Management Interface VLAN Identifier (0 = untagged): 0
Management Interface Port Num [1 to 4]: 1
Management Interface DHCP Server IP Address: 172.16.1.1
```

c.   Configure an interface to communicate with the access points. This will be in VLAN 100 and is tagged as such on the trunk.

```
AP Manager Interface IP Address: 172.16.100.100
AP Manager Interface Netmask: 255.255.255.0
AP Manager Interface Default Router: 172.16.100.1
AP Manager Interface VLAN Identifier (0 = untagged): 100
AP Manager Interface Port Num [1 to 4]: 1
AP Manager Interface DHCP Server (172.16.1.1): 172.16.100.1
```

d.   Configure the virtual gateway IP address as 1.1.1.1 (this is acceptable because you are not using this for routing). The virtual gateway IP address is typically a fictitious, unassigned IP address, such as the address we are using here, to be used by Layer 3 Security and Mobility managers.

```
Virtual Gateway IP Address: 1.1.1.1
```

e.   Configure the mobility group and network name as **ccnppod**. Allow static IP addresses by pressing Enter, but do not configure a RADIUS server now.

```
Mobility/RF Group Name: ccnppod

Network Name (SSID): ccnppod
Allow Static IP Addresses [YES][no]: [Enter]

Configure a RADIUS Server now? [YES][no]: no
Warning! The default WLAN security policy requires a RADIUS server.

Please see documentation for more details.
```

f.   Use the defaults for the rest of the settings (press Enter at each prompt).

```
Enter Country Code (enter 'help' for a list of countries) [US]: [Enter]

Enable 802.11b Network [YES][no]: [Enter]
Enable 802.11a Network [YES][no]: [Enter]
Enable 802.11g Network [YES][no]: [Enter]
```

```
Enable Auto-RF [YES][no]: [Enter]

Configuration saved!
Resetting system with new configuration...
```

Note: Wireless equipment varies from country to country. Make sure to use the appropriate country code.

Step 9: (Optional) Configure the prompt and access methods on the WLAN controller.

a. When the WLAN controller has finished restarting, log in with the username **cisco** and password **cisco**.

```
User: cisco
Password: cisco
```

b. Change the controller prompt to WLAN_CONTROLLER with the **config prompt** *name* command. Notice that the prompt changes.

```
(Cisco Controller) > config prompt WLAN_CONTROLLER
(WLAN_CONTROLLER) >
```

c. Enable Telnet and HTTP access to the WLAN controller. HTTPS access is enabled by default, but unsecured HTTP is not.

```
(WLAN_CONTROLLER) > config network telnet enable
(WLAN_CONTROLLER) > config network webmode enable
```

d. Save your configuration with the **save config** command, which is similar to the Cisco IOS **copy run start** command.

```
(WLAN_CONTROLLER) > save config
Are you sure you want to save? (y/n) y
Configuration Saved!
```

e. To verify the configuration, you can use the **show interface summary**, **show wlan summary**, and **show run-config** commands on the WLAN controller.

Lab 7-3, Voice and Security in a Switched Network - Case Study

Topology

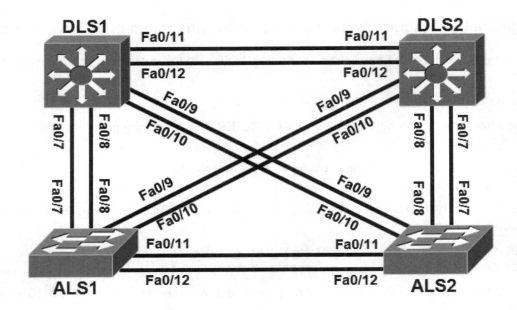

Objectives

- Plan, design, and implement the International Travel Agency switched network as shown in the diagram and described below.

- Implement the design on the lab set of switches.

- Verify that all configurations are operational and functioning according to the guidelines.

Note: This lab uses Cisco WS-C2960-24TT-L with the Cisco IOS image c2960-lanbasek9-mz.122-46.SE.bin and Catalyst 3560-24PS with the Cisco IOS image c3560-advipservicesk9-mz.122-46.SE.bin. Other switches (such as 2950 or 3550), and Cisco IOS Software versions can be used if they have comparable capabilities and features. Depending on the switch model and Cisco IOS Software version, the commands available and output produced might vary from what is shown in this lab.

Required Resources

- 2 switches (Cisco 2960 with the Cisco IOS Release 12.2(46)SE C2960-LANBASEK9-M image or comparable)

- 2 switches (Cisco 3560 with the Cisco IOS Release 12.2(46)SE C3560-advipservicesk9-mz image or comparable)

- Console and Ethernet cables

Requirements

The International Travel Agency has two distribution switches, DLS1 and DLS2, and two access layer switches, ALS1 and ALS2. Configure the switches as follows:

1. Disable the links between the access layer switches.

2. Place all switches in the VTP domain CISCO and set them all to VTP mode transparent.

3. Configure all inter-switch links statically as 802.1q trunk links.

4. Create VLANs 10 and 200 on all switches. Configure DLS1 and DLS2 SVIs in VLAN 10 and assign addresses in the 172.16.10.0/24 subnet.

5. Configure DLS1 and DLS2 to use HSRP on the 172.16.10.0/24 subnet. Make DLS1 the primary gateway, and enable preemption on both switches.

6. Place ports Fa0/15 through Fa0/20 in VLAN 10 on both access layer switches.

7. Enable PortFast on all access ports.

8. Enable QoS on all switches involved in the scenario.

9. Configure ALS1 Fa0/15 and F0/16 for use with Cisco IP phones with a voice VLAN of 200 and trust the IP phone CoS markings using AutoQoS.

10. Configure ALS1 Fa0/18 through Fa0/20 for port security. Allow only up to three MAC addresses to be learned on each port and then drop any traffic from other MAC addresses and set the violate mode to **protect**.

11. Configure ALS2 Fa0/18 to only allow the MAC address 1234.1234.1234 and to shut down if a violation occurs.

Notes:

_____

_____

_____

_____

_____

_____

_____

_____

_____

_____